GENDER AND HIGHER EDUCATION IN THE PROGRESSIVE ERA

L Y N N D. G O R D O N

Gender and Higher Education in the Progressive Era

Y A L E U N I V E R S I T Y P R E S S
N E W H A V E N A N D L O N D O N

Designed by Nancy Ovedovitz and set in Galliard type by The Composing Room of Michigan, Inc. Printed in the United States of America by BookCrafters, Inc., Chelsea, Michigan.

Library of Congress Cataloging-in-Publication Data

Gordon, Lynn D. (Lynn Dorothy), 1946–
Gender and higher education in the progressive era / Lynn D. Gordon.
p.   cm.
Includes bibliographical references.
ISBN 0-300-04550-6 (cloth)
0-300-05255-3 (pbk.)
1. Women college students—United States—Case studies.   2. Women—Education (Higher)—United States—History.   3. Progressive education—United States—History.   I. Title.
LC1757.G67   1990
376'.973'09034—dc20   89–78032
                                                        CIP

A catalogue record for this book is available from the British Library.

The paper in this book meets the guidelines of permanence and durability of the Committee on Production Guidelines for Book Longevity of the Council on Library Resources.

10 9 8 7 6 5 4 3 2

In loving tribute
to the courage and devotion of
Margaret Roberta Gordon (1951–1988)
and
J. David Richardson

And in memory of Daniel

CONTENTS

Contents

ACKNOWLEDGMENTS

The image of the solitary scholar bent over notes and documents, emerging from her study with a completed manuscript, does not accurately reflect the community of support behind research and writing. This book owes its existence as much to the generosity of archivists, teachers, colleagues, friends, and family as it does to my own efforts.

No historian can function without the knowledge and skill of librarians. Because a book on student life requires the use of obscure sources, I made many demands on their time and resourcefulness, and I was rarely disappointed. Kathleen McGowan, Mary Huth, Karl Kabelac, and the staff of the Inter-Library Loan Office at the University of Rochester; Albert Tannler at the University of Chicago; J. R. K. Kantor and Marie Thornton at the Bancroft Library, University of California at Berkeley; Frances Goudy and Eleanor Rogers at Vassar College; the late Doris Antin at Tulane University; the staff of the Agnes Scott College Library; and Barbara Haber and Karen Morgan at the Arthur and Elizabeth Schlesinger Library of Women's History, Cambridge, Massachusetts, efficiently guided my research.

During my undergraduate days at Barnard College, I first learned about the importance of women's colleges and the connections between higher education and social activism. I wish to thank my classmates, the Barnard-Columbia Friends of the Student Nonviolent Coordinating Committee (SNCC), the Columbia-Barnard Democratic Club, Students for a Democratic Society (SDS), and my teachers, particularly Nina Garsoian, Patricia

Acknowledgments

❖

Albjerg Graham, Suzanne Wemple, Chilton Williamson, and George Woodbridge, for the inspiration they provided.

My interest in the intersection between the social justice movements of the Progressive Era and the history of women's education began in the courses and seminars of Arthur Mann, Preston and Sterling Morton Professor of History at the University of Chicago. As my teacher and dissertation adviser, he set the same high standards for me that mark his own work. His support and concern in the years since I finished graduate school have meant a great deal to me.

I am fortunate that Steven Schlossman was on the Chicago faculty during my years of graduate study. His course in the history of women's education offered me the opportunity to relate the literature in women's history and women's studies to the history of education and American social history. As a member of my committee, his help in conceptualizing and organizing the dissertation and his continuing encouragement have been invaluable.

Additional faculty at the University of Chicago also helped me develop the resources I drew upon to write this book. I thank Akira Iriye and Emmet Larkin for their interest, patience, and example. William Veeder first taught me about the relationship among popular literature, women's history, and cultural ideologies and remains my model for combining path-breaking scholarship with outstanding classroom teaching.

At the University of Rochester, my colleagues in the Graduate School of Education and Human Development have probably heard more than they ever wanted to know about the history of women's education and of college students—and about the dilemmas of writing. My thanks to Barbara Agor, Craig Barclay, David Bleich, Dale Dannefer, William Lowe, the late Jack Miller, William Pinar, Judith Smetana, Joan Stone, Tyll Van Geel, and Arthur Woodward for their patience and support. I especially thank Philip Wexler, my colleague, chair, and dean, for his interest in the intellectual and political issues raised by my work, and his concern for my professional development.

An exceptional staff, including Assistant Dean Dirk Wilmoth, Director of Administration Betty Pool, Margaret Davidson, Betty Drysdale, Donna Femiano, Mary Haslam, Elizabeth Simpson, and Catherine Stark, made it possible for me to handle the varied responsibilities and the voluminous paperwork involved in producing a book. Margaret Zaccone's organizational efficiency, hard work, sharp wit, and warmth made my work easier and my days brighter.

As an associate of the Susan B. Anthony Center at Rochester, I have

benefited greatly from the opportunity to present my work and to participate in the research seminar given there. My colleagues in women's studies
have played a significant role in my intellectual development. I am grateful
to the directors, Barbara Ilardi and Bonnie Smith, and to Mary Young for
their interest in helping junior faculty and for reading my work; and to
Elizabeth Faue, Associate Provost Ruth Freeman, Ayala Gabriel, Grace
Harris, Kathryn Hunter, Nan Johnson, Brenda Meehan-Waters, Deborah
Modrak, and Marjorie Woods.

The earliest institutional support for my research came from Bowdoin
College, where I spent a year replacing a faculty member on sabbatical. I
thank the college for its grant, which allowed me to undertake the archival
research at the University of California at Berkeley and Sophie Newcomb
College, and the faculty and administrators, especially Ann Pierson, for
making me part of a very special community.

Friends and mentors at a host of other institutions lent time and energy to
read my chapters or extend my contacts with colleagues in the history of
education and women's history. Joyce Antler's contributions to my thinking
and writing, in this book and elsewhere, go far beyond my ability to thank
her. For some years, Rosalind Rosenberg has served as a sounding board for
ideas. Nancy Weiss Malkiel read an early version of my manuscript; her wise
suggestions formed the basis for many revisions. Jennifer Nedelsky and
Barbara Nelson helped this book grow and also helped me to survive the
process. From the time we formed a dissertation support group to the
present, Patricia Palmieri and Sally Schwager have shared with me a commitment to writing the history of women's education. Their critical reading
of this book focused and strengthened my arguments and clarified my
writing. My thanks also to Barbara Kuhn Campbell, Dina Copelman,
Natalie Zemon Davis, Hasia Diner, Steven Diner, Lewis Erenberg, Ellen
Fitzpatrick, Madeleine Grumet, Stephen Hansen, Debra Herman, Linda K.
Kerber, Ellen Condliffe Lagemann, Ellen More, Frank Ninkovich, Linda
Perkins, William J. Reese, Joan Shelley Rubin, Ellen Schrecker, Jordan
Schwarz, Ella Schwartz, Jonathan Sperber, Ellen Umansky, Kathy Waldron,
and Mary Ellen Waller-Zuckerman.

I also wish to acknowledge the support of the Woodrow Wilson Founda-
tion for a Dissertation Fellowship in Women's Studies and the able research
assistance of Ellen Bell Clements, Thomas Beck, Judith DeGroat, Laura
Smith Porter, and Susan Watson. Catherine Kelly was first my student at
Rochester, then my research and teaching assistant, and is now my friend.
Her excitement about this project, her knowledge of cultural history, and

her editing skills helped me a great deal in the final stages of writing. University of California alumni Irene Coffin '10, Mila Clearley Parrish '15, Ella Barrows Hagar '19, and James Edward Drew '21 shared their memories of student life with me in a series of interviews, providing fascinating information and important perspectives. Professor and Mrs. Lee Cottle of Decatur, Georgia, provided a welcome introduction to southern hospitality during my research time at Agnes Scott College. Charles Grench and the staff at Yale University Press helped this book become a reality and made the process relatively painless. I thank my manuscript editor, Karen Gangel, for her enthusiasm, skill, and patience. G. K. Hall and Company graciously permitted me to quote from an essay of mine previously published in *Woman's Being, Woman's Place* (1979).

My students—from those in the social studies classes I taught at Sweet Home Junior High School in Buffalo, New York, to undergraduates and graduate students at Chicago, Bowdoin, Northern Illinois University, Princeton, and Rochester—and the social studies teachers in the History Teachers' Institute at the University of Rochester have been a generous and appreciative audience for the ideas in this book. I thank Rachel Herzog, Michael Pliss, Eric Rakowski, Judith Resutek, Eric Rosenbaum, Anil Rustgi, and David Schiller, who sparked my thinking about the history and meaning of education, and Joseph Griffo and Robert Kramer, who, as department chair and principal, allowed me to teach critically and with autonomy.

Without two very special day care providers, Roxann Ross and Laura Hopkins, this book could not have been written. If all parents had such remarkable caretakers for their children, day care would be viewed as a positive good rather than as a necessary evil.

Others whose assistance and empathy made my task easier include Victoria Bigelow, Denise and David Goffman, Gene and Sue Golan, Rosemary Griffo, Mark and Micki Iris, Tracy King, Bryna Leeder, Carol Ninkovich, Robert and Deborah Rothman, Joyce and Christopher Saricks, Linda Schwarz, Marcia and Richard Stern, Linda and John Wallen, Lila and the late Arthur Weinberg, and Diane Swartz Williams.

Numerous aunts, uncles, and cousins have provided meals, lodging, warnings about the instability of academic life, and large measures of love. Stephen Shamberg, John Shamberg, and Judith Rose shared their home with me for several long stretches while I began my research. Lori Jaffe remained convinced of my eventual success, even when the evidence pointed in the other direction. Patricia Rosenzweig was always available to re-

Acknowledgments

❖

mind me that intelligent people can discuss things other than history. Elaine and Sanford Jaffe, Ruth and Charles Provow, Diane and Ed Mehlman, Jamie Leaf and Kim Eschelbach, and all their children kept my spirits up.

The burdens of this book and its often cranky author have fallen heavily on my immediate family, who rarely complained and always cheered me on. To Judith Factor, Carol Gordon, John Kohnke, Elaine and Lester Plotkin, David Richardson, Abigail Wechsler, Goldie Wechsler, Robert Wechsler, and Samuel Wechsler go my deepest thanks. I wish that my father, Thomas Gordon, and my grandparents, Sam and Dora Jaffe, who first taught me to appreciate books and to argue about history, could have seen this book.

Harold Wechsler took on far more than his share of domestic and family responsibilities so that I could finish my task. He has read drafts of chapters until his eyes glazed over and had the unenviable task of teaching me to use a word processor. Our shared intellectual and political commitments, as well as our disagreements, have given life and depth to many of the arguments in these pages. Beyond all that, I thank him for the joy and excitement he brings to my life just by walking in the door.

Introduction

In this book I analyze the education of the remarkable and highly significant generation of women students who attended American colleges and
universities during the Progressive Era, from 1890 to 1920. Coming of age
during the years when nineteenth-century women's culture, based on the
gender ideology of "separate spheres," reached the height of its influence,
experienced a backlash, and declined, college women of the Progressive Era
constituted a transitional generation, a bridge between Victorian and modern America. As such, their college experiences reflect the exhilaration,
possibilities, conflicts, and disappointments of a critical era in American
culture and in the history of American women.

Between 1890 and 1920, these women established a unique campus life,
linking the curriculum to the extracurriculum and demonstrating the
importance of higher education in women's lives and to the progress of
womanhood. Female separatism, social activism, and belief in a special
mission for educated women characterized their activities. Female communities created a climate of opportunity for women as students and as graduates. For both sexes, but especially for women, student life during the
Progressive Era reflected off-campus political and social reform movements
and closely linked collegiate activities to preparation for leadership in those
areas.

Historians have largely minimized or misrepresented the story of college
students. Some scholars write about higher education as a tale of institu-

tional development and leadership, devoting their attention to the "rise of universities" and to a "culture of professionalism" in the late nineteenth and early twentieth centuries. They sometimes discuss how students were shaped by these processes, without considering in turn the effect of students on institutions or the larger society. Others have treated campus life as consistently oppositional to academic culture, stressing men students' hedonism, and women students' interest in attracting men, without making distinctions in student behavior during different periods.[1]

Yet college women at the turn of the century were not simply a small and marginal group of elite women preparing for teaching careers or marriage. They made up an important and growing percentage of undergraduates (see table 1) and a much-discussed vanguard in the world beyond the campus gates. Their success in formulating and acting upon a well-defined educational and social mission led to on- and off-campus protests over the "effeminization" of universities and the professions. Throughout the period, this on-going debate about women in higher education was closely related to more general controversies about changing constructions of gender and appropriate roles for educated women in society.

Women attending college between 1890 and 1920 were not isolated

TABLE 1

Women Enrolled in Institutions of Higher Learning, Regular Session, 1870–1958[a]

Year	Number of Women Enrolled (thousands)	Percentage of All Women 18 to 21 Years of Age	Percentage of All Students Enrolled
1870	11	0.7	21.0
1880	40	1.9	33.4
1890	56	2.2	35.9
1900	85	2.8	36.8
1910	140	3.8	39.6
1920	283	7.6	47.3
1930	481	10.5	43.7
1940	601	12.2	40.2
1950	806	17.9	30.2
1956	1,019	21.0	34.6
1958	1,148	23.0	35.2

Source: Mabel Newcomer, *A Century of Higher Education for American Women* (N.Y.: Harper, 1959), 46. Courtesy, Harper and Row.
[a]Data from *Reports of the Commissioner of Education* and the *Decennial Census.*

behind ivy walls but took part in the political and intellectual ferment of the Progressive Era. Historians disagree about the nature and meaning of progressivism. Some have said that nostalgia for simpler values and times or the desire of reformers to halt a decline in their social status lay at the heart of the movement; others have stressed its modernizing, efficiency-oriented aspects. But however one characterizes this era, optimism and energy pervaded middle-class America. Progressives exuded confidence that human beings could ameliorate the deficiencies of the national life, while remaining within a traditional American framework.[2]

By offering intellectual laboratories for reformers and their programs, universities and colleges became an important arm of American progressivism. Research on social problems took place in new departments of sociology, psychology, and anthropology. Philosophers explored the nature of community, democracy, and society, while historians and theologians applied critical and hermeneutical techniques to ancient texts and documents. The undergraduate curriculum broadened to include courses in the social and natural sciences, modern languages and literatures, and history, while the elective system made it possible to study socialism, municipal housekeeping, urban politics, and economics. In addition to research and teaching, faculty participated in the good government movement, the reorganization of school boards, the development of watchdog commissions, woman suffrage, and settlement work.[3]

Expanded course offerings, professional reform activities, and the ideals of progressivism affected the extracurriculum, as students and faculty shared interests in politics and social reform. Male administrators, faculty, and students worked together to establish self-government associations, honor systems, service honor societies, and the organized and regulated competitiveness of football and debate. Although not completely successful in uprooting earlier, more violent patterns of student behavior, such efforts opened the doors to women's participation in college life.

In spite of opportunities for a truly coeducational extracurriculum during the Progressive Era, men's and women's student lives proceeded along separate, although parallel, paths. Aided by newly hired female faculty and administrators (graduates from earlier years), coeducated women students in the 1890s set up their own campus communities, with organizations and activities similar to the men's. At the women's colleges, the 1890s marked the beginning of a new era, as faculty and students demanded an end to "seminary-like" regulations from the 1870s and 1880s, established extracurricular activities similar to those at the men's colleges, and created reform organizations, such as settlement associations, corresponding to off-campus groups.

College women's separatism was not only a response to exclusion from men's colleges and men's campus activities but also a positive statement about gender distinctiveness. Victorian culture had defined separate spheres for the sexes—domesticity for women and public life for men. Although such prescriptions never fully described the realities of life, even for the white urban middle classes of the northeast, they represented important cultural norms. Out of women's domestic work and family concerns grew a women's culture, oppositional to the cult of the self-made, individualistic, aggressive nineteenth-century American male.

Victorian women's culture upheld religion, emotion, community, and the ties among generations of female relatives and friends. Eventually, some used the values of women's culture to enter social reform and women's rights movements by arguing that women's values would benefit the larger society as well as the home. Victorian separatism thus provided a power base and rationale for middle-class women's entrance into public life.

During the Progressive Era, the world beyond the college gates seemed particularly open to womanly influence. The culture of professionalism, with its defining characteristics of individual success, financial gain, and reliance on technology and science, had not yet cut off other models of professional achievement, especially the emphasis on service and reform. Women physicians, settlement workers, academics, and government officials often had a gender-related perspective on their work and its relationship to larger social concerns. Separate female communities at single-sex colleges or within coeducational institutions served as crucibles for the creation of attitudes, values, and practices, thus establishing a microcosm of the world students expected to enter after graduation.[4]

The Progressive Era, however, also constituted a time of profound social and cultural change. Throughout those thirty years, American attitudes, values, and styles slowly and gradually transformed; as they did so, younger women, the inheritors of progressivism, changed with them. Women students' separate organizations and spirit of social meliorism looked much the same in 1895 and in 1920, but their personal concerns and conceptions of gender politics evolved over time into a new cultural consciousness.

Scholars examining different generations of women college students have categorized the post-1890 group as frivolous and socially preoccupied, contrasting them unfavorably with the serious and dedicated pioneer generation of 1865 through 1890. Certainly the second generation demanded more purely recreational activities and more contact with men than their predecessors. Their life histories, especially of those who graduated after 1905, demonstrate that domesticity had a great deal of appeal to these young women. Their story, however, is far more complex than their proclivity for parties and their subsequent marriage rates indicate.

What truly distinguished the second generation from its predecessor (and its successors) was the linking of gender consciousness to campus life and to postgraduate plans for social activism, a growing commitment to egalitarian rather than separatist feminism, and a simultaneous interest in marriage. Until the 1910s, female students rarely talked of combining career and marriage, but the anguish over choosing between the two characterized the college years of women from the 1890s through the 1910s and can be found throughout the documents they left behind.

These shifts in students' attitudes and values and the higher marriage rate for graduates after 1905 lead some historians to offer a different conceptualization of the history of women college students. They identify a pioneer generation attending colleges and universities from 1865 to 1890, a second generation between 1890 and 1905–10, and a third during the 1910s. They further argue that second- and third-generation women students, having come from wealthier, more socially elite homes, had less interest in their studies and fewer reasons to prepare for self-support. In this interpretation, the 1910s becomes a singular and exceptional decade, marked by dramatic changes in dress, courting behavior, politics, and the deterioration of faculty-student relationships.5

The third-generation hypothesis, however, while distinguishing sharply between students of the era before 1890 and students of the 1910s, has little to say about the intervening years, 1890–1910, and what defines this supposed second generation. Furthermore, this analysis fails to account for continuities in student life, the common spirit of the thirty-year era, and the on-going congruence in political-reform goals between women students and faculty. The fascination and significance of the Progressive Era, on and off campus, lie in the way Americans of that period bridged and merged the culture of the past and that of the future. Under the aegis of progressivism, women college students balanced Victorian ideals with newly emerging beliefs and behavior.

Evidence on the issue of social class is scanty, but what there is argues against major changes in the student population between 1870 and 1920. During those years, American college women were overwhelmingly white, Protestant, and from middle-class homes. At state universities, women with fathers who farmed, clerked, or worked at other lower-middle-class occupations constituted a sizeable minority; but the majority came from the professional and entrepreneurial class. At the eastern and southern women's colleges, high tuition and residence costs limited attendance almost exclusively to those with fathers who were professionals and businessmen. The small numbers of Jewish, Catholic, and black women in higher education did not increase appreciably until the 1920s.[6]

In addition to passing over the story of the second generation as not worthy of the attention due the pioneers, histories of women's higher education and women college students have focused on the Seven Sisters colleges, which, although highly significant institutions, did not educate even a large minority of women students. In fact, coeducation was the fastest growing segment in higher education during the Progressive Era. The largest percentage of students going to women's colleges came as early as 1879–80 (28.3 percent); by 1920 the figure was down to 9 percent (including Catholic women's colleges). Only 29 percent of four-year colleges and universities were coeducational in 1870; but 43 percent admitted women by 1890, and 58 percent by 1910 (see table 2).[7]

A thorough examination of Progressive Era student life requires breadth, to explore the different types of institutions women attended, and depth, to uncover the rich details of students' experiences. To avoid portraying one institution as typical or, alternatively, relying solely on published sources to analyze many campuses, I took the middle ground by looking closely at five colleges and universities, some single sex and some coeducational, in the North, South, Midwest, and West.

Profound differences marked the lives of women students at single-sex and coeducational institutions. Regional differences, although less significant than the presence or absence of male students, also affected college women. The University of California and the University of Chicago provided important contrasts for the study of women at coeducational universities of the Progressive Era. Both universities were unusual in admitting women with little internal discussion and no public controversy, and at both institutions women students had a separate structure of social and extracurricular activities, approved by administrators, fostered by women faculty, and enjoyed by the students themselves.

Despite their similarities, however, California's relative isolation from urban progressive reform and the limited numbers and effectiveness of its female faculty contrasted sharply with Chicago, where strong women administrators and teachers and the joint involvement of faculty and students

❖

TABLE 2

Women Enrolled in Institutions of Higher Learning According to Type of Institution,
1869–1957[a]

			Women's Colleges				
Year	Total	Coeduca-tional Institu-tions	Total in Women's Colleges	Public Four Year	Private Four Year: Non-Catholic	Private Four Year: Catholic	Normal and Junior: Public and Private
Thousands of Students							
1869–70	11.1	4.6	6.5	—	2.2	0.1	4.2
1879–80	39.6	23.9	15.7	—	11.2	0.1	4.3
1889–90	56.3	39.5	16.8	—	11.9	0.2	4.7
1899–00	85.4	61.0	24.4	0.2	16.3	0.2	7.6
1909–10	140.6	106.5	34.1	0.1	20.8	0.4	12.8
1919–20	282.9	230.0	52.9	6.4	24.7	2.5	19.4
1929–30	480.8	398.7	82.1	18.3	36.5	10.1	17.2
1939–40	601.0	494.9	106.1	24.5	37.2	26.5	17.9
1949–50	806.0	709.1	96.9	9.2	30.8	35.2	21.7
1956–57	1019.0	920.7	98.3	11.1	30.9	42.9	13.4
Percentage Distribution							
1869–70	100.0	41.1	58.9	—	19.8	0.9	38.2
1879–80	100.0	60.4	39.6	—	28.3	0.4	10.9
1889–90	100.0	70.1	29.9	—	21.1	0.3	8.5
1899–00	100.0	71.4	28.6	0.3	19.1	0.2	8.9
1909–10	100.0	75.8	24.2	0.1	14.8	0.3	9.0
1919–20	100.0	81.3	18.7	2.3	8.1	0.9	7.5
1929–30	100.0	82.9	17.1	3.8	7.6	2.1	3.6
1939–40	100.0	82.3	17.7	4.2	6.2	4.4	3.0
1949–50	100.0	88.0	12.0	1.1	3.8	4.4	2.7
1956–57	100.0	90.4	9.6	1.1	3.0	4.2	1.3

Source: Mabel Newcomer, *A Century of Higher Education for American Women* (N.Y.: Harper, 1959), 49. Courtesy, Harper and Row.

[a]Data from *Biennial Statistics of Education,* Office of Education. The distribution of students among different types of institutions has been partly estimated for the earliest years. The coordinate colleges have been included with women's colleges if they have separate classes, at least in part, and with the coeducational group when all classes are coeducational.

in social movements produced a better climate of opportunity for women students.

Separatism on coeducational campuses demonstrated not only its critical role in promoting women's advancement but also its limitations when not combined with a strategy for equality. At Berkeley, coeducated women used separatism creatively to make a place for themselves at the university but found that men, using a "separate but unequal" frame of reference, objected to their very presence. Ultimately, women turned to the rhetoric of equality, asking why they should not have the same campus privileges as men. At Chicago, separatism worked simultaneously for and against women students. Women's prominence on the Chicago campus in the 1890s caused concern that they would dominate the undergraduate college. Over the vehement protests of women students, faculty, and alumnae, President William Rainey Harper instituted instructional separatism, or "segregation," to solve the problem of "effeminization."

While coeducated women struggled to establish and maintain their campus position, female students at single-sex colleges had, from the earliest days, enjoyed the advantages of sisterhood and community. At the eastern women's colleges, students and faculty fought together against the limiting popular conceptions of women's sphere and women's education and against restrictive institutional regulations.

In the 1890s, the Seven Sisters colleges (although they were not so termed until 1926 with the founding of the Seven College Conference)— Vassar, Wellesley, Smith, Barnard, Bryn Mawr, Mt. Holyoke, and Radcliffe—came of age, as they abandoned preparatory departments, attracted a better-educated and more distinguished faculty, set up student self-government associations and honor codes, founded campus branches of settlements and other reform organizations, broadened their perspective on women's careers, and competed with each other in athletics and debate. Founded in 1861 by a Poughkeepsie, New York, brewer, Vassar College had the curricular strength and endowment to become the first nationally recognized women's college. Located just north of New York City, with a faculty steeped in progressive reform ideology, Vassar women, as a community, displayed a particularly strong sense of social mission.

Generalizations about college women of the Progressive Era need modification when considering the experiences of southern white women. Southern women had only limited access to their state universities, and legitimate women's colleges did not develop there until the 1890s, some twenty years after the founding of most eastern single-sex institutions. Until

1905–10, the quality of faculty, curriculum, and student work did not match collegiate levels elsewhere in the country. And, steeped in their region's conservative social attitudes, southern students of this period had far weaker ties to progressivism, reform, women's rights, careers, and the world of single professional women than their northern counterparts.

In spite of these difficulties, southern college women of this era established organizations and fostered institutional allegiances. Steadily, although more slowly than their sisters at Vassar, they developed extrafamilial concerns, a sense of educated women's social and cultural mission, and an interest in careers and social service work. Sophie Newcomb and Agnes Scott Colleges exemplified southern women's colleges between 1890 and 1920. Named, respectively, after a dutiful daughter and a model Christian mother, both institutions had difficulty establishing and maintaining a collegiate curriculum and persuading parents to let their daughters participate in campus life. By the turn of the century, however, their students took great pride in being college women and slowly expanded both their undergraduate and alumnae activities.

Historical analyses of student life have generally relied on campus newspapers. These are indeed excellent sources for details about the lives of male students or of female students at women's colleges; but at coeducational institutions, the newspapers featured mostly men's athletics, male student politics, and obscure jokes, and I had to look beyond them to find out about women. Alumnae memoirs, letters, scrapbooks, diaries, photographs, and interviews; the papers and letters of faculty; annual reports by presidents and deans of women; yearbooks; and files of newspaper clippings pertaining to an institution's history told me about the day-to-day operation of student organizations and campus life.

For students' views of women's higher education and of its relationship to careers and marriage, their fiction, published in yearbooks and literary magazines, proved an invaluable resource. Students (mostly female) used short stories to try out various scenarios of "boy meets educated girl and complications ensue." Sadness about women's limited options and occasionally self-mockery about their aspirations pervade this student fiction. Most of the stories display no literary merit but evidence college women's strong consciousness and accurate perceptions of the cultural and social barriers they faced on and off campus.

Optimism and self-confidence characterized the campus lives of women college students during the Progressive Era, as they tested the utility of gender separatism and planned to make their mark on society. Only their fiction revealed private longings, doubts, and concerns about what lay ahead; unfortunately, however, these subterranean fears were well founded.

Even during the Progressive Era itself, the national debate over gender issues and negative reactions to single professional women condemned the effect of higher education on family life. Subsequent decades of political conservatism and national crisis between 1920 and 1960 did not favor either women's advancement or the renewal of an active feminist movement. Moreover, the decline of separatism, women's culture, and women's reform networks as organizing principles for public life had serious consequences. The achievement of suffrage and access to formerly all-male schools, businesses, and professional associations did not bring about gender equality; nor did egalitarian marriages prove easy to find and sustain in twentieth-century America.

Many women college graduates of the second generation combined work and marriage, but few had significant careers in higher education, the professions, or politics. The second generation found that higher education provided a liberal and nurturing environment, raising expectations that society did not fulfill. For women at the turn of the century, colleges and universities were special places—as one dean put it, "little Edens of liberty." Unfortunately, the social context of their adult lives contained little to sustain their idealism and enthusiasm.[8]

College women of the Progressive Era were not the first, and certainly not the last, students to be educated for a world that ceased to exist. Social psychologists tell us that attitudes and values acquired in college tend to persist throughout life. If so, the disjuncture between education and society must have been particularly painful for the second generation of college women—but may be illuminating for the researcher. We need to modify our assessment of higher education as a conservative force for social and cultural reproduction, by giving more attention to historical specificity, the tensions between school and society, and the campus experiences of diverse student groups. This book demonstrates that during certain historical periods college attendance expanded many students' social consciousness and desire for change.[9]

The study of women's campus experiences unfolds a new aspect of the history of American higher education at the turn of the century. Although some Progressive Era institutions immersed themselves in a male-oriented academic and professional culture, others served as the stage where women developed an alternative model of student life and professional goals. Facing heavy opposition from the educational establishment, this model became the "road not taken" for colleges and universities. After 1920 the domination of higher education by technologically oriented research universities and the resurgence of male student life successfully contained the threat of effeminization. Yet an examination of the existence and possibilities of alternatives helps us understand the history of higher education as a process of choice, not inevitability, and the importance of distinctive groups in providing those choices.

Finally, the campus life of this generation has contemporary relevance for student life and for women's higher education. We can look back on the Progressive Era as a time when faculty and students worked together for the good of the campus community and viewed higher education as intimately connected with larger social issues. Surmounting barriers of age, faculty interest in research, and students' devotion to athletics and Greek life, the two groups developed a common agenda of political and reform concerns and organizational structures reflecting that commitment. Knowledge about the history of American campus life may guide our sense of what is possible for today's collegiate communities.

Just as they did at the turn of the century, contemporary young women attend college during an era of changing gender roles and confusion about the meaning of those changes. The verbal harassment and shutting down of opportunities for coeducated women students during the Progressive Era seem mild compared to today's obscene phone calls, threatening graffiti, and date rapes. Yet the source of these practices is the same—fear of effeminization or, in more modern terms, fear that women's presence threatens male dominance of social and institutional life, on and off the campus. This book shows us how women students and faculty banded together to meet challenges and address fears. Combining ideas of female distinctiveness with a commitment to equality, their experiences provide not blueprints but suggestions for addressing our current concerns.

CHAPTER ONE

From Seminary to University: An Overview of Women's Higher Education, 1870–1920

VICTORIAN CULTURE AND WOMEN'S EDUCATION TO 1870

The conventions of middle-class Victorian culture prescribed separation of the sexes. The public, political, and economic world belonged to men, whereas women's sphere was limited to household and children. This ideology of separatism described middle-class life in nineteenth-century urban northeastern America: men worked for wages outside the home, while women toiled within it. But even outside the cities and in other regions of the country, Victorians accepted scientific and theological theories of profound, inherent male-female differences.

Victorian sex roles, and in particular the cult of domesticity, glorified the responsibilities of home and sentimentalized motherhood. Separate spheres allowed women no political voice, limited economic options, and few legal rights, even concerning their sacred duty of mothering. Clearly, men held the reins of power. Yet domesticity gave homebound women moral and spiritual authority within the family, and thus a role in urban, bourgeois society.

Historians have also noted that separatism promoted the development of a women's culture. In their domestic lives and intimate same-sex friendships, Victorian women embraced religious, moral, communal, and emotional principles opposed to the competitive materialism and individualism of nineteenth-century American life. Moreover, although confining women within the home, the cult of domesticity laid the ideological groundwork for their leaving it. The very qualities attributable to good wives and mothers—purity, piety, moral superiority, and gentleness—made women necessary actors in the public arena. The notion of "social housekeeping" and the idea that suffrage itself extended domestic duties to the world outside the household did not fully develop until the turn of the century, but began in the northeast during the antebellum era, with women's participation in missionary work, teaching, temperance, moral reform, and abolition.

In practice, then, the lives of Victorian men and women resembled overlapping circles more than separate realms. The incessant public discussion and debate over sex roles throughout the nineteenth and into the early twentieth century reveal that separatism was difficult to maintain, its definition and implications troubling men and women alike. As women moved beyond the home, albeit proclaiming their actions as logical extensions of domesticity, male and female critics complained that such behavior destroyed family life and ruined the health of women and children, thereby undermining the social order. These fears surfaced time and again as Victorian women challenged sex role boundaries, defining and redefining the meaning of masculinity and femininity and the interplay between public and private life. Conservatives, who insisted on a narrow, household-bound definition of women's roles, as well as liberals, who argued that femininity was not incompatible with certain public activities, believed that the sexes had inherently distinct natures.[1]

Even before the Victorian era, education was an important arena for the expansion of women's sphere under the rubric of improving family life. Since the mid-eighteenth century, reformers and radicals, including Mary Wollstonecraft, had asserted that lack of education made women frivolous and socially irresponsible, unfit to be companions to their husbands, good mothers to their children, or self-supporting in the absence of a male provider. The ideology of the American Revolution suggested the importance of family education for the creation of good "republicans," and Americans came to agree that educated mothers raised better citizens. Between 1780 and 1830, this association of women's education with family needs opened the doors of primary schools to girls. And in the nineteenth century, evangelical Christianity sanctioned education for women as a means of enhancing and enforcing their spiritual authority within the home.

In the antebellum North, economic issues also advanced the cause of women's secondary education. The exodus of labor from households into shops and factories meant that older children had to earn a living outside the home before they married. Northern women who remained single, through choice or necessity, turned to teaching as a "respectable" way of supporting themselves. The growth of primary education in the North and West during the antebellum era led districts, desperate for teachers, to hire women at half the salary paid to male teachers. Moreover, teaching as a female occupation represented one of the first cases of domesticity extended. Proponents argued that women made better teachers because they could draw upon innate maternal instincts in dealing with students.[2]

Thus, many women who attended seminaries, academies, or normal institutes did so in preparation for running their own classrooms. The need to train women to earn a living caused northern schools to emphasize professional courses as much or more than preparation for domesticity. Prominent women's educators such as Emma Willard, Mary Lyon, and Catharine Beecher claimed that women's secondary education enriched home life and enhanced Christian practice but also channeled their efforts into the development of a teaching profession.[3]

The quality of seminary education varied greatly, but some of the best schools, including Willard's Troy Female Seminary and Lyon's Mount Holyoke, offered a rigorous curriculum, featuring reading, writing, study of the Scriptures, grammar, mathematics, composition, arithmetic, history, geography, French, Latin, and natural history. The devoutly religious founders of many women's academies and seminaries demanded high standards of conduct and disciplined students sternly. Students observed the Sabbath, attended prayer meetings, and followed a schedule of bells indicating classes, study times, recreation periods, and sleep. Antebellum academies trained women to think and reflect, gave them access to books, companionship, and the example of their teachers, while preparing them to earn a living. Studies of individual institutions show that graduates worked at a variety of jobs and participated in community activities throughout their lives.[4]

Southerners also believed that women's education would uphold, not subvert, their slaveholding patriarchal culture. In the South, the high cost of a seminary education (around $150 a year for two to five years, with extra charges for music, dancing, drawing, and needlework) limited attendance to women who would not have to support themselves. Graduates of southern seminaries returned home to marry, raise children, and assume the duties of running a plantation or urban middle-class household. The diversity of denominational allegiances, the male-dominated hierarchy within evangelical Protestant churches, and the isolation of white women on farms and plantations kept antebellum southern white women from developing the bonds of womanhood, and thus the intimacy necessary for the creation of a separate women's culture. As Catherine Clinton put it: "Antebellum southern women were confronted by the irony of their education." Exposed to new forms and varieties of knowledge, they were nevertheless confined to the same domestic duties as their uneducated mothers and grandmothers.[5]

For some southern women, however, education may well have bred high expectations and ultimately dissatisfaction. The courtship of Bessie Lacy and Thomas Dewey in the 1850s offers one such example. At Edgeworth Female Seminary in Greensboro, North Carolina, Lacy became part of a world with larger concerns and possibilities than her parents' household. Her friendships with other women led her to hope that marriage would be a similar meeting of intellect and sensibility. In his analysis of Bessie Lacy's letters to her parents, friends, and Dewey, Steven M. Stowe demonstrates her gradual though reluctant acceptance of the nineteenth-century realities and constrictions of male-female relationships.[6]

By proving women's intellectual mettle, maintaining the rhetorical connections between domesticity and schooling, and training some young women to support themselves, nineteenth-century seminaries and academies expanded woman's sphere, paving the way for higher education. Indeed, the boundary between nineteenth-century secondary schools and colleges remained indistinct, particularly for women's education. Willard's and Lyon's schools compared favorably to the men's colleges of their day; several southern institutions even called themselves colleges.

Institutional distinctions were nonetheless clear to Americans of that era; and in the 1830s and 1840s women's desire to attend college inaugurated a century-long debate over female higher education. Once again, neither side refuted gender distinctiveness. Conservatives claimed that higher education would destroy women's desire to remain within the home, while liberals asserted that colleges would produce better wives and mothers. Yet women students and their families had their own agendas. They made the decision for higher education independently, often in opposition to the rhetoric around them, and many did not define their purposes in terms of domesticity.[7]

WHY GO TO COLLEGE? THE PIONEERS

Nineteenth-century advocates of women's higher education linked their cause to enhanced domesticity and "cultured motherhood." Protests came from doctors, clergy, and writers already uneasy about the expansion of women's public roles. Opponents claimed that by going to college, women would sever the tenuous connections between education and domesticity and enter the domain of men. In these years before the founding of well-established women's colleges, conservatives mixed arguments against female college attendance with objections to coeducation.

By the mid-nineteenth century, most Americans accepted coeducation in primary or secondary schools. As Victoria Bissell Brown has pointed out, Victorians were so sanguine about inherent sex-based characteristics that they did not believe prepuberty association of boys and girls endangered the formation of gender identity. Higher education, however, was another matter. As the final stage before the assumption of adult roles, collegiate coeducation put issues of separatism to the forefront. Most contemporary adult social institutions and organizations either excluded one sex or separated the two; coeducational colleges and universities were a major exception. How would students and faculty cope with such a situation, requiring them to treat men and women in the same manner, and simultaneously observe sex-role norms? And, most important, what effect would such associations have on the long-term relations between the sexes? Many feared that women educated with men would seek more than access to liberal culture and teacher training and want the privileges and duties of men. Would not collegiate coeducation, by its very nature, move women outside the home, their proper sphere?[8]

In the antebellum era, a few private colleges, notably Oberlin (established in 1833) and Antioch (1853) pioneered collegiate coeducation. Early in their histories, these institutions, both founded by Christian social reformers, struggled with the definition and implications of coeducation. Oberlin women studied the Ladies' Course (although they were permitted after 1841 to elect the men's course if they so wished). They were not allowed to deliver graduation orations, or any other public speeches, and were expected to perform domestic work, while male students did the heavier chores. Oberlin's first president, evangelist Charles Finney, and future administrators and faculty felt that coeducation provided a healthy social atmosphere, as well as practice for future ministers in dealing with women who would one day be their congregants or spouses. Social and extracurricular organizations and activities were sex-segregated; relationships between men and women took place in an atmosphere of evangelical piety and propriety. Similar conditions prevailed at Antioch, where President Horace Mann separated men and women completely except in the classroom. Women students and women faculty at both colleges resisted separatism. Oberlin students and future women's rights activists Lucy Stone and Antoinette Brown opposed their college's policies, while at Antioch women students broke the rules of social propriety so dear to Mann's heart by attempting to combine their literary society with the men's.[9]

In contrast, Lori Ginzberg's reinterpretation of Oberlin's early history depicts a more benign separatism, emphasizing the college's positive view of womanhood. Ginzberg maintains that the founders of Oberlin wanted men to live up to women's higher social and moral standards; separatism indicated respect for women's special qualities. She points out that male as well as female students performed the college's domestic work; that both sexes founded separate moral reform societies; and that the presence of women, according to contemporaries, inspired piety and correct behavior. Although Antioch and Oberlin administrators and faculty strictly limited women's roles on the campuses, the religious, reform-oriented atmosphere at these schools favored the presence of women and the development of their intellect. Women's rebellion against restrictions demonstrates self-confidence about their place at Oberlin and Antioch.[10]

Women's higher education continued to be controversial, despite the success of Oberlin and Antioch, Congress's passage of the Morrill Act (1862), providing for the establishment of state universities, and the founding of authentic women's colleges in the 1860s and 1870s. Harvard's Dr. Edward Clarke fanned the flames of opposition with his popular books, *Sex in Education, or a Fair Chance For the Girls* (1873) and *Building A Brain* (1874). Adding the authority of science to older arguments that religion and morality prescribed "woman's proper sphere," Clarke maintained that biology was destiny. Too much study, he said, drew blood away from the ovaries to the brain, particularly if the female student overtaxed herself during the "catamenial function" (menstruation). College women thus endangered their health and perhaps rendered themselves incapable of bearing healthy children. Although he particularly opposed coeducation, Clarke also condemned women's colleges like Vassar for educating women in the same manner as men.[11]

Given the controversy and the possibility of long-term deleterious effects, why did women want to go to college during the latter half of the nineteenth century? After all, domestic enhancement and even a teaching career were possible through a normal school, high school, seminary, or academy education. Why risk social opprobrium or one's health to go to college?

Some families apparently did not believe the "experts." The mother of young Martha Carey Thomas, future president of Bryn Mawr College, reassured her daughter that neither she nor her friends knew any women like those Clarke described in his book. For other families, rhetoric about domesticity took second place to ensuring their daughters' future; college was a good investment. Many families preferred state universities as a less costly educational choice; seminaries and normal schools were usually private and not universally available. Most states did not have significant licensing laws for teachers until the early twentieth century, but university credentials quickly became a useful asset for landing a more prestigious or better-paying urban teaching position. Families sometimes relocated near a state university, so that their children could live at home and attend classes.[12]

White southern women had little access to higher education until the 1880s and 1890s, almost a generation later than their northern counterparts. Yet arguments promoting their education had begun earlier, after the Civil War left many white women without husbands or financial resources. For these women, and subsequent generations caught in the throes of the modernizing and urbanizing southern economy, teaching became the road to self-support, as it already was in the North. And like northerners, southern proponents of women's higher education emphasized its applicability to Christian home life.[13]

If most aspiring college women equated the impetus for higher education with the need to earn a living, others had a wider, more idealistic vision. Although most advocates of women's higher education did not support women's rights, the Declaration of Sentiments, written in 1848 by the first women's rights convention in Seneca Falls, New York, listed lack of access to colleges on its roster of gender inequalities. In succeeding years, women's rights periodicals promoted higher education as the key to full social and economic participation. After deciding to devote her life to the women's rights movement, Kentuckian Laura Clay spent a year at the University of Michigan in preparation for her work in the cause.

Women's rights advocates sometimes played a leading role in women's admission to specific campuses and in refuting Dr. Clarke's theories. The *Woman's Journal,* the leading women's rights publication, printed highly critical reviews of Clarke's book by distinguished doctors and nonmedical authorities. Three volumes of essays, edited by suffragists Julia Ward Howe, Eliza B. Duffey, and Anna C. Brackett, proclaimed Clarke's ignorance about women's health and education. College women were certainly conscious of the women's rights movement, if only because critics of women's higher education usually linked the two causes. And whatever their political views upon entering college, some alumnae went on to become prominent in suffrage organizations and other women's rights causes.[14]

Higher education also offered intellectual and aesthetic fulfillment. Women's clubs, amateur scientific societies, home study, lyceums, and lectures provided forums for discussion and companionship outside the academy, but many women found that only in universities and colleges could they stretch their minds and test their capabilities. Writing about her experiences at Cornell, Florence Kelley said, "My freshman year was one continued joy. Anhungered and athirst for learning . . . here was indeed delight. Little did we care that there was no music, no theater, almost no library; . . . Our current gossip was Froude's life of Carlyle . . . I embarked upon a schedule of twenty-five hours a week of ancient and modern languages and mathematics . . . I listened and recited, studied, memorized, and acquired."[15]

In the nineteenth century, the "family claim" often kept unmarried women of the middle classes at home to look after parents and siblings, but some families supported their daughters' efforts to get the best education possible and move into the professions. In her analysis of Wellesley College's all-female faculty, Patricia Palmieri has described the nurturing and enabling New England family culture of the late nineteenth century. The women in Palmieri's study learned to value books and education early in life, and parental encouragement continued after graduation. In 1890, Wolcott Calkins successfully negotiated with Harvard's president, Charles William Eliot, for the admission of his talented daughter, Wellesley professor Mary Whiton Calkins, to the university's graduate psychology program.[16]

Nor was this phenomenon confined to potential Wellesley professors from New England families. A survey of Vassar alumnae from the classes of 1865 through 1890 (most of whom were from the New York–New Jersey–Pennsylvania area) revealed that these women had attended college because their parents wanted them to. Fathers were mentioned five times more frequently than mothers as sources of inspiration for college attendance.[17]

Less frequently, families outside the northeast also adopted progressive ways of raising daughters. William Campbell Preston Breckinridge, Kentucky lawyer, congressman, and Confederate colonel, was initially dubious about the decision by his daughter, Sophonisba, to attend Wellesley in 1884. He worried about the consequences, for her and for the family, of life outside their close-knit network of friends and relatives. "You have been tenderly reared & always treated with rather peculiar and affectionate esteem," he wrote to her. "Dutiful, loving, and unselfish; you were appreciated and perhaps a little spoilt in our not very large circle. At Wellesley you are but one of five hundred—a new, unknown one at that." On another occasion, he wrote: "One of the best results of education at home is common friends—that all the members of a family have in a certain sense mutual friendships & common associations . . . I doubt if what you gain compensates for this."

Breckinridge, however, was an empathetic father who had assumed responsibility for his daughter's care in infancy and nursed her through childhood illnesses. Above all, he wrote, "[I] persisted in my purpose to give your brain a fair chance to show its power." He urged Sophonisba to make the most of her opportunities at college, to explore Boston, accept the proffered class presidency, and remain for the full four-year course of study. Finally, the colonel reminded his daughter that "you ought to look squarely in the face that if I die, you will have to make your own living: & if I live you may have to do so anyhow . . . God preserve you . . . from the aimless . . . life of the young girls you would associate with here."[18]

For the first generation of college-educated women, the choice between single-sex and coeducational institutions determined the nature of their campus experiences. Most students, male or female, attended the tuition-free or inexpensive state universities. Yet as American higher education expanded and research universities developed, faculty involvement with scholarship left students without caretakers. Violence, indifference toward academic pursuits, an obsession with class competitions, and increased distance from faculty marked male student life in the 1860s, 1870s, and 1880s. Struggling for intellectual acceptance and social survival, the female pioneers of coeducation formed literary societies and other clubs but existed only on the social margins of college life.

WOMEN AT MEN'S COLLEGES, 1860–1890

Colleges and universities did not enthusiastically open their doors to women in the late nineteenth century, overwhelmed by egalitarian considerations. A few private men's colleges admitted women for local, idiosyncratic reasons or when pressured by women's rights advocates to do so. Women gained access to state universities, however, when parents, teachers' associations, or women's organizations, using the rhetoric of domesticity, petitioned legislatures and boards of regents to provide vocational preparation for the daughters of taxpayers.

At the secular state universities, founded outside the aegis of reformers, women encountered limitations similar to those at Oberlin and Antioch, but fewer mitigating circumstances. Hostility, ridicule, and neglect characterized the experiences of pioneer women students at Michigan, Wisconsin, and Cornell.

In 1855 the State Teachers' Association of Michigan proposed admitting women to the state university. Throughout the 1850s and 1860s the regents, legislature, and people of the state debated the issue. In 1858, responding to the application of three young women for admission, the regents appointed a committee to study the advisability of coeducation. Supporters of women's admission claimed that the university's charter required it to accept all "persons" residing in the state who met certain academic qualifications, and that "the basis of our national and state system is equal rights." The regents agreed that future mothers and teachers needed a good education and indignantly denied reports of a "women's rights" influence among female applicants:

> Woman is the parent and nurse of the human race. . . . Our statesmen and scholars, our moral and intellectual teachers, and our spiritual guides . . . receive from her their earliest and most lasting impressions. . . . We give no heed to those who attempt to connect or identify the application of the young ladies . . . with the political or social movements known as "women's rights," "Free Love," etc. etc. This application has no such connections in our minds, and we would not have the question prejudiced or the request of these young ladies spurned because some persons who advocate the Free Love Movement or attend Women's Rights conventions may also advocate coeducation of the sexes.[19]

The regents' committee wrote for advice to college administrators across the country. Not surprisingly, officials at the all-male eastern colleges replied negatively to the question of admitting women, but Oberlin's Finney and Antioch's Mann also issued grave warnings (influenced, no doubt, by women's resistance to regulation on their own campuses), indicating that they, at least, considered unsuccessful the attempts to elevate college life through women's superior morality. Mann stated that the administration of a coeducational college required "constant vigilance." Michigan authorities should be prepared, he said, to provide separate dormitories and eating places and to supervise women students. Finney doubted the success of coeducation in any atmosphere less evangelical than Oberlin's.

These reports reinforced the opposition of Michigan's faculty and administrators, and the regents declined approval of coeducation, concluding that it would, as a local newspaper reported, "unwoman the woman and unman the man." Advocates of coeducation did not give up, however. Stalled during the Civil War, the movement to admit women to the University of Michigan regained momentum shortly thereafter. The resignation of President E. O. Haven and pressure from taxpayers, women's organizations, and James and Lucinda Stone, teachers at the university's preparatory college in Kalamazoo, opened the doors of the university to women in 1870. Although the state of Michigan would have preferred to educate women separately, it could not afford to do so.[20]

Consideration of coeducation at the University of Wisconsin began in the 1850s, also inspired by the state's teachers. The regents established a normal department in 1863, when the Civil War took away so many male students that they feared for the university's survival. In 1867, after the war, President Paul A. Chadbourne (1866–1870), who opposed coeducation, established a female college. During the early 1870s, however, after Chadbourne's departure, the university gradually abolished separate instruction; the 1874 commencement was the last at which men and women graduated separately. Although an 1877 report by a Board of Visitors stressed the adverse effects of coeducation on women students' health, a faculty committee disputed the report. Objections to coeducation appeared from time to time in the university's publications, but women students remained.[21]

At newly founded, private Cornell University, not the state's taxpayers and teachers, but reformers and women's rights advocates, especially Elizabeth Cady Stanton and Susan B. Anthony, pushed for coeducation in the belief that it would form the basis for healthier relationships between the sexes and for marriages based on mutual intellectual interests and respect. They pressured founder Ezra Cornell, first president Andrew Dickson White, and trustee Henry Williams Sage to admit women. Mary Ann Cornell and White's first wife, Mary, and his second, Helen Magill (who held the first Ph.D. ever awarded to an American woman), also urged the higher education of women (although Susan Linn Sage, Henry's wife, did not).[22]

Ezra Cornell's motto, "I would found an institution where any person can find instruction in any study," encouraged the application of women students, but White was not eager to confront the difficulties of coeducation. He asked women to stop seeking admission until the university weathered an initial storm over its nonsectarian character. When women students continued to come to Ithaca, demanding admission, he relented and began construction of a dormitory and social hall for them.[23]

In Rochester, New York, women's organizations struggled for thirty years to coeducate the University of Rochester, a private men's liberal arts college. In 1898 the trustees bowed to community pressure, agreed to admit women if they brought with them a "dowry" of $100,000 to pay for additional faculty and classroom space, and imposed a two-year deadline for raising the funds. By the spring of 1900, the women of Rochester had raised $40,000. The trustees agreed to reduce their demand to $50,000, but in September the women still lacked $8,000. At that point, Susan B. Anthony, a Rochester resident, took a direct role in the struggle. Although long an interested observer and behind-the-scenes participant in the campaign for women's admission to the university, she had not openly associated herself with the cause, for fear of damaging it with the taint of women's rights. During the waning hot days of the summer, Anthony dashed around the city in her carriage, collecting pledges. Ultimately, she put up her only personal financial resource, a life insurance policy worth $2,000, purchased for her by the suffrage associations, in time to meet the deadline. The first women students entered the University of Rochester a few weeks later, in time for the fall semester of 1900.[24]

The interest of older women in seeing the next generation go to college is a highly significant feature in the history of women's access to coeducational institutions. Collegiate coeducation usually did not come about naturally or because of American democratic traditions. For nineteenth-century Americans, there was nothing "natural" about young men and women of marriageable age associating as equals. Despite the arguments that college-educated women would thereby make better teachers, and ultimately better wives and mothers, conservatives believed that collegiate coeducation had the potential to alter gender roles. Access to higher education in the North, Midwest, and West became a reality when women themselves— mothers, civic leaders, potential students, or women's rights advocates— pressured state and university officials to open the doors of colleges and universities. And with one exception (the University of Arkansas in the 1880s), southern state universities, too, coeducated because women campaigned for admission.[25]

Pioneer women students rejoiced at their new-found opportunities. Women like Martha Carey Thomas, Alice Freeman Palmer, and Elizabeth Cady Stanton (who wanted to send her daughter Harriot to Cornell but had to settle for Vassar) believed that coeducational schools represented social freedom and intellectual excitement, as opposed to the new women's colleges, which they regarded as little better than seminaries.

But even when access was no longer an issue, the appropriate relationship between men and women students was as troublesome at the new universities as it had been at Oberlin and Antioch a generation earlier. During the first thirty years of widespread collegiate coeducation (1860–1890), women students were ignored, ridiculed, and isolated from campus life. This hostility sometimes extended to the classroom, where male instructors, themselves educated at single-sex schools, had neither experience nor interest in teaching female students.[26]

In her novel, *An American Girl and Her Four Years in A Boys' College* (1878), Olive San Louis Anderson (Michigan '75) discussed the situation of women students at her alma mater. The book dealt with problematic issues and significant themes for the first generation of college women: the purpose of women's higher education, relationships between women students and their families, the uneasiness of male and female students with each other, and women's experiences with male faculty.

Anderson's heroine, Wilhelmine Elliott, struggled to define herself—to create a new image of womanhood—in a world with strictly defined gender roles. With her masculine nickname, "Will," her robust health, tomboy activities, distaste for organized religion, and high scholastic standing, Elliott was the very prototype of the "New Woman"—that masculinized female much feared by late nineteenth-century Victorians. She was also, however, startlingly beautiful, warm, and loving, with both male and female friends.[27]

Women liked and admired Will even when they did not understand her; men's feelings were more complex. Some had difficulty treating "Miss Elliott" as just another student, whereas others felt that if she were a student, she could not also be a lady. After her entrance examinations, a classics professor "conditioned" her acceptance until she did further work in Greek. He recommended a tutor, a young man working his way through college, but remarked: "If Jerry Dalton can be closeted for an hour a day with that face and eyes and never think of anything but 'The Retreat of the Ten Thousand,' he is a very remarkable young man." The professor's prediction proved accurate. Carried away by Will's beauty, the tutor tried to make love to her, and she walked out in disgust. In another incident, on her way to class, Will got caught in a "rush" (fight) between freshmen and sophomore men and received a bloody nose. The men ignored her plight, but the other women students helped her get home. As she put it, "There is not one of those boys but, if you find him out of college, would have run to a lady's assistance and begged a thousand pardons for having had any hand in such an accident; but, would you believe it, not one of those two hundred and fifty boys offered any help or sympathy, simply because they feel that we are trespassing upon their domains."[28]

Will's college experiences contrasted sharply with those of her friend Mary Palmer ("Mame"), who went to Vassar College. In their letters, Will adopted the stereotypic attitude toward women's colleges popular among women's rights advocates of her day when she referred to them as "boarding schools," and argued that the students should live with families in the town where it could be taken for granted that they would "conduct themselves properly without surveillance, and have the college provide for nothing but their intellectual wants." She praised coeducation for providing women with both social and intellectual freedom and claimed that the presence of "boys" taught "girls" about competition, achievement, and enthusiasm. Ironically, however, the early women's colleges, although they did institute social restrictions, taught women far more about "competition, achievement, and enthusiasm" than Will learned in her male-dominated environment.

WOMEN'S COLLEGES: MOVING BEYOND THE SEMINARY, 1860–1890

The percentage of women nationwide attending single-sex colleges peaked in 1879–80 (28.3 percent), then declined to 19.1 percent in 1899–1900 and to 8.1 percent in 1919–20 (with an additional .9 percent in women's Catholic colleges). Women's colleges had the greatest impact in the East and the South, where the strength of prestigious men's schools, and local or regional preferences for single-sex education, barred women from many private and state institutions until well into the twentieth century. Although they borrowed from the traditions of both men's colleges and female seminaries, women's colleges created unique institutional forms and practices.[29]

Founders and supporters of the eastern women's colleges, later known as the Seven Sisters, argued that their schools met the demand for women's higher education without sacrificing femininity. At single-sex colleges, women, they promised, could develop their minds without becoming like men. From the beginning, women's college administrators identified institutional intellectual goals with men's colleges, though their social aims remained conservative.

Late nineteenth-century American colleges and universities debated the merits of the traditional classical curriculum, with its prescribed courses and emphasis on Latin and Greek. Few institutions went to the extreme that

Harvard did under Charles William Eliot (1869–1909) in abolishing all requirements for the bachelor's degree. Most steered a middle course, expanding the percentage of electives in a student's program and gradually modifying the curriculum to emphasize laboratory sciences, social sciences, modern languages, and fine arts. Although they made it a point of honor to offer Latin and Greek courses, the eastern women's colleges also taught an impressive array of natural and social sciences and pioneered in the development of fine arts. Determined to prove the inaccuracy of Edward Clarke's theories, the colleges included hygiene and physical education in their curricula.[30]

To fulfill their promises that college women would remain womanly, founders and administrators looked to successful, well-established female seminaries like Mount Holyoke, instead of to men's colleges, when building their campuses and regulating students' lives outside the classroom. In her study of campus architecture at the Seven Sisters colleges, Helen Lefkowitz Horowitz noted that Vassar and Wellesley initially expected students to live in one main building, under the close surveillance of resident teachers, and to follow the rigid daily schedule made famous by Mary Lyon at Mount Holyoke in the mid-nineteenth century. Women's college founders continued the seminary's association of women's education with religion, requiring chapel attendance, prayer meetings, Bible study and placing heavy pressure on students to "convert."[31]

Discipline, religiosity, and the lowering of academic standards for a preparatory department caused women's rights advocates and some prospective students, like the fictional Will Elliott, to prefer coeducation in the late nineteenth century. And the students and faculty at women's colleges cast aspersions on female seminaries, resentful about their legacy of regulations and religious dogmatism. Yet the new institutions also adopted positive seminary traditions. Long before Progressive Era college students became interested in social reform, female seminaries had promoted an ethic of social service, passing it on to their institutional successors. Women's colleges thus combined insistence on collegiate level instruction with a commitment to social amelioration.

We can see these themes most clearly in the higher education of Jane Addams, who would have preferred to attend Smith College but, at her father's insistence, entered Rockford Seminary in 1877. Finding Rockford's religious atmosphere oppressive, Addams resisted pressures from faculty and from the school's founder and long-time principal, Anna Peck Sill, to convert and become a missionary. She did not, however, reject the push toward social service permeating Rockford, the "Mount Holyoke of the West." In a speech delivered during her junior year, Jane Addams revealed her philosophy of higher education. She sympathized with the intellectual aims of the women's colleges but emphasized her desire to combine these with an ethic of secular social service. Speaking of the modern woman's educational agenda, she stated:

> She wishes not to be a man, nor like a man, but she claims the same right to independent thought and action. On the other hand, we still retain the old ideal of womanhood—the Saxon lady whose mission it was to give bread unto her household. So we have planned to be "Breadgivers" throughout our lives, believing that in labor alone is happiness, and that the only true and honorable life is one filled with good works and honest toil.

Although women could, of course, be breadgivers in their traditional do-mestic capacities, Addams and other college women of her generation sought to be breadgivers for all of American society. In later life Addams continued to support research, scholarship, and higher education and to urge that college women (and men) use their knowledge for the greater social good.[32]

Early in their history, the eastern women's colleges functioned as closely knit communities serving students' and faculty's needs, often in defiance of administrators and trustees. These institutions provided professional homes for talented women academics who could not have found jobs in men's or coeducational colleges. And, as that faculty's sole constituency, women's college students did not have to compete with men for attention and recog-nition; their work and aspirations were taken seriously. Extracurricular activities, with or without administrative sanction, provided leader-ship opportunities. Moreover, students and faculty engaged in constant questioning about women's issues and the future of educated women, in-cluding the publication of serious and thoughtful articles on such subjects in their campus newspapers. Although such discussions undoubtedly took place among coeducated women, they did so privately, without the advan-tage of public campus forums for debate and sharing viewpoints.

At the women's colleges, the community was more socially homoge-neous, and thus more cohesive than at coeducational institutions, particu-larly the state universities. Female seminaries had educated women from a wide variety of backgrounds; some, like Mount Holyoke, made it a point to offer an education to the daughters of farmers and the "middling classes." In contrast, Seven Sisters students came from upper-middle-class households, with fathers who were professionals, merchants, or businessmen. With financial aid very limited, few women from less comfortable homes could afford the tuition, living expenses, and foregone income to attend a private college.[33]

The history of the founding and earliest years of Wellesley College shows the determination of first-generation women faculty and students to make these institutions their own. Bostonians Henry Fowle Durant and his wife, Pauline, evangelical social reformers whose children died quite young, wanted to create a family and community for themselves and their "Wellesley daughters." The Durants believed higher education would strengthen women's minds and bodies, prevent sentimentality and idleness, and prepare them to make the world a better, more Christian place. They hired only women faculty to exemplify the qualities they wanted students to emulate. Determined that his students would have all the advantages of young men attending Harvard, Henry Durant purchased the latest scientific and library resources for Wellesley. Forced to open a preparatory department when only thirty of the three hundred initial students met standards for college-level work, the Durants closed it within ten years.

Notwithstanding Wellesley's ambitious programs, rigorous academic standards, and highly intellectual women faculty, the Durants, partly from personal inclination and partly to demonstrate the propriety of women's higher education to a dubious public, cast college life in the seminary mold. Henry Durant, a Mount Holyoke trustee, admired the seminary's religious discipline and well-ordered daily life. He was particularly eager to convert Wellesley women to his own brand of evangelical Christianity. Although he changed the institution's name from Wellesley Female Seminary" to "Wellesley College" before opening its doors, the first students found themselves in a closely and carefully regulated environment.

Wellesley students and faculty defied the Durants and first president, Ada L. Howard, creating instead a true college community with few vestiges of the seminary. They resisted attempts to convert them, broke college rules, and staged a rebellion in 1876 (the year after Wellesley opened) following Durant's dismissal of three popular teachers for refusing to interrupt their classes to provide an exhibition before the Board of Visitors. This incident led to the loss of Durant's authority over the college, and he gradually withdrew from its affairs. Ada Howard retired after Henry Durant's death in 1881 and was succeeded by Alice Freeman, a young University of Michigan graduate with a secular, intellectually ambitious plan for Wellesley's development.[34]

Similarly, at Mount Holyoke Seminary, the transition to collegiate status pitted a modernizing elite of teachers and students against trustees and administrators who wished to maintain the seminary's reputation for offering a Christian education, oriented toward enlarging, but maintaining, woman's sphere. In the 1880s, Mount Holyoke students complained about required prayer meetings, domestic work, the self-reporting system for transgressions against the rules, lack of free time, and the difficulty of developing friendships in an environment where every hour of every day had its assigned purpose.

Teachers like Lydia Shattuck, a seminary alumna from the class of 1851, began to change Mount Holyoke's curriculum. Shattuck, whose personal acquaintance with founder Mary Lyon gave her much prestige, taught science, introduced laboratory experiments and discussed the theory of evolution in her classes. When queried about the compatibility of her work with the seminary's religious ethos, she replied, "Perhaps your question means to ask whether we have thrown the Bible overboard. I reply; we never did use it as a textbook for science, and we do not now."

The establishment of Vassar (in 1865), Wellesley, and Smith Colleges (both in 1875) challenged Mount Holyoke's primacy, not only within New England, but as the nationally acknowledged leader in women's higher education. In 1884, changes in the composition of the Board of Trustees and the selection of a new principal, Elizabeth Blanchard, swung the pendulum toward change. Although insisting that Holyoke had a unique mission, namely, the education of Christian women for social and religious benevolence, officials agreed to institute a college department. Many faculty responded by seeking college and graduate degrees themselves; by 1893 the transition to college was complete.[35]

THE FIRST GRADUATES:
AFTER COLLEGE, WHAT?

Both contemporary observers and modern scholars have viewed this first generation of women college students, educated between 1860 and 1890, as a serious and dedicated band of pioneers, eager to prove themselves intellectually, and with little time or inclination for frivolity. Before the ink had dried on their degrees, social commentators began scrutinizing the marriage and career patterns of these graduates. Unfortunately, most colleges did not keep alumnae records. Thus, we have no comprehensive survey of this group's choices; nor can we say a great deal about differences between women's college graduates and coeducated alumnae.

Most researchers who went beyond analysis of a single institution's alumnae took their data on college women's lives from members of the Association of Collegiate Alumnae (the ACA, founded in 1881). Since this organization admitted only the graduates of fifteen select colleges, the statistics did not represent a typical group. Whatever the average college graduate of the 1860s, 1870s, and 1880s did with her life, several trends became clear. First, although some women returned home to marry, raise children, or care for aging parents, higher education did not necessarily lead to quiet but enriched domesticity. Second, college graduates married later and less frequently than their counterparts in the general population, and had fewer children. And finally, higher education became, for some women, the prelude to prominence in the public sphere and to professional achievements.

Working alumnae made their influence felt mostly as teachers at all levels of the educational system, raising academic standards at schools across the country and inspiring their female students to go on to college themselves. Alumnae also staffed the women's colleges as deans, administrators, and occasionally professors at coeducational institutions. Less frequently, college women went into medicine, law, the ministry, and business. By the turn of the century, 12 percent of Vassar alumnae held graduate degrees from Yale, Cornell, Chicago, Columbia, Harvard, and Bryn Mawr. The class of 1891, with thirty-six members, had five Ph.D.'s. Finally, the unpaid labor of college women, as members of school boards, college trustees, organizers and directors of societies and charity groups, constituted a major social contribution.[36]

For some ambitious graduates, however, the world outside the campus gates remained the province of men. In their early postgraduate years, women such as Jane Addams, Sophonisba Breckinridge, Julia Lathrop, and Florence Kelley, wanting to carry out their college ideals, unsuccessfully sought socially significant work. Depressed and floundering, they ultimately found a home in the social justice movements of the Progressive Era and established the modern profession of social work. Combining masculine expertise and training with the attitudes and values of women's culture, these college graduates drew national attention to the need for social reform, formulated and campaigned for legislation to ameliorate the problems they identified, and served as officials to enforce it.[37]

Women who did not go to college also made their mark on the world, but increasingly college women led others in achievement. Of the entries in

Woman's Who's Who In America (1914), 63.4 percent had some advanced education, 43.8 percent had bachelor's degrees, and 22.7 percent had done postgraduate work. The correlation between higher education and achievement becomes even more impressive when we recall how few women actually attended college in the late nineteenth and early twentieth centuries.[38]

The pioneers often chose nontraditional personal lives as well. Although a precise accounting is impossible, it seems likely that half of them did not marry. In 1895, using a sample of 1,805 alumnae from the ACA register, one researcher reported that 28.2 percent of the women were married, compared to a rate of 80 percent for women over twenty years of age in the general population. When she restricted her sample to women over forty, the numbers changed, but the trend remained the same: 54.5 percent of the college graduates were married, compared to 90 percent of women in the general population. Undoubtedly, most of the career women in the group had remained single, for various reasons. Some prominent professional women, such as Dr. Alice Hamilton, felt that a mother could not adequately attend to both her children and her job. And Martha Carey Thomas, struggling with her attraction to an interesting man, prayed to overcome her feelings so that she could get on with her career. Still others may not have wished to assume the burdens of marriage in a patriarchal society in an era when divorce was difficult or impossible; or they did not find men who wanted intelligent, professionally active wives.[39]

Unmarried women college graduates did not necessarily lead lonely lives; many found emotional fulfillment and familial attachments in relationships with each other. Carroll Smith-Rosenberg has written compellingly about these intimate friendships, flourishing within the homosocial women's culture of Victorian America. As college women of the pioneer generation moved into social activism, professional careers, and suffrage work, they carried these friendships with them, maintaining lifelong partnerships and family ties with other women.[40]

Victorian reticence makes it difficult to know whether these friendships, many clearly erotic and sensual, were sexual as well. In the 1920s Katharine Bement Davis (B.A. Vassar, Ph.D. Chicago), head of the Bureau of Social Hygiene, surveyed twenty-two hundred "normal" middle-class women, most of them college graduates. She found intense same-sex friendships to be common among all her subjects, though most prevalent among the alumnae of women's colleges. Respondents differentiated between emotionally close relationships and those with a strong erotic component (expressed or not) but moved easily between the two, making rigid categorization of nineteenth- and early twentieth-century college women as homo- or heterosexual difficult as well as ahistorical.[41]

The first generation of college women realized some, though not all, of the conservatives' fears, as they demonstrated the potential of higher education to alter gender roles. Yet despite their boldness, ambition, and successes, the pioneers did not completely abandon woman's sphere. Many regarded their careers as successful precisely because they brought the values of women's culture—empathy, nurturance, compassion, and concern for the community—into the public arena. Women's personal and professional networks shaped their lives and were of critical importance to their achievements. Because higher education had meant so much in their lives, they served as mentors to the young women who succeeded them on the college campuses of the Progressive Era. For some, however, this was a disappointing and disillusioning project. Alumnae, women faculty, and administrators frequently complained about a lack of purpose and direction among the young women they advised.[42]

Historians have also taken the second generation to task for not carrying forward the aims of its predecessors, noting the flowering of student activities and the rise in the marriage rate for college women after the turn of the century. They concluded that these women came from a higher social class than the pioneers and attended college to have fun, participate in student life, and meet eligible men.[43]

Evidence below and in subsequent chapters, however, demonstrates a great deal of continuity from the first generation to the second, as well as highly significant changes. Although sharing the intellectual and political goals of their predecessors, the second generation gradually shifted its vocational orientation from service and social reform to individual achievement. And, more strongly than their mentors, Progressive Era college women felt the competing pulls of marriage and motherhood.

CONTINUITY AND CHANGE: COLLEGE WOMEN AND STUDENT LIFE DURING THE PROGRESSIVE ERA

By the turn of the century, American women had greatly modified the practices if not the ideology of Victorian gender culture. Living in a less isolated and self-contained female sphere than had their mothers, they entered and influenced the male worlds of higher education, the professions, and politics. The ideas and behavior of Progressive Era settlement workers, academics, and physicians had several sources and emphases, including a growing reliance on science, efficiency, and technology. Still, the values of women's culture, particularly concerns with democracy, community, compassion, and social gospel Christianity pervaded the rhetoric and informed the activities of many reformers and professionals. Suffragists argued that women's enfranchisement would further extend female cultural and moral influence to all segments of American life.[44]

American college campuses during this period reflected the social and cultural values of the progressive middle classes. Disturbed by the violence and elitism among male collegians of the mid-nineteenth century, and unable to rely on an increasingly research-oriented faculty to curb student excesses, presidents hired personnel administrators, such as deans of men or women, vocational counselors, and other support staff. Changes in the tone of campus life, however, came more from the students themselves than from administrative initiatives. Men de-emphasized brawling, hazing, and fighting to become involved in student self-government, honor systems and honor societies, civic and political clubs, and the regulated, organized competition of debate and intermural athletics. Such activities allowed individual recognition and achievement but also focused on service to the university community. White Protestant male college students used the extracurriculum as preparation for professional, business, and civic leadership in the larger society.[45]

The growing numbers of women college students found that the social and political climate of the Progressive Era provided a rationale for their own participation in student activities, while the presence of the first generation as faculty, administrators, and visiting alumnae smoothed their path. Women faculty and deans of women invited prominent reformers, civic activists, and feminists to visit the campus as speakers and to meet with students, and eagerly promoted female students' participation in campus activities. In their view, student life helped women transfer energies from the family to the more public world of the college community, where they learned leadership, organizational skills, and developed friendships. Without the extracurriculum, women students, especially at state universities, took courses and went home at night, or perhaps attended an occasional dance, untouched by the special experience of higher education and unprepared to assume postgraduate social and civic leadership. The importance women faculty and students attached to college activities demonstrated their expectations that alumnae would take on public as well as private responsibilities.

The curriculum, the example of their women teachers, and the social reform climate on and off campus encouraged female college students to bring womanly influence to bear in the public sphere. Like men of that era, they used collegiate culture as a blueprint for their future, a way of trying out their social responsibilities as educated women. Activities organized around women's rights did not attract many students, but reform and feminism shaped the second generation's aspirations and achievements. In the North, students participated in the social reform programs of campus Young Women's Christian Associations (YWCAs), the Settlement League, Consumers' League, suffrage clubs, and the Intercollegiate Socialist Society. Southern students also expressed interest in progressive social justice reforms, although more often in church or education-related activities than through suffrage or settlement work.

Women faculty and students argued for the adoption of courses on settlement work, socialism, sociology, and particularly sanitary science, or home economics, which was not always a nuts and bolts subject. Women scientists and social scientists of the Progressive Era, whose research focused on women, children, families, and communities, often became home economics professors, sometimes because they could not get positions in conventional science departments. Women studying home economics usually planned to teach the subject or work in federal and state institutions, as dietitians, food chemists, and county agricultural agents. In the attempt to place women's concerns into the curriculum, sanitary science of the Progressive Era resembles today's women's studies programs.[46]

The demand for home economics courses reflected another common concern of women faculty and students. By the turn of the century, college women found it desirable and necessary to seek jobs outside of elementary and secondary education. Through speakers, articles in campus publications, vocational conferences, job counseling, campus employment bureaus, and alumnae networks, the two generations of college women worked together to create and exploit women's career opportunities. Themes of service or nurturance continued to characterize most jobs considered appropriate for women. Increasingly, however, women took pre-business courses, planned graduate study, or attended professional schools. And the professionalization of such occupations as social work, medicine, and education required a bachelor's degree and postgraduate training.[47]

Women students of the second generation did not spend all their free time soberly pursuing social reform and careers. Yet even their purely recreational activities challenged the boundaries of Victorian gender roles, combining features of both men's and women's spheres in their campus lives. Women students formed and ran self-government associations, voted in campus elections, held mock political campaigns in presidential election years, debated, played basketball or soccer with teams from other schools, and put on plays in which women played men's parts. At women's colleges, students created class traditions: sophomores gently harassed freshmen, and juniors served as "sisters" to freshmen, just as seniors did to sophomores. Designed to initiate newcomers into the community and increase campus privileges as students became upperclasswomen, class activities had been largely the province of men until women's colleges adopted such practices at the turn of the century.

In her analysis of student life at Bryn Mawr College, folklorist Virginia Wolf Briscoe described a year-long cycle of class traditions, practiced since the early twentieth century, incorporating freshmen into the community and bidding farewell to seniors. In Briscoe's view, these class customs are significant, rather than frivolous, helping women find places and status in a public, nondomestic world.

In an elaborate ceremony at the beginning of the school year, freshmen receive lanterns, symbols of wisdom and of the intellectual prestige of women's higher education. Immediately afterward, the fun of Parade Night teaches them to combine work and play at college. During Hell Week, freshmen carry out the silly requests of upperclasswomen. Finally, on Flower Day, freshmen receive flowers and cards, symbolizing their acceptance into the community and completing the cycle. Lanterns at the beginning of the school year signify the entry of Bryn Mawr women into the formerly all-male world of intellect and study. The flowers in the spring show that studying like men need not bar women college students from the more traditional aspects of female lives. After Flower Day, attention turns to the seniors, honored on May Day with gifts, dancing, and awards ceremonies, while they distribute their college possessions to underclasswomen. In this sequence of traditions, seniors are "noticed, given precedence, admired, and finally symbolically excluded from the community." In the final ritual of the year, seniors roll hoops away from the center of campus, toward the world they will soon face.[48]

When Patty Went To College by Jean Webster detailed the lighter side of college life. Written by a Vassar alumna of the class of 1901, the novel had the ring of authenticity, and students called it "realistic" and "clever." The book depicted women students, like their male counterparts, developing a group identity and defying official attempts to control them and subdue

their youthful good spirits. Patty Wyatt's college career consisted of esca-
pades to outsmart teachers who wanted her to study, of evading rules,
playing tricks on friends and underclasswomen, and treating outsiders to
baffling but dazzling displays of Vassar wit. In one such episode Patty met
her visitor in the college parlor, where he sat in the middle of the annual doll
show. Each Christmas, the Vassar Christian Association asked students to
dress dolls as presents for children in the slums. Before sending the dolls off,
the association held a show to benefit the College Settlement Association.
Mr. Todhunter asked Patty about the dolls:

> "I say, Miss Wyatt, do—er—the young ladies spend much time playing with
> dolls?"
> "No," said Patty candidly: "I don't think you could say they spend *too* much.
> I never heard of but one girl actually neglecting her work for it. You mustn't
> think that we have as many dolls as this here every night," she went on. "It is
> rather an unusual occurrence. Once a year the girls hold what they call a doll
> show to see who has dressed her doll the best."
> "Ah, I see," said Mr. Todhunter. "A little friendly rivalry."
> "Purely friendly," said Patty.
> As they started for the dining room, Mr. Todhunter adjusted his monocle
> and took a parting look at the doll show.
> "I'm afraid you think us rather childish, Mr. Todhunter," said Patty.
> "Not at all, Miss Wyatt," he assured her hastily. "I think it's quite charming,
> you know, and so—er—unexpected. I had always been told that they played
> somewhat peculiar games at these women's colleges, but I never suspected they
> did anything so feminine as to play with dolls."

Mr. Todhunter appeared ridiculous not only because he did not recognize that Patty was mocking him but also because he thought of women
students as feminine children who dressed dolls in preparation for lives of
postgraduate domesticity. Any Vassar insider reading the book would find
that presumption especially amusing, given the socially activist nature of
their own Christian Association and of the national College Settlement
Association.

As the book progressed, Patty outgrew her student pranks and learned a
code of communal honor and service. She shammed illness to avoid a test
but confessed to the professor after she realized her high mark on the makeup examination would raise the grade curve, thus hurting her classmates'
standing. She successfully pleaded with the faculty to give Olivia Copeland,
a talented but failing freshman, another chance. When she overcut chapel, a
visiting bishop persuaded her to report herself to the Students' Association,

and she did so, although it cost her the right to chair the Senior Prom Committee.[49]

Women students' activities, organizations, and sometimes their courses thus mirrored the complexities of their lives and their hopes for the future, as they sought to perpetuate the new type of womanhood created by the pioneers. They combined beliefs in female distinctiveness, moral superiority, and the social service imperative with attitudes and activities said to be the province of men—namely, an intellectually rigorous education and political activism. And, with the example of the pioneers before them, Progressive Era college women expressed great interest in postgraduate professional and political activities.

But despite shared projects, social goals, and a common culture, the two generations of women on the college campuses of the Progressive Era discovered important differences between themselves and gradually drew apart. This generation gap began off-campus, in northern and western middle-class homes, with changes in child-rearing practices. Benefiting from a half century of health reform, education, and public discussion of women's rights, girls born after 1880 enjoyed more personal and social freedom and shared more activities with boys, including attendance at coeducational high schools. As they experienced greater closeness with and greater likeness to boys and men, educated women of the second generation found heterosexual intimacy and sexual expressiveness more desirable than had their predecessors.[50]

Less progressive values also led to the new popularity of marriage among educated women. Whatever the social benefits of woman's expanding sphere, many feared a resulting effeminization of American life and institutions because of the entry of women's culture into the public domain. Thus, during the very period when women's progress and influence reached its height, a cultural backlash appeared. Through "muscular Christianity," the Boy Scouts, wild West dime novels, competitive athletics, quotas for female admissions to colleges and graduate schools, and other measures, Americans reasserted the masculinity of their society. Unmarried career women living as female couples or in women's communities seemed particularly threatening, and a negative appraisal of women's homosocial relationships and networks accompanied reactions against women's culture. Modern marriage became the only socially and psychologically correct choice for the college woman.[51]

Finally, Nancy Cott has pointed to the growing individualism among feminists who attended college in the early twentieth century. For these women, the nineteenth-century woman movement with its emphasis on the shared identity and culture of all females, was a less important frame of reference than the equal rights of individuals, regardless of gender, to fulfillment in both their personal and professional lives.[52]

These changes became most evident on college campuses during the 1910s, as women students and faculty sharply disagreed about appropriate clothing, social regulations, and above all, male-female relationships, while continuing to cooperate in political and vocational enterprises. Contemporary charges of frivolity and lack of purpose made against women students of the Progressive Era stemmed from their elders' perception that these young women were entirely too concerned with what men thought of them. For their part, women students began to view their unmarried teachers as unfulfilled or even sexually deviant old maids.

Even earlier than the 1910s, however, the short stories of Progressive Era women college students revealed their hopes and fears. Like the pioneers, they looked forward to lives of purposeful social, civic, and professional activity, bringing women's culture into the public sphere; at the same time, this generation longed for heterosexual romance and marriage. In stories coming from coeducational institutions, the men usually appeared as attractive, superior creatures who knew best what would make women happy, and whose wishes prevailed. In stories written by students at women's colleges, the men were often foolish or unworthy. Regardless of the depiction of male characters, however, the stories rarely had happy endings; usually the female protagonist lost man or job.

In the South, students experienced this transition somewhat differently. White southern college women of the Progressive Era constituted a first generation, struggling to establish some independence from the family claim. Although they acknowledged the need for women's higher education, southern parents tried to minimize its effects. With exceptions like Colonel Breckinridge, most southern families clung to their daughters and to conservative notions of southern womanhood. Short stories by southern college women stressed themes of separation; often a fictional family member became ill or died when the daughter went to college.

Southern women's separate networks, organizations, and cultural influence began only after the Civil War and were less powerful and effective than in the North. Independent spinsterhood and women's communities never became the significant alternatives to traditional families that they were elsewhere in Progressive Era America. By the 1890s a small group of unmarried northern women faculty with impressive professional credentials held positions at southern women's colleges, but their students, while fond of them, did not regard them as role models. In her research on Greenville, North Carolina, and the East Carolina Teachers' Training School during the Progressive Era, Sally Brett found an "estrangement of female professor and female community member." Women professors were, by definition, not southern ladies; as such, their students could not identify with them. Although southern college women expressed interest in graduate study and careers, for the most part they functioned as wives and mothers, looking to married alumnae for guidance on performing the special social obligations of educated womanhood.[53]

Although region played an important part in setting campus trends and agendas, the choice of a single-sex versus coeducational college was, as it had been for the first generation, the most significant predictor of a woman's campus experiences. At Progressive Era coeducational institutions women, excluded from men's student life, created a world of their own and wrestled with the meaning and consequences of separatism as a cultural and political strategy for women's advancement in the modern world.

SEPARATISM AND THE ROAD TO EQUALITY: COEDUCATIONAL CAMPUSES OF THE PROGRESSIVE ERA

With the cooperation of male students, Progressive Era college and university presidents tried to curb violence and rechannel student life. They sought the development of a true university community, appealing to new national middle-class ideals of service, democracy, and self-government. Competition between institutions, usually in athletics or debate, replaced destructive interclass wars on campus. Fraternities took on new importance as organizations in which members of all four classes mingled freely, but they did not dominate college life. Instead, the community ideal became the focus of student activities. Service clubs, YMCAs, and political groups provided alternatives to fraternity life.

Building a progressive campus community seemed to resolve the social problems of coeducation. Beginning in the 1890s, coeducational institutions hired women as deans, physicians, hygiene and physical education instructors, and sometimes faculty. Just as older women had helped the pioneers gain access to higher education, so these new administrators and teachers, mainly first-generation college graduates, improved the second generation's campus experiences. They created important alliances with club women, reformers, suffragists, and alumnae. Their own status as college graduates, often with advanced degrees as well, was the most crucial element in their success, winning them at least the grudging respect of male colleagues. These women helped the second generation on coeducational campuses build a separate structure of social and extracurricular activities, rivaling the men's in number and variety.

The social and extracurricular separatism of Progressive Era college women may be viewed in a number of ways. As Harold Wechsler has wryly observed, "The arrival of a new constituency on a college campus has rarely been an occasion for unmitigated joy." When rich and poor male students coexisted at antebellum colleges, males and females at coeducational universities of the late nineteenth century, Jews and Gentiles in the 1910s and 1920s, and, more recently, whites and blacks, social separation has alleviated fears on both sides of conflict or amalgamation. Women students were not welcome in men's campus organizations; rather than accept exclusion from university life, they formed their own groups. At all times, however, men students dominated coeducational institutions, holding exclusive control over publications, student government, competition with other schools, debate, and campus politics. The growing importance of men's athletics, particularly football, further diminished the status of women on campus.[54]

Although separatism did not constitute equality on campus, anymore than it did elsewhere, it gave coeducated women a power base, drew them together to form a community, connected them with older women on and off campus, helped them to develop leadership skills, and provided forums for discussion of career opportunities. Moreover, separatism calmed fears about the possible negative effects of overly close associations between men and women. Both sexes felt more comfortable with some degree of separation, thereby ratifying Victorian notions about the unique capacities and possibilities of men and women.

Women faculty and administrators promoted and encouraged separation in campus life, not finding it inconsistent with intellectual equality. Lois Kimball Mathews, dean of women and associate professor of history at the University of Wisconsin, had previously taught at Vassar, and wanted coeducational universities to provide women with the same self-assurance promoted at single-sex institutions. Mathews explained her support of women's separate self-government as contributing to female independence and supporting the values of women's culture: "The young men's standard of judging their fellow students among the young women is commonly that of social availability, and that only. Young women judge one another by a quite different measure."[55]

❖

At its best, separatism attempted to put women's values at the center of university life. Even when separatism was solely a response to exclusion, it often developed into a positive force, as women pushed their fellow students and the university to acknowledge that separate should mean complementary, but equal. In the process, many came to a new understanding about their own lives and prospects. During the 1910s, as the off-campus movement for women's rights gathered momentum, culminating in the federal suffrage amendment in 1920, women college students on some campuses openly challenged men's right to shape and dominate campus activity.

In spite of their high ideals and substantial achievements, women's campus communities had serious flaws, especially their exclusion of students from the "wrong" backgrounds. The daughters of farmers and the less well-to-do made up a significant minority of women students at state universities. These women had to work their way through school or live at home while attending college. They had neither the time nor the right clothes to participate in campus activities and were rarely elected to sororities or special honor societies. Jewish, Catholic, and black students, also socially disadvantaged, sometimes had to form their own organizations, or have no stake in campus life.

Faculty behavior further isolated minority women, exacerbating the treatment meted out by their fellow students. When Laura Zametkin (the future Laura Z. Hobson, author of *Gentleman's Agreement*) entered Cornell University in the fall of 1919, she enrolled in a "baby Greek" course. After several months of hearing the instructor address her as "Miss Zamooski," "Miss Zimenky," or "Miss Djimorskey," she decided to speak up. "Professor Jones . . . if we're supposed to pronounce names like Clytemnestra correctly, and Iphigenia, and Agamemnon, and Aeschylus, don't you think you could say Zametkin? It's really quite easy." Zametkin's assertiveness saved her from further embarrassment in Greek class, but she could not prevent what she later described as "the great wound of my youth." Eligible for Phi Beta Kappa, she was denied the key because of the faculty's fear that too many "greasy little grinds from New York" had altered the honor society's "character" in unacceptable ways.[56]

Black women suffered the most from the intolerance of other students and faculty. And the small numbers of black students on northern and western coeducational campuses made it difficult for them to develop alternatives to the white social structure. When Gregoria Fraser entered Syracuse University in 1901 as a music student, the dean told her that dishwashing and scrubbing floors would make her hands unfit for piano practice. After she assured the dean that she had never done such work, the chair of the music department "informed me that ambition was a dangerous thing; some had to be hewers of wood and drawers of water." Fraser found the students equally unwelcoming; only a German man, a Jewish woman, and a Catholic woman, also marginal to campus life, spoke to her.[57]

Then too, the very success of social separatism and its promotion by college women themselves, inspired male administrators and faculty to use it as a precedent for academic separation. The growing numbers of women attending college and their considerable academic achievements alarmed the male educational establishment. After years of coeducation, many universities and colleges considered banning or limiting women's access; others established a separate women's college or segregated classes. As part of the general backlash against women's culture at the turn of the century, concern over possible effeminization of the university and its men, and masculinization of women students created a furor in the popular press as well, rivaling the outcry over Clarke's work in the 1870s and 1880s.[58]

Female faculty had favored social and extracurricular separatism, believing that women brought special gifts to the university and had, in turn, special needs to be fulfilled, but they vehemently opposed classroom segregation. In this respect they resembled women doctors and suffragists; the former felt that gender-specific qualities made them different and better physicians than men but nonetheless wanted coeducated medical schools; the latter argued for equality in political power so that women might bring their unique perspective to the electorate. Women faculty, alumnae, students, club members, suffragists, and reformers believed that classroom separation would erase gains of the past fifty years, during which women had struggled to prove their intellectual and physical fitness for higher education.[59]

Women's successes on the coeducational campuses of the Progressive Era proved their undoing. The numbers of female students rose steadily throughout this period, until, by 1920, they constituted 47.3 percent of American undergraduates; over 90 percent attended coeducational schools. Women's culture influenced student life, and women's campus communities flourished. Inspired by the fear that women were overrunning the campuses of America, dominating the liberal arts courses, and effeminizing higher education, male educators tried to curb this dangerous phenomenon.

Between 1902 and 1915, Wesleyan College banned women students; the University of Rochester, Tufts University, and Western Reserve University set up women's coordinate colleges; and Stanford and Michigan adopted quotas for women's admission. Chicago established separate classes for freshmen and sophomore men and women, while Wisconsin reluctantly decided that it was too costly to do so. On campuses with no formal barriers, educators and male students made it clear that they would not tolerate equality, even the equality of separate, complementary spheres. At some institutions, these restrictions on women lasted until the 1950s or 1960s.[60]

Growing differences between the first and second generations of college women represented a third problem for the cohesion and success of campus women's communities. Older women worried about what they viewed as a lack of educational and professional commitment in the second generation, while students moved away from their women teachers, and toward more intense relationships with men.

The following two chapters describe and analyze women's experiences at Berkeley and Chicago during the Progressive Era. The chronicle of the University of California illustrates the growth of a female community and the resulting empowerment of women students, which eventually led to their demands for equality. At Chicago in the 1890s, women of both generations quickly built such a strong campus life that male faculty and administrators moved decisively in 1902 to weaken its influence with classroom segregation. At both institutions the two generations of college women defined common educational, political, and reform purposes, but the younger women began to assert new personal priorities.

The pioneers had found coeducational universities liberating, but female students discovered, early on, that single sex colleges had many advantages. These advantages, derived from institutional assumptions about the importance of women's intellectual development and faculty commitment to women students, made single-sex schools, especially the eastern women's colleges, the leading national model for women's higher education during the Progressive Era. Women deans, faculty, and students at coeducational institutions consciously patterned their efforts to improve curriculum and extracurriculum on what women were doing at Vassar, Smith, Wellesley, Radcliffe, and Mt. Holyoke, and even at newly founded Barnard and Bryn Mawr (both opened in 1889).

"LITTLE EDENS OF LIBERTY": WOMEN'S COLLEGES OF THE PROGRESSIVE ERA

The Progressive Era brought recognition, expansion, and important changes to the eastern women's colleges. Freed from the need of members of the first generation to prove themselves, and aided by extraordinary women faculty and alumnae with graduate degrees from distinguished European and American institutions, second-generation students created a fascinating and intricate campus life. While popular literature continued to tout women's colleges as havens for the preservation of femininity, Progressive Era college life at the Seven Sisters schools offered women all the opportunities available to college men elsewhere. Self-government associations, athletics, and campus organizations flourished. The curriculum expanded to include courses in sociology, socialism, economics, and other topics with social relevance. Using faculty and alumnae as resources, students explored career and service options other than teaching. In 1912 graduates of women's schools in the East founded the Intercollegiate Bureau of Occupations in New York City. Social reform and political activity, including woman suffrage, became important features of campus life.[61]

Eastern women's colleges also served as the prototypes for a new form of women's higher education. Because reaction against coeducation during the Progressive Era made life at some universities difficult for women, some proposed "coordination," that is, the creation of women's colleges within universities. By linking a women's undergraduate college to a men's college or university, coordinate institutions represented a compromise between single-sex education and coeducation. Proponents of coordination argued that women students thereby received the advantages of both systems, but in fact the specifics of coordination varied widely. Barnard and Sophie Newcomb functioned largely as independent women's colleges with their own faculty, endowment, and campus. The women of Barnard and Newcomb fought to enhance their schools' standards and prestige. They used their endowment as leverage to gain access to the resources of Columbia and Tulane, while successfully protecting themselves against administrative interference from the universities.

In other cases, however, coordination simply excluded women, without offering them any advantages. Some coordinate colleges were founded and promoted by Progressive Era male educators eager to rid their universities of women's effeminizing presence. In 1900 the University of Rochester's new president, Rush Rhees, was dismayed to find himself at the helm of a coeducational university, following the successful campaign for women's admission. As English professor John R. Slater, Rhees' biographer, put it, Rhees determined to do his duty. "That he endured it," said Slater, "showed his patience and power of detachment, . . . for the women's mere presence in the crowded rooms and corridors conduced in the minds of some hostile critics to a high school atmosphere and hindered both study and college spirit." Male students at Rochester were equally unwelcoming, banging their feet loudly when a woman entered the classroom or slamming doors in her face. They sneered openly and formed crowds in front of campus buildings, forcing women to elbow their way through to get to their classes.

Rhees initiated a movement to replace coeducation with coordination and in 1912 threatened to accept the presidency of Amherst College unless the Rochester trustees agreed to his plan. In 1913 the Women's College of the University of Rochester opened its doors, with separate classes and social activities for female students. The situation quickly deteriorated as fewer resources were allocated to women students each year. When the men's college, graduate schools, and medical center moved to the new River Campus in the 1930s, women students had difficulty arranging access to advanced classes and libraries. The university did not reunite its undergraduate colleges until 1955.[62]

During the Progressive Era, the eastern women's colleges continued to be socioeconomically and ethnically homogeneous communities, admitting a few minority women but resisting significant diversification of the student body. College officials rarely discriminated openly; instead, they argued that applicants of a certain type would feel more "comfortable" elsewhere. In 1900 James Monroe Taylor, Vassar's president, explained to Harriet Giles, principal of Spelman Seminary, that he did not personally oppose admitting "colored girls" to the college but that white southern Vassar students would object, making normal campus life strained or impossible. Taylor told Giles that if a black woman applied to Vassar he would raise the matter with the trustees, but his lack of enthusiasm made such applications unlikely. Similarly, when Frances W. Williams sought admission to Mount Holyoke College in 1915, administrators told her mother that the academically talented young black woman would be happier at a different institution. Mrs. Williams, a Berea College graduate, replied: "Frances's happiness is none of your business; that's my business. I want to know if you will admit her." Holyoke did accept Frances Williams, who graduated Phi Beta Kappa four years later.[63]

In contrast, Wellesley continued to welcome a small number of black students, as it had during Alice Freeman's presidency, and supported their rights as members of the college community. Virginia Foster Durr, a white student from Birmingham, Alabama, who attended Wellesley from 1921 to 1923, enjoyed getting to know other southern students from Harvard and

Wellesley and joined the Southern Club to attend its dances. On the first night of her sophomore year, Durr saw a "Negro girl" sitting at her assigned table in the dining room. She promptly walked out and told the head of her house that she could not possibly eat with a Negro. The head crisply informed Durr that she could either abide by the rules of Wellesley College or withdraw from the institution. After much soul-searching, Durr decided that "if nobody told Daddy, it might be all right." She ate with her black tablemate and discovered that they shared certain southern tastes and distastes. Many years later, Durr, by then a committed civil rights activist, wrote: "That was the first time I became aware that my attitude was considered foolish by some people, and that Wellesley College wasn't going to stand for it. That experience had a tremendous effect on me." Wellesley became noted for accepting not only black but also Asian students and for insisting that they be well treated.[64]

Wellesley's record on the admission and treatment of Jewish women was less exemplary, possibly because their presence on campus challenged the opportunity to exercise the college's Christian missionary spirit. Like men's colleges and coeducational universities, the eastern women's colleges faced a "Jewish problem" from the 1910s until after World War II. The Ivy League and Seven Sisters colleges in particular felt that having too many Jewish students lowered the social prestige of their institutions. As with blacks, administrators did not like to speak openly about discrimination and restrictions. At Barnard College, whose New York City location and Jewish trustees prompted many applications from Jewish women, Dean Virginia Crocheron Gildersleeve (1911–47) denied that the college employed admissions quotas. However, Barnard's more subtle policies of "geographic diversity" and psychological testing effectively limited Jewish enrollment.[65]

Jewish women who did enroll at Seven Sisters colleges generally received courteous but aloof treatment. Ruth Sapinsky Hurwitz '10 praised Wellesley's commitment to intellectual, aesthetic, and altruistic values. While some girls, she said, came to college for fun and to pass the time before marriage, the majority were "training for some kind of service." Hurwitz immersed herself in the study of English literature, paying particular attention to the Victorians. Her interest in writing, developed through creative writing courses, blossomed into the publication of a prize-winning story in the *New England Magazine*. Under the influence of Professors Vida Dutton Scudder and Emily Greene Balch she volunteered for settlement work, relinquishing cultural and recreational excursions to Boston to do so, since she could not afford travel to the city oftener than once a week. She was "fascinated by the little Syrian and Italian girls I taught, and by the first-hand contact with problems of child welfare, housing and health." Not limiting herself to intellect and altruism, Hurwitz also attended dances at Temple Emanu-El in Boston, worked on the *Wellesley Magazine,* played basketball, participated in the class operetta and Tree Day dancing, and sang in the Glee Club.

A midwesterner from a progressive family, Sapinsky did not find Wellesley's Christian character offensive. She enjoyed the required Old and New Testament courses and found chapel services beautiful. She defended Wellesley when her Harvard friends told her about quotas at other colleges and the growing resistance to Jewish presence in the universities and the professions. Still, she acknowledged that Wellesley's Jewish women were not elected to important offices in student organizations or admitted to the secret societies; nor were they often invited to visit the homes of non-Jewish students. Stung by her growing awareness of Ivy League anti-Semitism, Sapinsky began to meet with Harvard students for discussions of Jewish life and issues and eventually married one of the participants, Henry Hurwitz, founder of the Menorah Society.[66]

Generational differences between the pioneers and women of the Progressive Era first appeared at the eastern women's colleges in the 1890s, as students sought increased opportunities to entertain young men on campus. During that decade the colleges began allowing students to dance with their male prom guests, instead of merely "promenading" with them up and down the college corridors. Students' growing interest in heterosexual relationships eventually created distinctions and distance between them and the women faculty, especially in the 1910s, when weekending at men's colleges became popular, thus modifying the close residential nature of Seven Sisters schools.

Founded mostly between 1880 and 1900, and modeled on the successful and prominent eastern women's schools, colleges for white southern women nevertheless had a distinctive atmosphere and followed a different timetable of educational development. In the South, the later founding of women's colleges and the shortage of good secondary education meant that academic standards remained an issue into the twentieth century.

Graduates of southern women's colleges before the 1920s often found it necessary to get a second bachelor's degree, from a northern college, before undertaking master's or doctoral work. In spite of her B.A. from Statesville Female College in North Carolina in 1889, Elizabeth Avery Colton could not be admitted to the freshman class at Mount Holyoke Seminary without a year of preparatory study. She subsequently chaired the English department at Meredith College in Raleigh, North Carolina, and founded the Southern Association of College Women (SACW) in 1903, which worked to raise academic standards in southern women's colleges. She surveyed southern colleges, normal schools, and seminaries for white women, publishing her evaluations in a series of bulletins between 1911 and 1916. The SACW did not achieve its major goal of obtaining state legislation to set minimum standards for chartering colleges, but did draw regional and national attention to the issues and influence curricular development. In 1921 the SACW merged with the northern Association of Collegiate Alumnae to form a new national organization, the American Association of University Women (AAUW).[67]

Formal denominational ties and required religious observances characterized southern women's colleges long after the Seven Sisters schools dropped such practices to identify themselves as secular institutions. Similarly, as Seven Sisters students and faculty successfully battled for relaxation of seminary-type rules, southern colleges maintained and even increased such regulations. In her study of campus life of the 1920s and 1930s at Hollins, Queens, Salem, Sweet Briar, and Wesleyan Colleges, Amy Thompson Mc-Candless found numerous social restrictions governing on- and off-campus behavior. In the 1920s, southern colleges warned students to avoid "extravagance and freakishness" in dress and not to wear jewelry. Drinking, smoking, and dancing were taboo, and chaperonage required. Queens College closed its campus to all visitors on Sundays, chaining the entrance and posting a sign proclaiming "Sabbath Day. No Admittance."[68]

Like Seven Sisters students, southern college women had homogeneous socioeconomic backgrounds. In her study of Wesleyan Female College and Randolph-Macon Women's College between 1893 and 1907, Gail Apperson Kilman called students "daughters of the New South." Wesleyan and Randolph-Macon students came from families in which fathers were involved in commerce or manufacturing (30.5 percent at Wesleyan, 24.8 percent at Randolph-Macon) or the learned professions (24.3 percent at Wesleyan and 30.3 percent at Randolph-Macon), or were white-collar workers (9.3 percent at Wesleyan and 10.2 percent at Randolph-Macon). Only 18.5 percent of the Wesleyan students and 13.3 percent of the Randolph-Macon students came from farming families; they were most likely the children of planters. Fewer non-Protestant women lived in the South than in the North. Thus, southern women's colleges never had many applications from Jewish and Catholic students, although they seem to have admitted those who did apply. The charters of these institutions explicitly limited them to "white women"; no racial integration occurred at southern women's colleges before the 1960s.[69]

Internally cohesive as these white women's colleges were, external ties hindered the growth of campus life. Parents wanted their daughters to become self-supporting but also expected them to retain close family loyalties. Throughout the Progressive Era southern educators strongly encouraged students to focus their attention on studies and campus life instead of on home duties and social obligations. These efforts were, for the most part, successful; between 1900 and 1910, southern women's colleges formed student governments, campus publications, debate teams, dramatics groups, and active alumnae associations.

During the Progressive Era students in the South constituted a first, not a second, generation, and as such had fewer opportunities to call on the support and advice of older college women. By the first decade of the twentieth century, the faculties of the best colleges included some northern-educated pioneer college graduates, although students did not develop a strong identification with these women. Given southern conservatism, it is hardly surprising that women's colleges of that region did not have the close ties to urban progressivism or the interest in women's politics that we find at the eastern schools. Yet, self-conscious about their status as educated women, southern college students explored avenues to make their mark on society, particularly through civic and religious activism. By the end of the Progressive Era, students had begun to demonstrate more interest in careers and in progressive social reform.

The following chapters examine the evolution of campus life at Vassar, Sophie Newcomb, and Agnes Scott Colleges. Common themes united these institutions, most notably the determination to make women's higher education the intellectual equivalent of the best available to men. All three began with preparatory departments and evolved into liberal arts colleges— Vassar in the 1890s, Newcomb and Agnes Scott by the 1910s. Founders and administrators proclaimed the most traditional purposes for educating women, namely the enhancement of domesticity, but students, faculty, and alumnae at all three schools shaped institutional purposes for their own ends, creating a rich campus life combining aspects of men's and women's spheres.

Differences among the colleges reflect varied regional and local societies. Social-justice progressivism, suffragism, interest in careers, and the closeness of students and faculty marked Vassar College during the Progressive Era. Working together, the two generations of college women utilized "men's" privileges but modified them to fit the imperatives of women's culture. Women students enjoyed the fun of competition, whether in hockey, debate, or class elections, but, with faculty assistance, tried to control its effects on friendships and community cohesion. They sought information on new professional careers opening up to women, such as law and business, but also looked for ways to implement social reform ideals. Conflicts over the role and conduct of heterosocial relationships did not prevent the two generations of college women from cooperating in political and reform projects.

Compared to their sisters at Vassar, students of Agnes Scott and Sophie Newcomb had fewer ties to faculty, less enthusiasm for careers, and little interest in suffrage. Yet the two southern schools also differed from each other. As an urban, nonsectarian, and nonresidential college associated with southern women progressives, Newcomb contrasted with Agnes Scott's Presbyterian character, more isolated residential life, and student interest in religiously based social service.

At the turn of the century, single-sex colleges allowed women the luxury of exploring curricular and extracurricular options without encountering, on their own campuses, the objections and resistance of men. However, even the dignity of a separate institution did not command equality for women outside its gates. When Vassar women, for example, challenged Princeton students to a debate, the invitation drew anger and outrage from the men, who did not consider the two colleges equal. Like coeducated women, women's college students found separatism an essential prerequisite, but not a guarantee, of gender equality in American society.

CHAPTER TWO

Women at the University
of California, 1870–1920:
From Pelicans to Chickens

In 1869, funds provided by the Morrill Act permitted the all-male liberal arts College of California (founded in 1855) and the Agriculture, Mining, and Mechanical Arts College (1866) to merge and become the University of California. Until the establishment of a second branch in Los Angeles in 1919, the northern university, located first at Oakland and then at Berkeley, was the only state-supported campus in California. Women had occasionally attended lectures at the College of California as special students but had never received degrees. Nevertheless, apparently without incident or comment, the Board of Regents resolved on October 3, 1870, that "young ladies be admitted into the university on equal terms in all respects with young men." Eight women registered for classes in 1870, forming 9 percent of the total enrollment. Ten years later, Berkeley had 241 undergraduates, of whom 62 (25 percent) were female. By 1893–94, women made up almost one third of the 751-member student body; and by 1900, 46 percent.[1]

The first generation of women students—the group that attended between 1870 and 1890—lived in isolation from each other and from the university community. During the Progressive Era, under the direction of older women benefactors, faculty, and administrators, California women made a place for themselves on campus, forming a separate and distinctive community. United in their own organizations, "the women of the university" maintained an uneasy, unequal, and frequently discussed balance of power with male students. Ultimately, women students used their separate power base to challenge men for control of the Berkeley campus and to demand a redefinition of gender roles.

THE EARLY DAYS: CLASS AND GENDER AT THE UNIVERSITY OF CALIFORNIA, 1870–1890

Berkeley's male students built their campus life around a structure of class traditions and interclass rivalry. Men were initiated, sometimes violently, into college rites as freshmen, gaining status and privileges with each year they spent at the university. Class members wore distinctive headgear for easy recognition: soft blue porkpie hats for freshmen; gray-checked caps for sophomores; gray top hats, or "plugs," for juniors; black for seniors. Freshmen could not use certain parts of the campus—benches, stairs, walks—and spoke to upperclassmen only when spoken to first. The sophomores acted as policemen, enforcing the codes restricting freshmen and also hazing, harassing and playing jokes on the unfortunate newcomers. Juniors, as the "brother class" of the freshmen, encouraged them to defy the sophomores, by force if necessary. The seniors, "brothers" to the sophomores, urged them to make outrageous demands of the freshmen. Tensions between freshmen and sophomores broke out into "rushes," or fights, some formally scheduled, others spontaneous. During a rush, each class tried to subdue and tie up members of the other class.[2]

Another kind of "class" also determined campus status. Statistics sporadically collected by administrators show that approximately half the students came from families of professionals and businessmen; the other half had fathers who farmed or worked in the mines, reflecting the merger of the liberal arts college with the agriculture and mining school. In *For the Blue and Gold,* a novel about Berkeley in the early days, author Joy Lichtenstein described the freshman year of James Rawson, a student from a small town in California. Sophomores gave him inaccurate directions to campus when he arrived at the Berkeley railroad station and tricked all the freshmen into lining up "to be measured for uniforms." Exhorted to get even by the juniors, the freshmen organized, electing Rawson rush chairman. They lost the rush, but Rawson so distinguished himself in the melee that his friends urged him to go out for football. Athletic success, and continued defiance of the sophomores, won Rawson election as class president. In his "finest hour" Rawson helped the freshmen win the Bourdon-Minto rush. Freshmen traditionally buried their Bourdons and Mintos (first-year algebra and composition textbooks) during the spring, signifying the end of their year as probationary college men. Sophomores watched carefully for any signs of the ceremony and halted it if they could. The Bourdon and Minto success assured Rawson's status as a big man on campus for his remaining three years.[3]

Lichtenstein repeatedly contrasted his hero's humble origins with the backgrounds of his wealthy, privately educated opponents, who dominated the fraternities. At least in novels, life at Berkeley provided opportunities for men like Rawson to achieve campus prominence. Class organizations and activities counteracted, for some, the influence of socially exclusive fraternities. Berkeley men developed an "old boy" network depending on strength, manliness, character, and loyalty to class.[4]

In contrast, class activities for women were limited to an occasional vice presidency or membership on dance and commencement committees. Although the men wore distinctive hats that identified the classes and set them apart from noncollege students, women wore conventional hats and gloves in public, to demonstrate their status as "ladies," whose appearance did not betray their roles as college women.

The physical nature of class competitions made it difficult for women to participate. Women watched rushes and football games from the sidelines. At class or athletic rallies the men cheered, sang, and demonstrated while the women students mingled in the crowd with other outsiders. They voted in class elections, but men considered them easy to fool. Rawson's friends assured him that his good looks would capture the votes of women students.

The university administration did not offer much support to women students. Until the turn of the century, Berkeley women had no athletic program, no facilities for social and cultural events, and no rooms for club meetings. Berkeley did not build dormitories for either sex until the 1920s, but women faced greater obstacles finding housing close to the university. Men formed chapters of national fraternities, banded together in residence clubs, and more easily persuaded parents to let them live in the "mixed" boardinghouses surrounding the school. Berkeley had no sororities or women's residence clubs until the 1890s, and ultimately fewer of each than did men. Unsure about the social standing and reputation of women college students, boardinghouse keepers often preferred to rent exclusively to men. Long after most men lived on campus, many women students still traveled to their classes every day, although families sometimes moved to Berkeley so their children would not have to make the difficult daily commute across the bay. Thus, males more easily found living quarters where they could associate with their classmates, develop mutual interests, and participate in common activities.[5]

The lack of social and extracurricular structures for women accentuated social class differences among them. James Rawson bridged the gap between men by leading rushes and playing football, but women had no such options. In a revealing scene from *For the Blue and Gold,* Rawson commiserated with fellow student Harriet Gray about the women's lack of social life: "But you women haven't the chance for outside activity that men have. You can't go in for rushes and Bourdons, nor play football, nor go out at nights." Gray replied: "But there are many things we could do to make life more cheerful . . . if we'd be to one another like men are. Women make it so hard for their sex.'

Berkeley's early classes produced some nationally prominent women, such as Milicent Washburn Shinn '80, who edited the *Overland Monthly,* a regional literary journal, for fourteen years. In 1898, Shinn became the eleventh person and first woman to receive a Ph.D. from the university. She published articles on child development, establishing an international reputation for her scholarly work, and held offices in suffrage organizations and in the Association of Collegiate Alumnae. Shinn never married and spent the last forty years of her life caring for her ailing mother, tending the family farm and finances, and nurturing her brothers and their children.[6]

It is impossible to say how representative Shinn was of Berkeley's first generation. But whatever the postgraduate accomplishments of Milicent Shinn and others like her, female students at Berkeley sparked no interest in the faculty or community, had no access to the main currents of student life, and did not, during the first generation, create a strong campus presence.

GENERATIONS WORKING TOGETHER: CREATING A WOMEN'S COMMUNITY AT BERKELEY, 1890–1920

Beginning in the 1890s, California college students, influenced by Progressive Era ideals of service chose activities benefiting the university community over class traditions, hazing of freshmen, and rushes. The most highly coveted campus distinction became election to an honor society, open to seniors who had served the university through athletics, debate, student government, student-faculty committees, philanthropic work, dramatic or musical achievement. Violence and pranks did not disappear, but students redirected aggression away from their own campus and toward the university's arch rival, Stanford. Fraternities took over freshmen initiation, confining it to the first semester. Freshmen and sophomores officially "buried" the rushes in 1905, building a concrete "Big C" at the top of one of Berkeley's hills to symbolize university unity. By 1911 distinctive class dress disappeared; all men wore "cords" (dirty corduroy pants). Even before then, however, the *Blue and Gold* hailed a new "corporate spirit involving loyalty, service, self-sacrifice, and reaching outward far beyond the pale of the University. It is as wide as humanity, for as a University we know nothing of political divisions or of role, or status, or sex."[7]

President Benjamin Ide Wheeler (1899–1919) encouraged the development of community. He believed in student self-government as preparation for life in a democracy, urged seniors to assume leadership roles, and consulted them frequently on university policy. One month after his inauguration, the faculty disciplined senior football player Jim Whipple, ordering him not to play in the "Big Game" against Stanford. Worried about his team's fate, Whipple played anyway. The faculty wanted to expel Whipple, but Wheeler instituted "senior control" over the case, asking senior men to help him arrive at a just solution. Together, the president and the seniors decided to award Whipple his degree, after a semester's suspension. Thereafter, senior men held regular meetings in a special senior men's building and set up a Student Affairs Committee to handle disciplinary matters.[8]

The new style of student life, begun before Wheeler's arrival, offered women more possibilities for participation than the rowdier pre-1890 era. Women as well as men could serve the university. They did so at Berkeley in their own organizations, with the indispensable support of older women. The generosity, concern, and leadership of Phoebe Apperson Hearst (1842–1919), first woman regent of the University of California, sparked the beginnings of increased activity among the women students. A Missouri schoolteacher before her marriage to future senator and millionaire George Hearst, Phoebe Hearst maintained a lifelong interest in education and had a productive career as an educational philanthropist. Her gifts to the university included sponsorship of a contest to select a comprehensive architectural plan for the campus, and funds for faculty salaries, research, biology laboratories, and the Hearst Memorial Mining Building. She is best remembered, however, for her impact on the lives of Berkeley women.

In 1891, after her husband's death, Hearst donated eight $300 scholarships for women, later increasing the number to twelve. Because students paid no tuition fees in those days, the scholarships covered living expenses and books. She invited women to teas, parties, and receptions at her Berkeley home, and sponsored European research for graduate students. In 1900 she donated the entertainment pavilion of her house to the women for a student center. The top floor of this building, named Hearst Hall, became a gymnasium so that women could at last have physical education classes; the remaining space was used for club meetings, social functions, storage for athletic equipment, and a women's lunchroom offering free tea. Later she donated additional funds for a women's outdoor basketball court and a swimming pool.[9]

Hearst's contributions and their impact on women students went beyond money; she also took a personal interest in their lives, meeting and corresponding with them and their parents. She requested information on how each woman financed her education, discovering their need for respectable part-time employment. Women who needed to earn their way through the university worked as household help for Berkeley families, encountering all the problems faced by working class and immigrant women who spent their lives as domestic servants. Those who managed to do the work, attend classes, and study had few connections to university life. Establishment of the Hearst Domestic Industries (HDI), in which college students earned money by sewing, alleviated the financial distress of some of the poorest women students and enabled them to feel part of the campus community. As Adeline Grace Smith noted, in a letter to Hearst, she worked at HDI a fixed number of hours per day, instead of "until the housework was finished." She could now attend church on Sundays and participate in some college activities. She no longer had to stay up late at night cleaning the kitchen after dinner, without time to do her personal laundry and make herself presentable for class the next day. Hearst also tried to ensure that HDI students would take some pleasure in their college days. She sent gloves and flowers to them, invited them to receptions at her home, and arranged for someone to read to them while they sewed.[10]

Other students received Hearst's attention as well. Christine Labarraque, a blind law student, wrote to thank her for the opportunity to continue in school. In addition Hearst paid the medical expenses to have Bessie Sessions's sight restored, sent Ella Castillo Bennett to a suffrage convention, supported Jeanette Shafer's graduate studies in social work at the University of Chicago, and helped launch the architectural career of Julia Morgan. At the request of Milicent Shinn, she met and talked with a young woman considering an imprudent (according to Shinn) marriage, and encouraged her to finish college instead. Alumnae recalled getting advice from Hearst about hairstyles and clothing; and on an unexpectedly wet day, she sent umbrellas to students attending a YWCA convention.[11]

Phoebe Hearst became the leader of a group of older women seeking to improve the lot of Berkeley's female students. In 1897, she was appointed to the Board of Regents. Although her letter of acceptance was appropriately deferential—"I trust that you will never have cause, through any lack of judgment in my official relations to the Board of Regents, to regret making the courageous departure of appointing a woman"—her social prestige, wealth, and example prodded the regents and the university administration to action. The California chapter of the Association of Collegiate Alumnae (ACA) rejoiced in her selection. As alumna May Treat Morrison told her: "The ACA has hoped for years for a woman regent. . . . The woman of their choice happens to be the governor's choice as well."[12]

Hearst's appointment also encouraged women students to urge the hiring of female faculty and staff. Katharine C. Felton '95, later an instructor in social work at the university, complained about this issue in the campus newspaper:

> For twenty-five years, the University of California has graduated women, many of whom have shown themselves eager and able to pursue the academic life. . . . The opportunity has been denied them. No woman has ever been appointed on the Faculty, and but one has been made a "fellow". . . . There is nothing so galling to a woman, so paralyzing to her effort, as to know that her capacity or incapacity is not taken into consideration, but that she is shut out from an intellectual field, merely because she is a woman. . . . The presence of women in the Faculty would be of inestimable benefit to the students, especially to the girl students. . . . They feel the need of someone whom they can consult freely and unhesitatingly. . . . Had women representation in the Faculty, a harmonious and fit relationship would be established between college men and women."[13]

The administration resisted naming female faculty, but had long agreed that women students needed a dean, and better physical facilities. In 1890, President Horace Davis unsuccessfully sought funds from the regents to provide women students with their own building containing "appropriate study and reception rooms." And in 1898, emboldened by Hearst's presence on the board, President Martin Kellogg argued:

> From thirty-five to forty per cent of the students at Berkeley are young women. Heretofore the policy of the Board has been to appoint no women to the teaching staff. Since the coming of Mrs. Hearst onto the Board of Regents, the question has often been asked, why not allow women a representation on

the Faculty? Without suggesting what the answer should be on broad lines, it does seem fitting that there should be a Dean for the young women of the University; an educated woman of such reputation, wisdom, and sympathetic personality as would make her a trusted counselor and guide. She should be able to teach, but teaching should be much the less important side of her work.[14]

In 1898, the regents permitted Phoebe Hearst to fund the part-time appointment of Dr. Mary Bennett Ritter as physician to women students and lecturer in hygiene. Since 1891 Ritter had volunteered to examine women students and provide them with certificates of fitness so that they could use the gymnasium. The students could not afford to pay her for the examinations, and the university would not do so, but Ritter donated her services, despite a busy private practice. As a part-time faculty member with a salary, she also taught a hygiene course, kept regular office hours for students, and found herself called upon to be an unofficial dean of women. A very popular dean, Ritter handled student problems with tact and dispatch, winning confidences from students and townspeople. She recalled:

On a few occasions, hasty marriages were arranged after too ardent love-making, but the standard of morality was very high. . . . The few cases which came under my care were those of young people, weak, perhaps, but not evil. One was a freshman boy, boarding in a family in which there was a young high school girl. One day this girl came to my office for an examination. After making the examination my first question was, "Have you a lover?" "Yes," she faltered. "Bring your mother to me tomorrow." The mother admitted she had been culpable in leaving the young people alone after she had retired. Both were under legal age. Consent of the parents to their marriage was obtained. A quiet wedding occurred in Mill Valley and the boy forfeited his college education.[15]

Phoebe Hearst paid Ritter's expenses to visit the eastern women's colleges, Cornell, the University of Chicago, and Wisconsin to study their dormitory systems. When Ritter returned in the summer of 1900, she persuaded Hearst to furnish women's club houses to be run like the Smith College cottage system, which provided respectable, attractive housing for women, without the social elitism of sororities. That autumn the Pie del Monte and Enewah clubs opened, with fifteen women students and a housemother residing in each. The California State Federation of Women's Clubs financed a third cottage. Eventually Hearst, Ritter, and male faculty formed a Club House Loan Fund Committee. Students of either gender could borrow from the committee to start a club, gradually paying the money back. Once paid for, the club might continue as a cooperative or reorganize as a fraternity or sorority chapter. By 1910, men students had twenty-three fraternities and nineteen clubs; women had nine sororities and twenty-three clubs.[16]

Encouraged by Hearst's and Ritter's efforts on their behalf, female students expanded their social and extracurricular life, with organizations and activities duplicating and paralleling those of the men students. They began by forming the Associated Women Students (AWS) in 1894. In 1887 men organized an all-campus student government, the Associated Students of the University of California (ASUC, still in existence today), but women, although members, felt that ASUC did not meet their needs. In founding AWS they also hoped that the new organizational structure, unlike the sororities, would draw Berkeley women together, regardless of social class. As the male-oriented student newspaper condescendingly suggested: "That the women of the University are misunderstood; that they misunderstand each other; that they are altogether too far from the Faculty wives just as the men are too far from the Professors; that many of them know little college spirit . . . are all considerations of importance . . . that should urge the women of the University to support the organization of their forces in such a way as will open roads to the improvement of conditions."[17]

Slow to begin, AWS had three committees, whose functions demonstrated the limited nature of women's campus life: a Ladies' Room Committee, a Lunchroom Committee, and a Lost and Found Committee. Eventually, AWS sponsored and supervised separate women's cubs—the Sports and Pastimes Association, all-female debating societies, women's drama and music groups, the YWCA—and selected candidates for the women's editorships on campus publications. Academic clubs also appeared: the XYZ Club, for women interested in higher mathematics, and the Chemistry Fiends. The Fiends' activities shed light on women's discomfort in certain fields dominated by men. To help women feel at ease, they brought domesticity to the chemistry building, making fudge and coffee over the Bunsen burners. In February of every year AWS sponsored "Woman's Day," during which female students took over the campus, holding athletic contests, a fair, a dance, and producing women's editions of the newspaper and literary magazine. Pleased with President Wheeler's ideas about senior control and student self-government, AWS found ways for women to manage their own relations with the university. Its leaders petitioned successfully for a Women's Student Affairs Committee, claiming it was improper for men to hear cases involving women. Senior women raised money for a senior women's building, Girton Hall.

In 1901 AWS president Agnes Frisius and senior Adele Lewis asked Dr. Ritter to help them establish an honor society comparable to the men's Order of the Golden Bear and Skull and Keys. The Prytaneans, as the new organization called itself, elected to membership women who had performed notable service to the university. Sorority and clubhouse presidents and the executive officer of every women's club automatically became members. Women could also be elected to the Prytaneans through outstanding work in the YWCA, the West Berkeley Settlement House, or athletics, music, and drama. The Prytaneans served as a link among the faculty, administration, and women students. The group held festivals, masques, plays, and parties to raise money for a student infirmary, a women's dormitory, the senior women's building, and the establishment of home economics courses. Membership in the Prytaneans became the most coveted honor for a woman student. Extraordinarily proud of their achievements, graduates continued their association with the university and its women students, and in 1936 organized the Prytanean Alumnae Association.

The appearance in the 1890s of four sororities—Kappa Alpha Theta, Gamma Phi Beta, Kappa Kappa Gamma, and Delta Delta Delta—had exacerbated social class distinctions by shutting out those whose social status or ethnicity did not qualify them for membership. Often, sorority members came from the same secondary school and had been chosen as pledges before their matriculation at the university. The new extracurricular structure increased social opportunities outside the sorority system. After the advent of AWS, however, women shut out of sororities could participate in university life through club and service work. To prevent a clique from monopolizing campus offices, AWS started a point system. The AWS presidency was worth ten points; the YWCA or Prytanean presidency, eight points; mass meeting chair, swimming manager and Newman Club vice presidency, six points, and so on. No AWS member could hold offices totaling more than ten points.[18]

In 1904, Phoebe Hearst told Ritter that she would no longer pay her salary. Whatever the reasons for her decision, they were not personal, because the two women continued to exchange friendly letters. Ritter at first agreed to work without salary until a replacement could be found, although she felt that the position should be funded by the university as a necessary resource for women students. In August, however, following a serious carriage accident, she wrote to Hearst that she could no longer forego the salary. Ritter asked President Wheeler to fund the position, but he refused, saying that Dr. Reinhardt, the men's physician, could take over her work.

Upset by the interview, Ritter hoped women students and alumnae would protest attempts to hire a man for her position.[19]

Following Ritter's resignation in autumn 1904, Hearst and the ACA tried to persuade Wheeler and the regents to appoint women faculty, "thus making the University of California co-educational both in name and in deed." Charlotte Anita Whitney (Wellesley '89), president of the local chapter of the Association of Collegiate Alumnae, was particularly disturbed about the cancellation of the hygiene course, the only curricular offering related to women and the home. The ACA committee formed to deal with the situation recommended to Wheeler that a woman be put in charge of Ritter's work, that she be measured by the highest academic standards and have strong enthusiasm for the work and its significance for women. "The fact that one third of the student body of the University of California is women," wrote Whitney, "and that these students are without a voting member of the faculty to represent them is sufficient explanation of the second condition."[20]

Hearst and the ACA had correctly foreseen that further recognition of women students depended on support by women inside the university structure—professional academics with impeccable credentials, rather than benevolent ladies. In 1904 Jessica Peixotto became Berkeley's first woman faculty member, and in 1906 Wheeler named Lucy Sprague dean of women. No direct evidence links Phoebe Hearst and the ACA to these appointments, but they undoubtedly created an atmosphere making them possible. And it would have been difficult for Wheeler to ignore Hearst's many and continuing gifts to the university; between 1900 and 1902, for example, her contributions totaled $203,000.[21]

Sprague and Peixotto shared the difficult experience of being the first academic women on campus; they were friends, housemates, and co-workers for women students. Both college graduates, they understood, as Hearst could not, the problems and possibilities of women's higher education. As members of the English and economics departments, respectively, neither attended faculty meetings. "Certainly we could have gone," Sprague said, "but I know that it would have prejudiced the men against us, and we already had enough prejudice to live down."

Daughter of a Portuguese Jewish merchant in San Francisco, Jessica Blanche Peixotto '95 entered the university at the age of thirty-one, over her family's opposition. A brilliant student, she received the second doctorate awarded by Berkeley to a woman in 1900. She became the university's first female faculty member as an instructor in political economy in 1904 and its first female full professor in 1918. Peixotto taught courses in contemporary socialism, poverty, the child and the state, crime as a social problem, and the household as an economic agent. As a member of the State Board of Charities and Corrections, she supervised California's juvenile penal system. In 1917 she developed a nationally recognized program for training war workers, which became the foundation for Berkeley's graduate school of social welfare.[22]

Peixotto brought the study of domestic science and social work to Berkeley, but it was Sprague, as dean of women, who had the greatest impact on the daily lives of students. Born in 1878 to a wealthy Chicago family, Lucy Sprague grew up during an exciting period in the city's history. Her father's money and social position enabled her to enjoy Chicago's cultural resources and to meet people like Jane Addams, whom she very much admired. Her family also knew and entertained faculty from the new University of Chicago; her sister Mary married economics professor Adolph Miller. Most important for Lucy's future, the Spragues became friendly with George Herbert Palmer, Harvard philosophy professor, and his wife, Alice Freeman Palmer, former president of Wellesley College and dean of women at Chicago. When Lucy reached eighteen, she wanted to go to college, but her parents' poor health and overprotectiveness kept her at home. The Palmers learned of the situation through Mary Miller and invited Lucy to live with them while she attended Radcliffe.

Existing on the fringes of the Harvard community, without its own faculty, Radcliffe lacked the social life of the other eastern women's colleges, and Sprague, dividing her time among Cambridge, California (to nurse her tubercular parents), and New England (to visit her emotionally disturbed sister, Nancy) had little time for fun. Still, she studied with the eminent Harvard philosophy faculty, played basketball, sang in a mixed chorus, and was class president her senior year. At the Palmer home, the center of her college days, she met distinguished and interesting guests, listened to Alice Palmer read poetry, and developed a taste for intellectual life. When she graduated magna cum laude in 1900, she wrote: "I was forever walking out of a world where I had found freedom—intellectual freedom, human freedom. A new world had opened to me, and now I thought it was closing forever."[23]

Upset by her family's continuing crises, and unwilling to become a permanent nurse to her father, Sprague remained with the Palmers while trying to determine her future. In 1902 she accompanied her mentors to Europe where, in France, Alice Palmer died following emergency surgery. Sprague returned to the United States with George Palmer and kept house for him for another year, realizing more than ever her need for an independent life. Looking for a dean of women, Benjamin Wheeler heard about Lucy Sprague from her brother-in-law Adolph Miller, now teaching at Berkeley. Palmer advised her to accept Wheeler's offer, and she did, though fearful of the job's challenges. As she put it, years later: "I wasn't quite twenty-five, had been trained at a small man-scared woman's college, and had worked there as a secretary. The University of California was co-educational, had nearly two thousand women students, and many more men students, and had never had a Dean of Women or a woman on the faculty. I marvel at my temerity, for I was thoroughly frightened. . . . President Wheeler was a gambler. I was a gambler too—a desperate one. I said I would come."[24]

Although she arrived on campus after women students had made considerable progress, Sprague found their situation disturbing. Her own alma mater lived in the shadow of Harvard, but the Palmers had provided her with a broader, richer college life than any experienced by her new charges. The attitudes of Berkeley males toward women surprised and dismayed her. And the lack of harmony between women students, despite AWS's efforts, confounded her. Although outshown by Harvard, Radcliffe, a smaller and more homogeneous institution backed by prominent Boston women, had not faced such problems. In her autobiography, written in the 1950s, Sprague recalled her initial impressions of the University of California:

> It came as a shock when I realized that most of the faculty thought of women frankly as inferior beings. The older men were solidly opposed to having any women on the faculty. Any woman who, intellectually, could hold such a position, must be a freak and "unwomanly." . . . To be sure, most of the Harvard faculty held the same opinion. . . . But few of the men I studied under had this attitude. . . . And I had lived with the Palmers. No one who had lived with Alice Freeman Palmer could believe that an intellectual career must make a woman unwomanly—or unfeminine, either.[25]

The new dean gave priority to four tasks: bringing women students closer together; using their moral influence to set standards for the university's social life; enriching women's educational and extracurricular experiences; and informing them about nonteaching careers. She began by attending meetings of AWS, Prytaneans, the sororities, the residence clubs, and other women's organizations to discuss campus life with the students and put groups in contact with each other. Concerned about the gulf between sorority members and other women, she suggested common projects.

Sprague had been at Berkeley only a short time, when women students noted the improvements she brought to their campus lives:

> The clubs were all languishing. The Mask and Dagger boasted of but four members, the athletic clubs were lagging, oppressed with difficulties; the Guitar and Mandolin Club consisted only of its name. . . . But now things wear a different aspect, and the change is due to the combined efforts of our able AWS president and the dean of women. And right here let us acknowledge that the best thing that ever happened to the women of this University was the creation of the office of Dean of Women, and that the best thing that ever happened to the office of Dean of Women was the appointment of Miss Sprague to fill it.[26]

Sprague rejected any role for herself as "warden of women" but nonetheless sought the elimination of potentially scandalous situations with the hope of preserving order and preventing limitations on the social freedom of Berkeley women. She moved first to regulate the mixed boardinghouses surrounding the campus. By 1908 she had inspected all of them, set standards for those housing women, asked proprietors to house only one sex, and mailed a list of approved houses to incoming freshmen women.

In setting social standards, Sprague had the cooperation of the women students, who were eager to exert their moral influence over the university. In 1910, with Sprague's approval, AWS proposed guidelines for student conduct. "The women of the University" put themselves on record in opposition to mixed boardinghouses, cheating on examinations, and leaving bleachers or meetings during the singing of the alma mater. They asked for a 10:30 P.M. curfew for callers at women's residences, 1:00 A.M. for dances, and quiet hours during the evening in student residences. They recommended that women leave word as to their whereabouts at night, come in from walking by 10:00 P.M., and only use two evenings a week for recreation. Organizations were to hold social functions only on weekends. Although women had no power to enforce these suggestions, the guidelines were printed in student handbooks and newspapers and discussed at mass meetings. Use of the phrase "women of the University" before each rule indicated a growing self-consciousness.[27]

Sprague broadened the horizons of her female students by strengthening their ties to older women—for example, by requesting that faculty wives invite freshmen to their homes. At her own Wednesday afternoon receptions she fed students sandwiches, chocolate, and cake and read poetry to them, as Alice Palmer had read to her. Discovering a lack of organizational experience among the women, she formed "Critics on the Hearth," a club to teach rules of parliamentary procedure. The lack of civic interest among Berkeley students shocked her, and she took groups into San Francisco to study prisons, schools, courts and asylums and to see connections between their education and the world. Sprague modified the hygiene course begun by Mary Ritter to include information on sexuality and venereal diseases. She found this aspect of her job important, but a little strange:

> The wave of sex hygiene—prophylaxis as it was first called—swept over the country when I was at Berkeley. It was then that [her sister] said that in order to be thought modern you must say "syphilis" once a day. . . . Dr. Reinhardt had begun lectures to the men, with terrifying reports about scores of boys fainting. What would the women students do? The trouble of course was that the taboo against mentioning sex was being first broken down through horrifying tales of disease. Both Dr. Bancroft and I felt that a positive approach must be made. So she began giving lectures to large groups of the women on sex physiology, including menstruation, pregnancy, and childbirth. Because of her wholesome personality, very few girls fainted, but I don't doubt we started some fancy complexes. My part was to follow up acquainting the girls with sex diseases. . . . Of all the queer things I was called upon to become at Berkeley at the age of twenty-seven, I think becoming a specialist on sex diseases was the queerest.[28]

When Sprague arrived at Berkeley, she polled women students about their career choices and discovered that 90 percent planned to become teachers. They attended the university for the prestige of its degree and for a fifth year of courses, making them eligible for high school positions. Sprague believed that most students chose teaching because they had no other options, and she set out to explore alternatives. Taking a leave of absence from the deanship in 1910, she went to New York City to learn about women's career possibilities, for herself as well as her students. At the Henry Street Settlement, she followed the daily activities of Florence Kelley (an exhausting task in itself), watched the visiting nurses go about their work, and helped to draft labor legislation. She worked next with Mary Richmond at the Charity Organization, investigating and reporting on individual cases. At the Russell Sage Foundation she helped Pauline Goldmark gather and interpret data on social problems. After three weeks as a Salvation Army worker, Sprague had extended conversations with educational reformer and school superintendent Julia Richman. Sprague's final report to President Wheeler has not survived, and we do not know what use she made of her New York experiences on the Berkeley campus. In fact, the trip may have done more for her own career development than for her students, by ironically confirming her personal commitment to early childhood education and school reform. In 1912 she married economist Wesley Clair Mitchell and moved with him to New York, where she founded the Bank Street College of Education and raised their four children.

Just before Lucy Sprague left the Berkeley campus in 1912, she initiated a women's pageant, the Partheneia, or masque of maidenhood. Modeled on similar events at eastern women's colleges, the Partheneia had two purposes: to unite women students through their work on a common project and to allow expression of creative and artistic talent. Women competed to produce the best original script on some aspect of the theme "from girlhood to maidenhood," and for the acting, dancing, and singing parts. Others wrote publicity, sold tickets, sewed costumes, composed music, painted scenery, and choreographed dances. The Partheneia drew audiences from outside the university and bridged gaps between the women who worked on it. Anna Rearden, author of the first pageant, dedicated it to Lucy Sprague, "the princess who makes dreams come true."[29]

In her biography of Lucy Sprague Mitchell, Joyce Antler has assessed the dean of women's relationships with her students. Young women did indeed regard Sprague as a beautiful and elegant princess who tried hard to "quicken their cultural lives" and to interest them in important issues of the day. In particular, Sprague spoke to them about the role of college women in social progress and kept the problems of working-class women in their consciousness. At the same time, Lucy Sprague could be insensitive about socioeconomic differences closer to home. Antler relates one such incident, in which the dean complained about a noisy campus bell awakening her each morning at eight o'clock. Students who had risen hours before 8 A.M. to commute to the university or to work resented her irritation. Yet whatever her personal foibles, Lucy Sprague persuaded women students that they had a contribution to make to university life. During her tenure as dean, women students became a self-conscious presence on campus, forcing male students, faculty, and administrators to acknowledge them, and claiming the right to exert "womanly" influence over the conduct of university life. The Partheneia, with its demonstration of "feminine ideals," including service, art, culture, and beauty, symbolized and culminated her efforts.[30]

After Sprague's departure, her fellow Radcliffe alumna and handpicked successor, Lucy Ward Stebbins, took up the question of future careers for women students. Dean Stebbins sent questionnaires to the thirty-seven academic departments of the university, asking faculty, "To what fields of paid work for women other than teaching does training in your department lead? What course should be pursued by the student who wishes to equip herself for any one of these fields? How many years of graduate or professional work is required in each case? What are the opportunities for advancement and the salaries paid?" Seventeen departments responded to Stebbins' inquiry, listing jobs for women as dietitians, physician's helpers, designers, professional shoppers, food analysts, landscape gardeners, supervisors in rural schools, art librarians, executive secretaries, caseworkers, buyers in department stores, and institutional workers.[31]

Concern about women's careers also sparked a campus movement for a Department of Home Economics. May Shepard Cheney '83, appointments secretary and teacher placement counselor at Berkeley for forty years, became interested in home economics as an area with exciting opportunities for women after summer session courses given by Ellen Richards and Sophonisba Breckinridge in 1910. Women students enthusiastically argued that home economics could be presented in a scholarly fashion to promote mental discipline and lead to an intelligent understanding of the place of the household in society. Through the efforts of Stebbins, Cheney, Peixotto, and the Prytaneans, domestic science courses were finally offered in 1912, and a department opened in 1916.[32]

Thus, with the aid of older women both on and off campus, women students at the University of California created a separate community that allowed them to do more than simply attend classes. In 1907 Lucy Sprague reported to President Wheeler that only 19 percent of the women did not participate in campus life, compared to 53 percent at the time of her arrival a year earlier. Still, students' backgrounds, sororities, and the lack of central residence facilities continued to divide women. In 1912 Lucy Ward Stebbins told President Wheeler: "The women students . . . are living in their own homes where their time and interest are justly demanded even at the expense of 'college life.' Many others who are self-supporting are without the time or energy or interest for anything beyond their personal needs or ambitions."[33]

Amy Steinhart, a student who experienced the divisiveness still present on the Berkeley campus, came from a wealthy German Jewish family in San Francisco. She applied to Vassar College in 1896 but chose Berkeley after her father's death made it important for her to remain at home. Steinhart credited her high school teachers with influencing her to go to college: "New teachers coming to the school were college women. . . . I think that made quite a difference. One teacher was a Vassar graduate. She was the kind of person on whom girls have crushes. . . . It was she who persuaded us that we ought to go to college. Then we acquired a Latin teacher who was a graduate of Ann Arbor."

Amy Steinhart's religion kept her out of the social world created by the sororities. As she put it, "It was the first time that I came face to face with anti-Semitism. . . . There were just three sororities on the campus at this time. And this very great friend of mine, with whom I had gone all through school, was rushed for all three, and I was left out." Her long daily commute, including a 7:30 A.M. ferry ride, further limited participation in the women's community, although she joined the yearbook staff and watched her brother, also a student, play football.[34]

Few black women attended the University of California, but those who did found no place in the women's community. Ida L. Jackson, who transferred to Berkeley in 1920 from New Orleans University and graduated in 1922, spoke of the pain it caused her to sit in classes every day next to students "who acted as if my seat were unoccupied, showing no sign of recognition, never giving a smile or a nod." Jackson and the seventeen other blacks on campus (eight women and nine men) organized the Braithwaite Club and later the Alpha Kappa Alpha sorority. Yet even separatism, a successful strategy for white women, granted blacks no campus status. The *Blue and Gold* refused to publish their club pictures, and the YMCA pool, open to white women students, remained closed to Jackson and her friends.

Jackson praised the friendliness and kindness of President Wheeler and Dean Stebbins, but they could not protect her from students' insults or faculty bigotry. After graduation, Ida Jackson received a master's degree from the School of Education. Her thesis, "The Development of Negro Children in Relation to Education," argued that factors other than inherent, inherited intelligence affected the development of IQ. She pointed instead, to the influence of sociological and environmental conditions in children's lives. Two of the faculty on her committee refused to approve her findings, and she received her degree only after an appeal to the Graduate Council.[35]

Women students had no other options than a separate social and extracurricular life; clearly male students would not integrate their organizations and activities. Yet women students rarely asked them to do so, probably because they too felt more comfortable with separation. Women declared their events off-limits to men, the Partheneia being a notable exception. Berkeley women believed their community, though different from the men's, should have equal rights and influence on the campus, but they quickly found that the men did not agree, and that even separation failed to diminish male hostility toward "coeds." The position and role of women students at the University of California remained unsettled through the Progressive Era. Some male students and faculty supported women's separate activities; others continued to deplore the very existence of coeducation. Women students themselves constantly pressed for a redefinition of their status and ultimately disputed men's domination of the campus. At the same time, as their short stories demonstrate, they wanted the romantic attentions of their male peers and worried that higher education would interfere with their prospects for courtship and marriage.

SEPARATE BUT NOT EQUAL: DEFINING COEDUCATION AT BERKELEY

Male students and faculty at the University of California shared the fears common on other campuses that women were driving men out of the humanities. Many believed that sexually segregated classes would prevent this effeminization of the university. The *Daily Californian,* a student newspaper published by the fraternities and other prominent men on campus, felt that separation benefited both sexes: "The minds of men and women are radically different so subjects could be taught to better advantage by so conducting the classes as to suit the needs of the students."[36] Professor Edward Clapp agreed, telling an alumni audience that coeducation should not mean "amalgamation" of the sexes. "The only result of such an effort is to produce a poor and feeble hybrid which is as unsatisfactory to the one side as to the other."[37] Or, as the *Blue and Gold* put it in 1905:

> Briefly, familiarity breeds contempt. . . . The intimate associations which go with co-education prohibit forming the idealism about feminine charms which makes them charming. . . . Woman, man's ideal, is immeasurably more powerful than woman, man's equal. . . . We don't want the unlikeness destroyed. . . . When woman becomes man in character, man must necessarily cease to be man. . . . Note how people living long among redskins acquire similarity of feature to Indians. . . . In such wise, co-education might destroy the dissimilarity between the sexes.[38]

Berkeley, however, never instituted separate classes. President Wheeler did not hold women responsible for men's desertion of the humanities, linking course choices, instead, to men's increased concern about careers: "The causes of the movement . . . lie deeper than the suggested palliative assumes. . . . The present day university student far more urgently than the college student of thirty years ago insists upon shaping his course in reference to a proposed life activity." Wheeler stated that mining, engineering, agriculture, business, and law drew more men away from the humanities than did the presence of women in their classes.[39]

Despite these remarks, Wheeler held traditional views of women's place in society. Although rejecting classroom segregation at Berkeley, he recommended the establishment of state junior colleges, assuming that women would be more likely to attend institutions closer to their homes than they would the university. When advising Lillian Moller '00 (later Lillian Gilbreth, the prominent industrial engineer) on the proper delivery of her graduation speech, Wheeler told her to wear a ruffled gown, avoid bombastic gestures, and above all: "Read what you have to say, and from small pieces of paper. Don't imitate a man." He approved of the separate women's community, advised and supported Lucy Sprague, and encouraged women students to form their own organizations and to prepare themselves for postgraduate domesticity, not for a role in public affairs or even teaching careers: "Women need different organizations from the men and ought to have them. Their standards are different. You are not like men and you must recognize the fact. . . . You may have the same studies as the men, but you put them to different use. You are not here with the ambition to be school teachers or old maids; but you are here for the preparation of marriage and motherhood. This education should tend to make you more serviceable as wives and mothers." By keeping themselves separate from the men, Wheeler said, women would be the cleansing, uplifting power in the university. Their superior morality and idealism would benefit male students.[40]

Notwithstanding their progress in establishing themselves on campus, Berkeley women found themselves excluded from most class offices, from intercollegiate competition, and sometimes from scholastic honors as well. Lillian Moller Gilbreth recalled that she was denied a Phi Beta Kappa key on the grounds that it would be of more use to a man. In 1910, the *Daily Californian* still used the word *students* synonymously with *men*, and in its columns discussed football and class politics almost exclusively. As Henry Morse Stephens, professor of history, described the situation: "At present the men students are in a majority, and in America, the majority rules; the men seniors control the men students, and where the senior men meet and make their public opinion and recognize their leaders is the Heart of the University."[41]

Despite the rhetoric about women's special place in university life, men resisted "womanly influence" over campus politics, athletics, and publications. When women asked for representation on the ASUC Executive Committee, the *Daily Californian* replied: "While in a general way the interests of the men and the women are the same, yet the activities of the two great divisions of the student body are so widely different that they must be directed by distinct organizations. . . . The principal function of the Executive Committee is the direction of athletics, concerning which nine women out of ten are so profusely ignorant that the judgment of their members on the committee in regard to it would be worse than valueless."[42] ASUC continued, however, to accept women's dues, returning to AWS only 20 percent of the money to use for its own work. And when women students, who sat separately at football games, wrote their own cheers and songs, the newspaper commented: "It is true that the university is the place for progressive ideas and if the time is coming when equal rights and privileges will be accorded everyone, California will want to be in the foreground. Even if that time were here, it would seem that a football game is distinctively a masculine event, and any demonstration by the women students would be not only untimely, but unbecoming as well. Theirs should be the passive part until the world has changed a little more."[43] To squelch a distressing rumor, the *Daily Californian* reassured its readers that no females besides the women's editor would be appointed to its staff.[44]

Men students made clear their distrust of female voters in university elections, insisting that women chose only handsome, glib candidates. The *Pelican,* a campus humor magazine named after the stereotypically ugly, bespectacled "coed," pictured a well-dressed young man standing on a large feminine hand labeled "Co-Ed Vote." Another cartoon showed cigar-chomping female ward bosses buying male votes, women proposing marriage to men, and soldiers dressed in fancy hats and high-heeled shoes. On the subject of woman suffrage, the *Pelican* satirized:

> Girls, it's perfectly silly to think that we can't vote just as well as the men. The idea! I was so ma-ad last night! My! I was perfectly wi-ild! That sarcastic Tom Wotsisname—he's a Pi I and the nicest man in the House, but he's so perfectly sarcastic. Still, you know, they say one has to be clever to be sarcastic; and he does so effect the blase; he's the best dancer in college: we were discussing Woman's Rights and all, and he said—imagine the nerve! "Why, Maybelle, if you women were allowed to vote, Landers Stevens would be President of the United States on the first ballot! Just imagine! I was perfectly cra-azy!"[45]

Most male students at Berkeley had probably attended coeducational primary and secondary schools and become accustomed to the presence of women there. Yet they clearly had difficulty dealing with college women simultaneously as intellectual equals and objects of romance in the Victorian tradition. In the world off-campus, men and women in their late teens and early twenties did not share pursuits and goals. At the university, however, they sat in classrooms together, studied, took exams, and were members of the same class. Berkeley women voted in college elections, a privilege not accorded adult female Californians until 1911. Women, too, had mixed feelings—not about coeducation itself, a right they jealously guarded, but about their proper relationship to classmates and the desired outcome of higher education. Did they, should they, share postgraduate goals with men? And if not, what did coeducation mean?

Men expressed doubts and hostilities about coeducation and women's campus status in student publications. The *Blue and Gold,* Berkeley's yearbook, began using student photographs in the 1890s. Frequently men's pictures were grouped by class, whereas women appeared in an undifferentiated section at the back of the book as coeds. Yearbooks and newspapers printed numerous jokes about the incompatibility of intelligence and personal attractiveness in a woman. Cartoons lampooned women students as "pelicans," skinny, ugly, "grinds," anxious to show off to the professors. Pelicans became, or already were, old maid schoolteachers, because no man wanted to marry them. The *Blue and Gold* warned that however pretty a freshman woman, if she studied too hard she would make her "pretty little nose very red," her "rosy cheeks" jaundiced, and her hair thin. Her ultimate fate, according to a cartoon, was that of an ugly schoolmarm. In the yearbook of 1893 men wrote in the "Farewell Address of the Seniors to the Coeds": "In your future careers as schoolmistresses some day, you push your spectacles upon your brows and dream of the past, think on us, your admirers and brothers. You never will forget us, we know full well, and believe fully that indeed, indeed we will be brothers to you. In fact, we desire nothing more."[46]

Berkeley males exempted themselves from the baleful social effects of a college education. The *Blue and Gold* of 1895 showed a pretty young girl "when she comes" next to a bespectacled, sour-faced woman surrounded by books "when she leaves." In contrast, the boy "when he enters" squinted at his books and dressed poorly, but left college a handsome, polished gentleman. In the yearbook's "Ye Rime of Ye Ancient Co-Ed," a pelican lamented:

> I have tried for twenty years to change my name
> But in spite of all my efforts 'tis the same
> But a masculine degree
> Such as B.L. or A.B.
> Turns an old maid to a bachelor of fame.[47]

Taught to idealize women as mysterious, different creatures, men felt uncomfortable with them as peers and competitors. As a Berkeley student from the class of 1900 wrote of his first love, nonstudent Miranda Brainerd:

> I fell deeply in love with her in what seems to me to have been a very spiritual way. She was very frail, tubercular. . . . To me she was a person from another world—more a spirit than a girl of flesh and blood, and my devotion to her was always of that character. . . . I shall always cherish the memory of that friendship as something quite apart from the rest of my life at that time. It was a sanctuary to which I could go and leave behind the rough and tumble and find inspiration from this strangely shy and spiritual contact. . . . This was a very perfect friendship and of tremendous value to me just then in fixing a certain idealism about women that has never been entirely lost.

In contrast, this young man treated his female classmates as "buddies," who shared too much of his everyday life to be invested with the spiritual, romantic qualities necessary in a love-object.[48]

Confusion about relationships between men and women students was a feature of life at Berkeley from the earliest days. In 1885, the *Occident,* a nonfraternity paper, published a humorous skit about a meeting of the glee club that serves as a metaphor for the social problems of coeducation. Club members, both male and female, were planning the annual concert and party, when "Miss N" remarked: "The young ladies must have escorts. Last term several of the young ladies were left unasked, and others were asked so late that they did not have time to make their cakes nor even to fix up pretty." Everyone faced a quandary in this situation. How should men treat female club members? As equals, with a common interest in music? As such, they surely had the right to attend the club's parties. And yet, they were "young ladies," who needed escorts and who baked cakes for the parties. Miss N and a male club member made up a list of the women members and assigned an escort to each. Unaccustomed to having their objects of romantic attention selected for them, most of the men balked at taking their appointed partner to the party. The women were equally uncertain. Wanting to attend the party, but unwilling to be humiliated, they discussed holding a separate event. Lack of unity prevented the women from holding their own party, because those invited by men were content with the situation. In the end, the arranged solution failed, and women club members without escorts missed the party again.[49]

The dilemma of the glee club illustrated college men and women's search for appropriate campus relationships. During the Progressive Era, however, student authors of both sexes described women's competing pulls toward coeducation and romance, or careers and marriage, certain that the two poles were incompatible. The *Occident* changed character several times between the 1880s and the 1910s, but as a nonfraternity and sometimes a literary publication, it printed short stories by both men and women demonstrating both their mutual attraction and the barriers coeducation placed in their way. Two stories about brothers and sisters urged college students to leave the ways of childhood, during which boys and girls played with relative equality, and to learn to be men and women. In "The Parting Paths," a twin brother and sister spent springs and summers on their grandfather's cattle ranch. The sister, who narrated the tale, said that up to their tenth year, she and her brother, Tim, had been equals: "But a few weeks before our eleventh birthday, the first narrow crack came in our little world, which was to widen into the deep chasm of dissimilarity which no clasped boy and girl hands can bridge." While horseback riding, she and her brother came across a camp of Indians, not hostile, but "lazy and cruel." One of the Indians grabbed her bridle: "I screamed wildly, dropped my reins, and stretched my arms to Tim."

Similarly, in "The Way of a Sister," Laura realized that she and her brother had grown up. When Thurston returned from college he was no longer willing to be her friend. Laura's mother advised her daughter to dress up, attend a neighborhood dance, and surprise Thurston. Astonished that Laura was so attractive and grown up, her brother danced with her and soon assumed an appropriately protective role. "I say, mother, I'd rather that Langland fellow didn't hang around here quite so much—you know sis is getting to be quite an interesting girl."[50]

Other stories show higher education altering the proper relationship between the sexes, and thus destroying romance. Tom Graham and Ethel Hayes grew up together and attended the same high school. Ethel dreamed of going to college and then becoming a trained nurse, but Tom, though he loved her and longed to follow her to the university, had no money to do so. He tried to tell her about his feelings, but she laughed and said she would never marry. Tom worked and saved until he could afford to attend Stanford, but collapsed from exhaustion during his first final examinations. Not knowing the identity of her patient, Ethel came to nurse him. As she took care of him, she realized that she loved him, but too late. Tom died in her arms. In another tale, Gwen became very angry when Ted told her that he had been assigned the negative side in a debate on coeducation. Determined to make him change his mind, she arrayed herself in her best and went to the debate with another man. She sat where Ted could see her, and he became so rattled that he could not make a coherent speech. Professor C, judge of the debate, nevertheless awarded the prize to the negative: "The whole point at issue seemed to be that woman hinders the intellectual development of man. The first speaker on the negative gave us the example of sweethearts biasing the speaker. The second speaker proved this by his inconsistency. The decision stands for the negative."[51]

Aside from the problem of campus relationships, men and women worried about what came after college. In "A Man's Work," an editor asked reporter Mary Hartley, dressed to attend a society tea, to interview a prominent businessman, Caspar Bartnett, instead. Hartley wanted to change her clothes and use the same approach to her assignment as a man would, but her editor and co-workers convinced her that pretty girls turned Bartnett's head, and she would get more information dressed as she was. Hartley got the interview, but Bartnett told her that in the future he would talk to her about business only when she was dressed for business. Hartley exulted in her scoop: "I've done it, . . . a really, truly scoop, the biggest in months. And the best of all is, I've done it like a man." Although on the surface the story had a positive attitude toward working women, the message had a twist to it. Women could not work as men did without losing their femininity.[52]

Sometimes the stories made fun of educated women who sought to exert their moral influence by becoming "social housekeepers." In "Little Miss Fixit," economics major Isabel Landis refused to marry Harold Jarvis. "I am determined upon a career, Harold. You know perfectly well that I majored in Economics in college. I shall go in for settlement work. In fact, I am already doing it." Her employer, a charitable society, sent Landis to investigate a case of reported child neglect. Unimpressed, Jarvis grumbled, "Why don't those old hens in that uplift society let mothers take care of their own babies?" He told Landis to call him at the Union Club if she changed her mind, and he would take her to lunch. Investigating her case, Landis found a rosy, healthy baby cared for by an elderly woman. The baby had given new meaning in life to his adopted mother, a young formerly flighty girl, and payment for his care kept the old woman from the poorhouse. Properly chastened, Landis made her call to the Union Club.[53]

"Three Maids Errant and a Blushing Knight" satirized the experiences of three graduates of eastern women's colleges who went west for government jobs and to make new lives for themselves. They had, as the narrator put it, "no idea what we could do." Finding the civil service jobs not to their liking, they unsuccessfully sought other work and lodging. Only when one of their number, "the Duchess," attracted the attentions of a personable young man did their luck change. The young man, who turned out to be wealthy and well connected, married the Duchess, found a job for Nan, and promised to introduce the narrator to his younger brother.[54]

In some cases higher education stood between women and the achievement of womanliness. In "Straws," college-educated Betty Jamison hated her job as a rural schoolteacher. When Lem, a young farmer in the valley, proposed to her, she considered marrying him so that she could have her own home and children. In the end, however, his grammar and manners repelled her, and she turned him down. Higher education had placed this young woman in an unfortunate role—that of being unable to find satisfaction with a man who loved her. Like many college women, she saw teaching as her only alternative. At the end of the story, she unlocked the schoolhouse door, opened the windows and watched the pupils come in, "watched them with eyes whose weariness saw unbroken stretches of rows, always wriggling, through unbroken stretches of years."[55]

The clearest conflict between higher education and traditional womanhood came in "How She Gave Her Consent," by Robert Hood '06. Edith Lorimer had become engaged to Harold Lacy in their junior year. On graduation day he came to her boardinghouse, jubilant at a lucrative offer to be assistant superintendent of a mine in South Africa. Harold was particularly pleased, because now he and Edith could marry immediately instead of waiting as they had expected to. Edith, however, refused: "Oh, don't tempt me, Harold. I couldn't—I couldn't go yet. You see, I always thought I'd like to make my own living for a while before I was married, and make a little money too. I wouldn't like to come to you with nothing at all, and I haven't enough to buy my trousseau now even." Harold dismissed her answer as "stuff and nonsense," but Edith stoutly replied: "A girl, you must remember, has her own notions of pride, just as well as a man. I would like to show that all these years of education have not been wasted, that I'm good for something in the world. Besides, we're both very young." Harold remained firm, and they quarreled. Edith's best friend, Helen Armstrong, learned of the problem and told Harold not to worry; she would arrange everything. She advised him to escort Edith to the 7:30 A.M. train taking her to her teaching job as though nothing had happened. When the couple arrived at the station, they were met by all their friends throwing rice, yelling congratulations, and decorating Edith's luggage with white ribbons. Bewildered, both denied that they had married, but no one believed them, and Harold was forced to get on the train with her. Edith burst into tears, and he comforted her: "'You don't believe that I'm to blame for all this, girlie,' he said tenderly, 'it's all that little witch Helen's doing. But you know, dear, there's only one thing that we can do now, and that is to make it all true.' And there came no word of dissent from the limp figure by his side in the intervals of her subsiding sobs."[56]

These tensions expressed in students' short stories found their way into daily life on the Berkeley campus, particularly in the debate over the proper relationship between AWS and ASUC. Women and men struggled over the meaning of separatism. As students they shared many concerns, but as men and women they were supposed to inhabit different worlds. How should campus life reflect those similarities and differences?

As student government developed between 1900 and 1910, AWS coordinated women's extracurricular and social life separately, turning over one fourth of their funds to ASUC, the organization nominally representing all students. ASUC, however, had no women officers and put few resources into women's activities. Many women students resented the situation but were divided as to a solution. No one suggested merging the two groups, partly because men would not have tolerated equality within one organization, and partly because neither sex considered it appropriate for men to supervise women's social life. Some women, however, argued that both sexes should feel their "first loyalty and interest in the large association [ASUC]." This would be possible if women were represented on the ASUC executive committee, instead of merely having the right to vote for men on it. Others felt that total separation benefited women. They wanted to sever all relations with ASUC and demanded that the group change its name to Associated Men Students of the University of California to reflect its activities more accurately. In a long article for the *Occident,* Annie Dale Biddle argued that "there is at California no field in which a true Associated Student body can exercise itself." She pointed out that athletic, disciplinary, social, and musical functions were all carried on separately, and recommended separate student associations, with a common committee of officers to handle "emergency situations" where men and women students needed to work together. Women would no longer pay 25 percent of their funds into the ASUC treasury, but "separation in student organization does not mean separation in college spirit."[57]

During the school year of 1907–08 the *Daily Californian* led a drive to exclude women from ASUC. Realizing that exclusion without other structural changes endangered their position on campus, women students held a mass meeting and recommended unanimously that men vote against the measure. In the January 1908 vote, only male members of ASUC cast ballots, deciding 135 to 92 that women should remain in ASUC. Discussions about representation and the relationship between ASUC and AWS did not disappear. Confusion over the role of separatism and the meaning of coeducation continued to plague organizational life, as it did romantic relationships.

PUSHING FOR EQUALITY: BERKELEY AND COEDUCATION IN THE 1910S

Before 1910, University of California students had few connections and seemingly little interest in the politics and excitement of the Progressive Era. As one woman student put it, "We were very much circumscribed—almost entirely—by just campus affairs, and the outside world didn't mean so much to us in terms of affecting our particular lives." During the 1910s, however, campus attitudes and events reflected heightened awareness of changing times. Women students became increasingly angry over their separate but unequal existence on the Berkeley campus. In this decade they challenged men students, sought respect for themselves and their activities, and achieved a new prominence in college life, while maintaining a separate power base.[58]

During the 1910s, the *Daily Californian* became more diverse in its choice of topics and more lively in its views, while alternative publications, such as *Student Opinion, Brass Tacks,* the *Pelican,* the *Dill Pickle,* and the *Raspberry Press,* also expressed opinions about the campus, the nation, the world, and the coed. Demonstrating a new awareness, women students complained that university officials ignored their needs and even their presence. An editorial in one of the new publications stated the case as follows:

> Slowly but surely the fact has been forced upon our minds that the University of California is merely tolerating co-education. We attended our first University meeting of the semester. . . . We heard advice heaped upon the heads of the '19 men, but . . . we didn't hear a word of welcome addressed to the Freshmen women. . . . A few days ago a large number of students enrolled in an English course limited to fifteen. The professor's method of elimination was brief and simple: "All the men in the class may remain," he said. Girls have found the problem in countless other courses.[59]

Female students also demanded a greater voice in class affairs, more publicity for their own athletic events, a women's rooting section at the football games, and less emphasis on male-dominated traditions. As a freshman put it in *Student Opinion:* "The other day I was tired, so sat down on the bench outside the co-op. A girl pulled me off and told me that girls aren't supposed to sit there or walk up the steps next to it. These are the traditions, but there aren't any traditions about what girls can do, and men can't. I thought that was pretty poor."[60]

In the spring semester of 1916, two incidents demonstrated the growing sense of injustice among women and the hostile responses of men. Desiring closer identification with the university community, women revived the discussion about AWS and ASUC. Most felt the time had come to merge the two organizations. The men approved the merger until the women asked for seats on the Executive Committee of the ASUC. The men told AWS officers they might run for election to the committee, but they would not designate seats for them. The women then declined the merger, fearing loss of control and funding for women's activities. The men responded angrily in the pages of the *Daily Californian*, criticizing the women's "lack of trust." "May AWS continue in its brilliant career, distributing points, devouring suppers, and providing facilities for the shining of dainty boots in private."[61]

That same spring, biology student Josephine Miller '16 inadvertently swallowed the contents of a pipette holding several million typhoid bacilli. She did not become ill, but the San Francisco papers, to President Wheeler's fury, made the most of the incident at the university's expense. The editor of the *Daily Californian* warned that Miller's experience highlighted "the whole question of feminism."

> Whenever we hear of a college woman who has entered the field of scientific research or is "the only woman in the College of Mechanics" we feel just a little regretful. When her photograph is featured on the front page of the pinksheet for swallowing microbes or being mixed up in a laboratory explosion, or otherwise making a faux pas in a usually masculine field of endeavor, we always feel a sneaking hope that the undesired publicity will prove a warning to other ambitious feminine endeavors. . . . We are glad to see women voting, and we would have them own property and be independent when they will. Yet when we hear the feminist resent the fact that men tip their hats to her and offer her seats in street cars and refrain from smoking and swearing in her presence, we must beg to differ. . . . Were we of another sex and if publicity were forced upon us, we hope that we might be pictured for adopting a foundling and not for operating a transit or imbibing too deeply in a typhoid laboratory.[62]

In previous years, Berkeley women had ignored editorials on the differences between the sexes, possible separate classes, and the like. But this time, Elsie McCormick '16, women's editor of *Brass Tacks,* replied sarcastically in her article, "An Etiquette for Coeds":

Do not swallow typhoid germs—it is unladylike. Do not study hygiene—it is not polite to be interested in the health of your family or the community. Be a man's comrade but do not compete with him. He knows that he will never hold his position if you do. Do not request men to swear in your presence. Only suffragettes do that. Always glare at a man in the streetcar until he gives you his seat. If you show any willingness to stand it proves you are a feminist, and hence ineligible for an M.R.S. degree. Do not be the only woman in the College of Mechanics. To know anything about the anatomy of an automobile is immodest. Pay your ASUC dues promptly, but do not be so bold as to ask for a place on the Executive Committee. If a man speaks to you, always preface your answer by "Tee-hee." If you make any other remarks, you will be considered unmaidenly. Do not study anything useful. Co-eds should specialize in English, and a diluted form of art history. Always look and act as silly as possible. If you can't think of anything else to do, giggle. Co-eds who live up to these rules will reach the man's ideal of the perfect college woman.[63]

World War I brought increased publicity and prominence to women students, further straining male-female campus relationships. Total attendance at the university fell 12 percent between 1916–17 and 1917–18, with the proportion of women increasing from 43 percent to 53 percent. Taking advantage of their majority to demolish old customs, women sat on the senior bench with their knitting, used the men's swimming pool when their own was closed for repairs, insisted on the right to patronize the Joint, a campus restaurant, and used stairs and lawns formerly reserved for the men. The *Raspberry Press,* a men's paper, bemoaned the situation in a cartoon entitled "From the Land of Womanhood to College Prominence," showing men uniting to block the road in the women's way. Another cartoon pictured a woman with "The Partheneia" under her arm knocking at the university door.[64]

Not all men retaliated so good-naturedly. Some made a point of gathering on well-traveled campus paths to make lewd remarks about passing females. When this practice drew complaints from women, the men responded: "Why do women come to a co-educational college anyway? Why don't they go into seclusion and never see a man in all their long and wearisome lives. . . . Forget it, girls, come down to earth and realize that the Senior Bench is a worthwhile tradition. . . . Tempt not the eyes, and they will see not. Also beware of her who speaks much of her virtue."[65] Don Abshire '18 protested that "piping the flight" (watching and commenting on women passing by) was the one remaining male privilege on campus: "Stripped of the sacredness of our bench, our steps, and our pool, we stand before the scornful and critical gaze of those, at whose shrines we have formerly knelt,—our faults and weaknesses in full exposed in the blinding light of the supreme 'co-ed'. . . . We cannot engage one another in light conversation, nor indulge in that glorious pastime of 'rating' without bringing down the wrath of that wild-eyed but determined throng, or the militaristic tendency."[66]

Berkeley students were not as involved in the war as those at eastern colleges, a trend that held generally for western college students. While Berkeley's enrollment fell by 12 percent during the war years, Harvard and Yale lost 40 percent of their students, Princeton 35 percent, and Cornell 27 percent. Regional considerations partially account for the greater variety of war work performed by eastern college women. Nevertheless, the attitudes of male students made it difficult for Berkeley women to do anything besides knitting and first aid. Ella Barrows Hagar '19, daughter of professor and future university president David Barrows, took what she described as a "man's job" chairing fund-raising and war-work committees on campus. When the newspapers published a picture of her on the telephone soliciting funds, the *Raspberry Press* "razzed" her for achieving such unladylike prominence. Unlike women at Vassar, Barnard, Sophie Newcomb, and Smith, however, Berkeley women sponsored no ambulance units and did no overseas relief work.[67]

Women students' battles to claim their rights extended into the social realm during the 1910s, as standards for clothing, makeup, and courting behavior changed dramatically. In her interview for the Prytanean alumnae book, Dorothy Rieber Joralemon '15 described the new social customs of her college days:

> Up to that time I think we were largely a puritanical group of boys and girls. It was all right for a boy to hold a girl's arm if he was helping her across the street, provided he held it just above or below the elbow. But if the hand crept down the arm and threatened to pass the wrist, then the girl could say, "I'm not that sort of girl." And the boys were very careful about where they put a kiss, because a kiss often meant a proposal of marriage in those days. . . . And after ragging, spooning—we called it then—became more prevalent and much more elaborate. And the boy could let his hand slip past the wrist with impunity, and often it would go much farther. And this was when our puritanical foundations really began to slip.[68]

Berkeley men acknowledged and applauded the disappearance of the "pelican" in favor of a more attractive, romantically inclined "chicken":

The pelican, a familiar type in an earlier college generation, was a pale, mournful creature, compounded of books and safety pins. . . . She offended the aesthetic sense of man. . . . Probably she couldn't help it. By the time she had fought with her family about the need of intelligence for women, and had seen her men friends take to their heels at the suggestion of it, she was reduced to books and safety pins . . . the acceptance of women as fellow workers meant adjustment of the most radical sort. At any rate, she was certainly a delightful source of material for the college funny paper. It was named for her. Of course there were attractive girls in college even in the hey-day of the pelican. But the pelican typified the college woman in mental attitude, if not always in appearance. And by her were they all judged. . . . The pelican is a nearly extinct species. She lurks in an occasional education class. She is no more typical than the dinosaur. She is not even fit for jokes anymore.[69]

In spite of their preference for the chicken over the pelican and their own participation in the new courtship styles described by Joralemon, men condemned women students for "permitting" such changes. Women should use their moral influence, they said, to keep men from patronizing the establishments of San Francisco's tenderloin district. When the tango and similar dances requiring close bodily contact between partners arrived in Berkeley in 1913, male students exhorted the women to take action against such behavior. Senior women, backed by Stebbins, did indeed issue a statement against "progressive dancing," but the men wanted individual women to exercise control for both sexes:

Anyone who has heard some men talk before or after or during a dance in regard to the clinging and so-called passion of some of their partners, or who has noticed the tendency of a large sixty per cent of the men to get as much loving as possible out of their dances, will agree that half of the dancing around here is not fairly and squarely decent . . . most girls are ignorant of the physical effect of indecent dancing on a man. . . . With the coming of feminism will disappear many of the protective barriers of convention which have shielded women in the past and the girl of the future who preserves a high moral standard must be able to stand up squarely on both feet and unassisted have the strength to say "no."[70]

The *Pelican* warned that men might run around with fast women, but they seldom married them.

> You add to your hair where it's lacking
> With some that you bought in a store,
> Those smiling red lips are made redder
> With a pencil, O, just a bit more!

There's something for those starry eyes too,
With which they can more starry be,
But I know that it's none of my business,
It really is nothing to me.

And your dress, too, has undergone changes,
It seems that you've lost modesty
From your ankles your skirt is still climbing
You'll soon cut it off at the knee.

Of course I still take you to dances,
For to dance one must have a girl,
But later, when you are through college
And somebody's wife you may be
I know I shall still be a bachelor.
That is some of my business, you see.[71]

More bluntly, the *California Alumni Fortnightly* blamed women students for the "subtle degeneration" of a once "frank and happy comradeship."[72] Through joking and teasing, men warned women about crossing boundaries and jeopardizing the balance between men's and women's spheres.

Berkeley women's separatism, beginning solely as a response to exclusion and proceeding to a vision of womanly influence at the university, ultimately became a means of pushing for equality and integration. At the same time, however, a freer sexual atmosphere, the growing cultural importance of heterosocial intimacy, new ideals and definitions of marriage, and eventually postwar conservatism made feminist protest and separatism seem outdated and unnecessarily confrontational. Shedding their image as pelicans, only to become chicks, and disbanding their separate organizational structure after the war, Berkeley women of the mid-twentieth century lost their bid for campus equality, their separatist feminist vision, and their power base as well.

"Politics is Politics," or The University Republican Club of the Future, *The Pelican,* c. November 1911. Courtesy, University Archives, Bancroft Library, Berkeley, California.

"The Dream of Derdra," Partheneia pageant, 1914. Courtesy, University Archives, Bancroft Library, Berkeley, California.

PELICAN

When Dolly used to go to Class to make an eight o'clock,
The blasé Seniors, sweater-clad, her passageway would block;
And smokers on old North Hall steps would never move their feet—
But crowd the sidewalk to the curb, so Dolly took the street.

For co-eds in the good old days walked by with modest mien;
They never were obtrusive, they were neither heard nor seen.
They dressed in khaki, greys and drabs; and powder? Not a grain.
They went in for that high brow stuff. (They made themselves quite plain.)

But now when Dolly goes, she's class! Her motor calls at noon.
She barely makes a one o'clock and thinks that quite too soon.
A Senior with her cigarettes, a Junior with her books.
With men the same, what is the change? Why, only Dolly's looks.

Now carmine lips and low done hair and costume from Lucille
Whose clinging chiffons hide her lines and likewise half reveal.
The streets are crowded to the walk; our Dolly knows the trick:
She goes in for that eye brow stuff, for Dolly is some chic.

L'ENVOI.

Since girls today have learned the way to make our pulses quicken
And changed the game—let's change the name from Pelican to Chicken!

Poem from *The Pelican*, April 1914. Courtesy, University Archives, Bancroft Library, Berkeley, California.

The women's building, Hearst Hall, 1901. Courtesy, University Archives, Bancroft Library, Berkeley, California.

Dean Marion Talbot's room, Green Hall, c. 1900. Courtesy, University of Chicago Archives.

Green Hall students knitting for the war effort, 1917–18. Courtesy, University of Chicago Archives.

Debate team, March 1908. Courtesy, Vassar College Library.

Sophonisba Breckinridge, J. D., Ph.D., and assistant dean of women, c. 1900. Courtesy, University of Chicago Archives.

Campus suffrage parade, c. April 1912. Courtesy, Vassar College Library.

Student socialists atop Main Building, Vassar College, March 1916. Courtesy, Vassar College Library.

Senior picture of Gertrude Homera Folks, *The Vassarion,* 1916. Courtesy, Vassar College Library.

Field Hockey team, c. 1906–16. Courtesy, Agnes Scott College Library.

Students at Agnes Scott Institute, 1902. Courtesy, Agnes Scott College Library.

Chemistry laboratory, 1911–16. Lowry Science Hall. Courtesy, Agnes Scott
College Library.

H. Sophie Newcomb Memorial College before move to Tulane campus in 1918. Note arcade in center where students gathered. Courtesy, University Archives, Howard-Tilton Memorial Library, Tulane University.

Pottery salesroom with faculty member Desiree Roman. Courtesy, University Archives, Howard-Tilton Memorial Library, Tulane University.

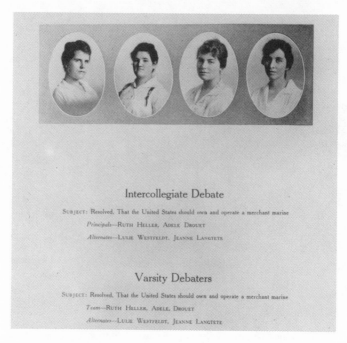

Intercollegiate debate team, *The Jambalaya,* 1916. Courtesy, University Archives, Howard-Tilton Memorial Library, Tulane University.

Domestic science class. Courtesy, University Archives, Howard-Tilton Memorial Library, Tulane University.

The University of Chicago, 1892–1920: The Western Yale and the Western Wellesley

The University of Chicago opened in 1892, after most major American universities had become established, and quickly became a leading center for graduate study. Unlike other coeducational campuses, Chicago offered unusual opportunities for women students and faculty. As a result, in the 1890s, women occupied so prominent a campus position that in 1902 the university sought to limit their influence by setting up sexually separated classes for undergraduates. The ensuing controversy attracted nationwide attention, raising fundamental questions about the nature of the sexes and the aims of higher education.[1]

The Baptist origins and funding of the school did not significantly affect the university's development, nor did Baptists dominate the faculty and student body. Although a Baptist himself, President William Rainey Harper (1892–1906) played the primary role in shaping the new university according to secular norms. Harper left a professorship of Semitic languages at Yale to assume the presidency at Chicago when founder John D. Rockefeller promised to establish a graduate school in addition to the proposed Baptist undergraduate college. Conscious of the need to find support for the university among prominent non-Baptist Chicagoans, Harper involved Marshall Field, Charles L. Hutchinson, and Martin Ryerson in fund-raising and governance.[2]

Harper modeled the new institution on eastern universities, wanting it to become the western Yale. Chicago initially required entrance examinations and would not accept certificates of graduation from accredited secondary schools for admission, as did most midwestern colleges and universities. To build a graduate school equal to those at Harvard, Hopkins, and Yale, Harper raided other campuses for his 123 faculty members. Tales of fabulous salaries circulated through the academic world, and job applications flooded Harper's office. He did not, in fact, have a great deal of money, particularly after giving seven-thousand-dollar salaries to some head professors and promising yearly increments to others, but Rockefeller rescued him with another large donation. When finally assembled, the western Yale had fourteen Ph.D.'s from Germany and over twenty American doctorates, including nine from Yale itself.[3]

In his roman à clef about university life in the early years, Robert Herrick, a professor of English, commented on Chicago's eastern bias: "The majority of the faculty belonged to the Yale camp; a few came from Princeton and Cornell, a number from small Western colleges, only a handful from Harvard. The Harvard representatives were not popular . . . because they expected all to bow down when they announced with an air of finality 'we do thus and so at Harvard.'"[4] Harper, however, went beyond eastern traditions to make Chicago unique, devising an elaborate institutional structure of graduate, undergraduate, and professional schools, an extension division, a press, and affiliated colleges and academies. He carefully arranged the faculty, assigning ranks of head professor, professor, nonresident professor, associate professor, assistant professor, instructor, tutor, docent, reader, lecturer, fellow, and scholar.[5] Other innovations dealt with students, as Harper tried to prevent the development of an undergraduate life reminiscent of Harvard and Yale. Differences in wealth and social class divided the student body at the eastern men's colleges. Although Yale was his model in other areas, Harper detested the social snobbery and class pranks associated with eastern student life. Could he have eliminated undergraduate education altogether from Chicago, he would have done so. As it was, he hoped eventually to move freshman and sophomore instruction off campus to the affiliated colleges. To minimize class identification Harper divided undergraduate work into the Academic Colleges (freshmen and sophomores) and the University Colleges (juniors and seniors). Later these divisions became, respectively, the Junior and Senior Colleges. Because of the quarter system, a student could graduate at any time during the year, further diminishing class loyalties. In Harper's university, the graduate school came first: "It is proposed in this institution to make the work of investigation primary, the work of giving instruction secondary." He hoped, too, to keep Greek letter societies off the campus, but in this he proved unsuccessful.[6]

The admission of women represented another departure from eastern custom. Midwestern and western institutions usually lacked the resources to indulge preferences for single-sex higher education. The original University of Chicago (1867–1886) had reluctantly admitted women in the 1870s in a vain attempt to stave off financial disaster. The new university's charter, written in 1889, stated that women should enter all departments on the same terms as men. Harper had misgivings but agreed to support coeducation.

> I would not be honest with you were I to conceal that all my feelings have been opposed to co-education. My own work has been done thus far in institutions open only to men. . . . In a new institution untrammeled by traditions and with the flexibility which it is hoped will characterize the University of Chicago, there seems to be no possible doubt that co-education will be practicable. At all events the matter has been decided. The charter admits persons of both sexes on equal terms. The desire of the founders and the requirements of the charter will be carried out in the letter and in the spirit.[7]

Characteristically, Harper sought the leading women's educator in the United States for the dean of women, former Wellesley College president Alice Freeman Palmer. She had retired from the presidency in 1887 to marry Harvard philosophy professor George Herbert Palmer but remained active in women's higher education. She worked with Elizabeth Agassiz to establish the Harvard Annex, later Radcliffe College; raised money as the president of the Women's Education Association; and served on the Massachusetts State Board of Education and the Wellesley Board of Trustees. Harper offered both Palmers faculty posts. Although reluctant to leave the East, and concerned about her health, Alice Palmer did not want to turn down the first full professorship at a coeducational university offered to a woman. She agreed in 1892 to come to Chicago as professor of history and dean of women, provided she could reside in the city for only twelve weeks a year. As her assistant and successor, she chose Marion Talbot, instructor of sanitary science at Wellesley and cofounder of the Association of Collegiate Alumnae.

Harper appointed seven other women, giving Chicago more female faculty than at any other contemporary coeducational institution. They included Julia Bulkley, associate professor of pedagogy and assistant dean of women; Martha Foote Crowe, assistant professor of English; Zella Dixson, assistant librarian; Alice Bertha Foster, M.D., tutor in physical culture; and some assistants in foreign languages. The university also opened competition for its graduate fellowships to women; in 1892–93, six of the forty-three fellows were female.

More than Harper expected, women and indeed all students at Chicago sh●ped the campus atmosphere. In its first decade the university was a particularly progressive place for female students. During the 1902 controversy, many faculty maintained that the considerable achievements of women at Chicago had come at the expense of male students and the collegiate life. Yet even after 1902, when traditional student life became stronger, women continued to maintain a favorable position. As at Berkeley, they benefited from the backing of prominent women in the city.

A SUPPORTIVE OLDER GENERATION

Between 1870 and 1890 Chicago's women organized themselves for cultural, philanthropic, and reform purposes. The Woman's Building at the Columbian Exposition of 1893 symbolized the generation's energy and determination. Designed by twenty-three-year-old Sophia Hayden, first female architecture graduate of MIT, the building was inspired by Susan B. Anthony, who resented women's exclusion from previous fairs and fought for an exhibit highlighting their achievements. Her prodding led to the creation of a Board of Lady Managers, chaired by Chicago society leader Bertha Honore Palmer. The board committed itself to financing a Woman's Building for displaying women's creative and humanitarian work. Bertha Palmer went to Europe to win support for the project, arranging for exhibits from England, France, and Germany.

Besides craft and industrial work, the Woman's Building had an organization room with displays by the YWCA, the WCTU, and other women's groups; a dormitory for single working women; a women's library; a child care center; and facilities for appearances by speakers, including Anthony. The board set aside funds for a permanent museum devoted to women's achievements, but the depression of 1893 made that impossible. So many people attended the events, especially the suffrage lectures, that building managers needed police assistance to handle the crowds. Anthony said that the exposition advanced the cause of women's rights farther in six months than had half a century of other efforts. Another contemporary wrote: "Never in the history of nations has there been such a revelation of women's capabilities and deeds as in this gala year. But commencement is almost over. The world has seen, heard, and applauded. With the end, comes the beginning."[8]

Founded in 1889, Hull House on Chicago's West Side represented another way for women to play a larger role in public life. College graduates Jane Addams, Florence Kelley, Julia Lathrop, Dr. Alice Hamilton, and Ellen Gates Starr sought to improve social conditions and family life in urban, industrial America. Compulsory education, child labor, mothers' pensions, parks and playgrounds, workmen's compensation, vocational education and guidance, protection of newly arrived immigrants, women's labor unions, and crusades against prostitution occupied the attention of the Hull House women. As social conciliators they drew together upper-class women with working-class leaders in a successful reform coalition. Hull House residents established close contacts with the new university, frequently appearing on campus as speakers and as guests at receptions, luncheons, dinners, and teas. They entertained faculty and students in their own homes or at Hull House. Graduate students—Sophonisba Breckinridge, Grace and Edith Abbott, and others—became involved in social reform work in the city. Jane Addams taught courses at the university. Undergraduates participated in settlement projects and raised funds at the annual Settlement Dance.[9]

Socially prominent Chicago women also expressed interest in the university. Harper appeared before the prestigious Chicago Women's Club to request donations for women's dormitories. The *Chicago Inter-Ocean* reported: "At a meeting of the Chicago Women's Club Harper made it clear that the University of Chicago was to be of the broad gauge order, and that the gentler sex was to come in on the same footing with its brothers; there was to be no annex or other attachment, but the woman's department was to be full-fledged, absolutely equal in all respects with that of the men. Now, what would the women do about it, queried Dr. Harper." Between 1892 and 1893 the Chicago Women's Club raised slightly over $1 million for female students. Contributions ranged from $25 to $10,000; Elizabeth Kelly and Nancy Foster each gave larger sums to build four women's residences: Kelly, Foster, Green, and Beecher Halls.[10]

Female faculty shared friendships and ideals with the city's women leaders. Alice Palmer and Marion Talbot expected women students to uphold high academic standards, create a democratic campus life, and become socially conscious citizens. They wanted students to enjoy the intellectual advantages of a large urban university, combined with the rich communal and social life of the eastern women's colleges. If Harper planned a western Yale at Chicago, Palmer and Talbot worked for a western Wellesley.

Born in 1855, Alice Elvira Freeman belonged to the first generation of college women, having entered the University of Michigan in 1871. At that time Mt. Hoyoke and Elmira were hardly more than seminaries, and Vassar had yet, in her view, to prove itself a true college. Freeman struggled to put herself through college, leaving school for a time to help her family financially by teaching. She sent her brother through medical school, and one sister to a seminary. She nursed another sister, Stella, until the latter's death in 1879 and supported her father when his medical practice flagged. She received a bachelor's degree from Michigan in 1876 and an honorary Ph.D. in history in 1882 after assuming the Wellesley presidency (she had completed every requirement for the doctorate except the thesis). Henry Durant, founder of Wellesley College, tried several times to hire Freeman as professor of history, but not until her sister's death did Alice accept the offer. Two years later she succeeded Ada L. Howard as president.

Aware from her own experiences of the need to maintain high intellectual standards and produce graduates capable of self-support, she turned Wellesley into a first-rate institution. In a posthumous biography of his wife, George Palmer summarized her achievements at the college;

> A scholarly, united and admired college was built up. Seeking to raise the rank of Wellesley until it should equal that of any New England college, she found herself hampered by lack of fitting schools, by a loose system of admission on certificate, by lack of accommodation in college buildings for suitable numbers, and by consequent lack of funds. She found her teachers too few, badly chosen and badly paid, burdened with excessive routine work, and needing to be more solidly organized into departments. She found meagre laboratories and library, no provision for physical training, and little connection between the college and the learned and social world outside. At the close of her administration, these deficiencies had disappeared, without leaving debt behind.[11]

Freeman's appointments raised the level of the faculty. The most outstanding were Katharine Lee Bates and Vida Dutton Scudder in English literature; Katherine Coman in political economy; and Mary Whiton Calkins in philosophy and psychology. After Freeman's presidency, but during her tenure as a trustee, the college hired Mary Emma Woolley, future president of Mount Holyoke College, and Emily Greene Balch, reformer and peace advocate. Woolley later modeled Mount Holyoke on Wellesley standards and traditions. The faculty inspired many students to do graduate work. Between 1892 and 1902, Wellesley and Vassar each sent more women to the graduate departments of the University of Chicago than any other institution except Chicago itself.[12]

Two Wellesley alumnae of the Freeman era had outstanding careers at the

University of Chicago; both had high praise for their alma mater and its influence on their lives. Elizabeth Wallace, born in 1865 to a missionary family in South America, came to Wellesley in 1882, after attending a number of female seminaries. Annoyed at the pettiness of seminary life, she applauded Wellesley's regulations as "wise and reasonable" but admitted that she frequently disobeyed rules prohibiting boxes of food from home. Wallace admired and respected her teachers, through whom she learned scholarly techniques and developed a talent for foreign languages. Wellesley taught students like Wallace to value intellectual achievement. "To fail in any study," she said, "was an unspeakable humiliation to a Wellesley girl of my day. It was kept a dark secret and her deficiency would be made up surreptitiously during an ensuing vacation." Wallace also mentioned the presence of distinguished visitors, such as Oliver Wendell Holmes, Matthew Arnold, Lyman Abbott, and Dwight Moody, part of Freeman's plan to bring students in touch with cultural and intellectual trends. After her graduation in 1886, she moved to Minneapolis to live with her family, taught secondary school, and then studied history at the University of Minnesota with Harry Pratt Judson. When Judson moved to the new University of Chicago in 1892, he urged Wallace to apply for a graduate fellowship. After a stint as a teaching fellow, Wallace earned a doctorate in romance languages, served as dean of women at Knox College in Galesburg, Illinois, and then taught at Chicago until her retirement in 1927.[13]

Sophonisba Breckinridge also attended Wellesley College during Freeman's presidency. Initially, Wellesley disappointed her, and she regretted not going to a more "progressive" college, like the University of Michigan. As Freeman made changes, however, Breckinridge warmed to the college and praised the excellent teaching of Latin and mathematics. Breckinridge also valued her leadership activities at Wellesley. As three-time class president, she learned to draft a constitution and administer parliamentary procedure—techniques, she said, that helped her later in life.[14]

She learned, too, how to live with other members of the closely knit female community. The day she arrived at Wellesley, Breckinridge discovered she had a black classmate, Ella Smith. When horrified friends of her Kentucky family protested, Sophonisba's father remarked: "She got on all right with the boys. . . . I think that she will get on all right with the colored"—as indeed she did. In Breckinridge's junior year, several students argued that Ella Smith's rights as a member of the Wellesley community extended only to educational experiences and that, contrary to tradition, she should not be permitted to invite her family to the prom. As class president and mistress of ceremonies for the prom, Breckinridge "with Miss Freeman's help . . . insisted that every experience at Wellesley was educational," and Ella Smith brought her guests. This sense of female solidarity carried over into Breckinridge's years as assistant dean of women at Chicago.[15]

Like many of her generation, Breckinridge initially went through a postgraduate period of doubt and drift. She became the first woman admitted to the Kentucky bar after reading law in her father's office, but finding it impossible to start her own practice, she remained uncertain about her future. A former Wellesley classmate, then living in Chicago, persuaded her to visit and introduced her to Marion Talbot. Talbot took the brilliant and talented Breckinridge under her wing, provided her with part-time work as her own assistant, and nominated her for graduate fellowships. Breckinridge earned her master's and doctoral degrees in political economy, followed by a J.D. in 1904 from the university's new law school. She taught at the university for many years in various departments, founded the School of Social Service Administration, and published studies of the effects of industrialization on family life.

Alice Freeman's Wellesley had promoted intellectual achievements and the desire to lead a socially useful life. She expected most of her students to marry but, having set the example, felt family life should not preclude their participation in public life. Besides promoting "sound learning" women's colleges sought to encourage idealism, build character, develop taste, and cultivate manners. A large coeducational university offered broader intellectual opportunities but did not provide social and leadership opportunities for women. At Chicago, Alice Freeman Palmer saw the chance to build a women's community within a large university, and thus to maximize the advantages of each form of higher education.

Palmer's close friend and successor as dean of women, Marion Talbot, also dedicated herself to serving women's needs within the university. Talbot's parents were upper-middle-class Boston reformers. Her mother, Emily Talbot, founded the Girls' Latin School because her daughters had been unable to find college preparatory educations in the city. Marion Talbot studied Greek and Latin with a private tutor, as well as other foreign languages in Europe, before entering Boston University, from which she received her bachelor's degree in 1880. Unlike Alice Freeman and Sophonisba Breckinridge, who needed money and entered the working world immediately after graduation, Marion Talbot found herself with nothing to do. After a few years of boredom and depression, she began the study of sanitary science with family friend and MIT professor Ellen Swallow Richards. A Vassar alumna and chemist, Richards developed sanitary science virtually in her own laboratory, applying scientific principles to the solution of industrial, social, and domestic problems. After Talbot received a second bachelor's degree, in sanitary science, Palmer appointed her to a Wellesley instructorship.[16]

Like Palmer, Talbot asserted women's rights to mental development, proud of her generation's achievement in establishing their intellectual capabilities. As she said in her book on women's education: "Women have proved their ability to enter every realm of knowledge. They must have the right to do it. No province of the mind should be peculiarly man's. Unhampered by traditions of sex, women will naturally and without comment seek the intellectual goal which they think good and fit. The logical outcome of the present status of women's education will be intellectual freedom on an individual basis."[17] She shared, too, Palmer's sense of adventure about the University of Chicago. The Midwest seemed a wild and faraway place. When she left Boston a friend gave her a piece of Plymouth Rock to take along. "The gift was rather symbolical of the attitude of Boston educators to the new undertaking," Talbot later wrote. "Those were shifting and perilous sands out there on the edge of the prairie."[18] Talbot made the eastern women's colleges her reference point, frequently visiting them to compare their residential life to Chicago's. When the question of admitting black students to the dormitories arose, she recalled Wellesley's attitude toward race relations and urged the administration to decide the issue in terms of what "our Eastern friends" would think.[19]

Like Palmer, Talbot knew that women would have no social life at a coeducational university unless they created their own. Toward that end the two deans made many plans for Chicago: a "house" system; elimination of divisive elements such as sororities; female control over campus social standards; umbrella organizations drawing together women undergraduates and graduate students; a strong female faculty; programs in household administration; respect and recognition for the achievements of university women. After Palmer resigned in 1895 to concentrate on her New England commitments, Talbot bore the responsibility of administering their plans until her own retirement in 1925.

At other universities, women students lived in boardinghouses, at home, or with relatives. Talbot wanted women to live in residence halls to promote communal spirit and social life. Until the women's halls opened in the fall of 1893, female faculty and students shared quarters in the Hotel Beatrice.

When southerner Elizabeth Messick arrived in Chicago in September 1892, not knowing the location of the university, but planning to register as a student, a helpful neighborhood druggist took her to President Harper, who turned her over to Marion Talbot. Talbot put Messick on a cot in her own room and took charge of her during those first difficult weeks. Freshman Demia Butler recorded in her diary her arrival on September 21, 1892, entrance examinations on the 22nd, and sitting on a mattress at the hotel while Palmer and Talbot explained how the women's halls would function. Women faculty and students dined with male professors, visited the Columbian Exposition as a group, and borrowed Snell Hall from the men students in the spring of 1893, when the Beatrice was needed for visitors to the exposition.[20]

When the women's halls opened, a female faculty member headed each one. Talbot herself began at Kelly and then became head of Green Hall, where she lived for many years. At various times Elizabeth Wallace, Julia Bulkley, Sophonisba Breckinridge, Gertrude Dudley (of the physical education department), and Myra Reynolds (of the English department) served as hall heads. Students ate dinner at tables presided over by women faculty or graduate students. The students themselves ran the halls, as part of the Palmer-Talbot plan to promote democracy and social responsibility. Each hall elected officers, set rules, gave parties and teas, and controlled its own social life. Incoming students were assigned to a hall for a six-month probationary period, at the end of which the permanent residents asked them to leave or voted them in as full members. To emphasize the distinction of hall residence, Talbot listed members in her yearly reports to the president. The student yearbook, the *Cap and Gown,* also published membership lists.

According to Sophonisba Breckinridge, assistant dean of women, student-initiated regulations concerning quiet hours rarely needed enforcing, because residents respected each other's privacy; nor did the faculty presence become intrusive. Breckinridge explained the 10:15 P.M. curfew, one of the few faculty-sponsored rules, as a convenience rather than a restriction.

> One thing was fixed by domestic arrangements. The maids came on duty at seven and went off duty at 10:15. That meant that the halls were closed at 10:15 because the only way anyone could get in was by ringing the bell, in which case the head of the house had to open the door. This meant restriction if the student did not want the embarrassment of being "let in" by a Head who had perhaps been in bed. If the student was going to be out later than 10:15 she could get the key. If she got caught and knew that she would be late, the nice

thing was to telephone in advance, in which case the Head would be prepared. This arrangement did not seem suitable for mature women, and so I undertook to remain available with my door open so that whether it was a guest who stayed later than 10:15 or a student who stayed out later there was no inconvenience or restriction.[21]

Not all women students could afford to live in the halls, or wished to do so. In 1908, at Talbot's urging, the university set up a housing department to inspect student boardinghouses, place some off-limits, and ensure that men and women did not reside at the same address. Talbot required all approved boardinghouses to provide a sitting room for callers, so that bedrooms would not be used as substitutes for parlors.[22]

Talbot emphatically disapproved of male students' control over campus life. Like many nineteenth-century Americans, she believed women to be better qualified than men to set social standards. Harper's lack of interest in undergraduate life allowed Talbot to exercise unusual power and influence for a female faculty member on a coeducational campus. In *The Education of Women* (1910), Marion Talbot set forth her theories about men, women, and social controls: "This (control of social affairs by men) is a condition so at variance with what is desirable and even necessary that too much emphasis cannot be placed on the importance of readjustment. One of the greatest gains needed in the education of women is a revival, through adequate training, of their peculiar influence in unorganized social activities, and then out and beyond into the organized social activities in which they are destined to play an increasingly prominent role."[23]

Talbot's duties as dean of women went beyond supervision of the women's halls to include the registration and approval of all campus social functions; directing the social calendar; conferring with social committees and officers of organizations; assisting fraternities in maintaining good social standards; advising the Board of Student Organizations (the board had the power to grant or withhold approval to new campus organizations); setting standards of dress, dancing, conduct, and manners; and supervising "the conduct of men in the Women's Quadrangle."[24] When Harry Pratt Judson, president of the university following Harper's death in 1906, wanted to give Talbot an office in Lexington Hall, a women's building, she objected: "I think it imperative that my office should be situated where men will feel perfectly free to come to it. . . . The direction of the social life means that I must have frequent and easy conference with men, in fact my duties . . . bring me in contact with at least as many men. . . . My duty is to the University and not merely to the . . . women."[25]

In policing student conduct, Talbot relied on private persuasion rather than on regulations. As Judson told George MacLean, president of the State University of Iowa: "We have very few rules bearing upon social affairs; we assume in general that they will be conducted according to recognized canons of good society which are practically the same the world over. In cases of ignorance or carelessness the Dean of Women uses her judgment in making suggestions."[26]

Cases from Talbot's files demonstrate her tactful handling of "ignorance or carelessness." Wanting to preserve the social freedom of women students, she avoided scandals that might lead to restrictions. On one occasion, men students invited the women to a dance at a neighborhood public hall. Talbot commented: "Let us find out how parties are given and invitations issued by the people who are showing great interest in the University. I have no inclination to force on the community the standards to which I have been accustomed, but I do not think we are compelled to accept the standards of Podunk." Eventually Talbot decided that undergraduate women should not go, but graduate students might do as they pleased. Demia Butler noted in her diary that the women were disappointed but felt better when Talbot wrote notes to their escorts, explaining the situation. Butler's escort, Mr. Stone, "took it beautifully. He talked with Miss Talbot, and then understood." Talbot suggested that the men come to the Hotel Beatrice in the evening and "dance a little" instead. On another occasion, a female graduate fellow wanted to have a wine party for other women graduate students. Her guests accepted the invitation, but with qualms. Finally, in an appeal to stop the party, they turned to Talbot who called in the hostess for a discussion.

> When I told her that I thought it might prove very damaging to the University and the status of women scholars if it should be known that such a gathering were to take place and that I would like to have her help avoid such an outcome by recalling her invitations, she became very angry and said she had had wide experience in educational institutions and had never experienced such interference with personal liberty. . . . The gathering for the sole purpose of drinking up wine left over from another function . . . could not be allowed. She asked by what authority I thought I could prevent it. I replied, "By the authority of the Dean of Women responsible for the good name of the women of the University."[27]

Talbot could also be tough with the fraternities when necessary. Harper referred to her a request from a student to let the Phi Kappa Psi dance go on until 2 A.M. instead of the traditional midnight curfew. Her reply: "Very few University men have been invited to this dance outside of the fraternity and I

I think the effect on city people of changing the hour would not be desirable." On another occasion she wrote to Harper that the Beta Theta Pi house "hardly seems a proper place for our young women to visit until a better report comes."[28]

Parents and students occasionally complained about Talbot's strictness. Dorothy Van Slyke's parents objected to their daughter's expulsion from the university, saying she had had their permission to visit a "Mr. Young" in the city. Ethel Strauchon's family wanted her reinstated at Green Hall, claiming that Ethel had only been involved in a "frolic that went a bit too far." In his novel, *Chimes,* Robert Herrick dubbed the dean of women "Gertrude Porridge," saying she acted like a warden in restricting women students.[29]

Others, however, descried Talbot's leniency. In 1896, Harper wrote to her: "May I ask you to suggest to Miss Josephine Allen greater prudence in her public conduct. . . . I am wondering whether it is in accordance with the wishes of the house committee of Kelly that young gentlemen should come in on a Saturday afternoon and dance. I am under the impression that a report to this effect would not be beneficial to the best interests of the University."[30] Professor James R. Angell complained that boys and girls loitered in the corridors together and chattered in the libraries. Talbot received a letter from "A Senior," who, when asked to look after a friend's sister at the university, found the young woman "ruined." He traced her downfall to Talbot's permissiveness in allowing students to dance the seductive tango at university parties: "I am sure that no woman who has reached the age of discretion would condone the Tango if she had seen it danced as it is at University functions or other dances. . . . Is it fair to the fathers and mothers who entrust their pure and innocent daughters to your care to permit this to go on? . . . No one will ever make me believe that the majority of girls who dance this know why it is they prefer this type of dancing to any other and why it is that you see people 'Tango' where there is no music and not even a floor . . . for instance at beach parties."[31]

Students countered Talbot's Gertrude Porridge image with stories of her graciousness and praised her for ignoring minor infractions. In her memoir of Talbot, Irma H. Gross told of one such incidence: "Where freedom for women was concerned, she could conveniently close her eyes to petty rules. In a period when smoking in women's dormitories (but not in men's) was forbidden, one day she smelled cigarette smoke coming from behind a closed bedroom door. She commented, 'Oh, a popcorn party!' and went her way."[32] Talbot also exercised compassion in dealing with her charges: "My next duty last night was to accept the confidences of a dear sweet child, not yet 21, but married at 15 to a roue. She is now divorced, with a three year old boy, and has come here to study Greek and Latin and fit herself to teach. She is a flirt out-and-out and can't help it anymore than she can help breathing . . . but Mrs. Palmer and I, after very serious talks with her, believe in her fully. Her position is a very hard one, but she wants to come to me freely for advice, and I have her confidence."[33] On the whole, Talbot managed her disciplinary duties well, avoiding scandal and allowing students a maximum of freedom. Had she not done so, the university might well have imposed strict regulations on its women students.

Since the residence halls housed only 20 percent of the women, they did not draw together the whole female population. To remedy this, Talbot sponsored "umbrella organizations" open to all university women: the Neighborhood Clubs, the Club of Women Fellows, and the Woman's Union. She also promoted the activities of the University of Chicago Alumnae Club. The Neighborhood Clubs—Northwest, Northeast, Southwest, and Southeast—organized the 40 percent of female students commuting to the university from their homes in or near the city. The clubs provided these women with rooms for resting, eating, and socializing during the day and gave teas, receptions and parties to make them feel at home on campus and part of university social life. Most important, perhaps, they arranged for their members to attend evening functions at the university in groups and to be escorted home, so that commuters could share in all activities.

Talbot herself served as president of the Club of Women Fellows. She wanted this group to link women faculty and undergraduates and consulted members on such issues as the admission of national sororities to campus. At club meetings the group discussed women's careers and professional development. The graduate and professional orientation of Chicago brought issues of careers to the campus sooner and more seriously than at Berkeley. Their topics included: "Requirements for the Doctorate," "Life in German Universities for American Women," and "Value of Graduate Study for the Secondary School Teacher." Male professors addressed the group on: "Capabilities of Women for Scientific Work," "The Relation of Women to the New Education," and "Women as University Fellows." In addition to its intellectual purposes, the club held parties and luncheons for women graduate students.[34]

In 1904, Talbot founded and presided over the Woman's Union. Open to all university women, with its headquarters in Lexington Hall, the Union offered lunchrooms, meeting rooms, and philanthropic activities. Talbot also saw the union as a meeting ground for university students and promi-

nent women from the city. Ella Flagg Young, Harriet Van Der Vaart, Jane
Addams, and Florence Kelley gave Wednesday afternoon lectures on educational and reform issues. The Union provided meeting rooms for the
Chicago branch of the ACA and the National Council of Jewish Women and
sponsored exhibits by the Illinois Consumers' League. Additionally it channeled women students into working for the University of Chicago Settlement, headed by social reformer Mary Eliza McDowell. In a remark directed
against undergraduate snobbery, Talbot commented on the purpose of the
Woman's Union: "An attempt is made to contribute in a democratic way to
the recreation and uplift of all the women in the University."[35]

Talbot persuaded the university that the women needed a larger clubhouse, and in 1915 Ida Noyes Hall (a gift of LaVerne Noyes) containing
clubrooms, a gymnasium, a swimming pool, and lunchrooms, replaced the
Woman's Union. Wanting students to have an organizational structure, she
set up the Woman's Administrative Council to run Ida Noyes Hall. After the
war, the Federation of University Women replaced the council. So long as
Talbot remained dean of women, she sponsored some sort of organization
open to every woman on campus.

Founded in 1898, the Chicago Alumnae Club enjoyed Dean Talbot's
patronage. The club held social functions, gave theatricals to benefit the
University Settlement, and set up a library to rent textbooks to students.
They maintained a resident fellowship at the settlement and sent representatives to the Chicago Collegiate Bureau of Occupations, designed to place
college women in fields other than teaching or social service. The Alumnae
Club fulfilled Palmer's and Talbot's ideals for the activities of educated
women and, much to President Harper's annoyance, took a major role in the
1902 controversy, defending women's educational rights.[36]

Eager for the university to hire additional female faculty, Talbot pushed
for more appointments and higher salaries. She strongly urged the promotion of Sophonisba Breckinridge, sought permission for physical education
instructor Gertrude Dudley and her students to use the university pool, and
issued teaching recommendations for women graduate students. She could
and did feud with other women but on the whole showed her students a
good example of the female solidarity she wished them to practice.[37]

All her life Marion Talbot supported the educational and intellectual
equality of men and women. Believing, however, that most women of the
second generation of college graduates would become homemakers by
choice, she argued that the curriculum should fit them for their careers: "So
far, then, as the social and economic arrangements of society allot to men

and women different tasks so far must the educational machinery be developed differently for the two sexes. That both shall be treated according to sound psychological principles, while to each is given the opportunity for being trained for such social tasks as await the well-educated member of a modern democratic community, is the ideal to be sought."[38] College women, she said, should understand the application of chemistry, biology, sociology, economics, and the law to their homes and families. Unlike their mothers and grandmothers, they lived in an era when the modern household required an educated person to run it properly. They should also use their training outside the home to deal with community problems, becoming "urban housekeepers" and social reformers. During the Progressive Era these ideals had wide appeal as suffragists, including Talbot, argued that women voters would provide an important moral and reform influence on American society.[39]

In 1892, fourteen institutions of higher education offered courses in sanitary science, household administration, domestic science, or home economics.[40] Talbot initially taught sanitary science at the university as an assistant professor in the Department of Sociology and Anthropology. In 1904 she and Breckinridge became the only full-time faculty in the newly created Department of Household Administration, which established a rigorous program, solidly within the liberal arts tradition. In addition to the seminars of Talbot and Breckinridge, the department cross-listed courses in chemistry, biology, sociology, and anthropology. Talbot's own work stressed the intellectual aspects of sanitary science. According to her student Irma H. Gross, Talbot "early saw that understanding consumption in and by the household was increasingly more vital than productive skills in the household. Especially she viewed the household in its social and community relationships."[41] The special seminar in sanitary science dealt with "new and unsettled problems whose solution will help place the subject of public health on a more secure scientific basis. The topics assigned will be chemical, physiological, economic, or social according to the preference and training of the individual students. . . . This work will be designed only for students capable of carrying on independent investigations."[42]

Breckinridge covered such topics as women and the law, the economic, legal, and social position of the family, and the effects of industrialization on domestic and working life. She and Talbot collaborated on *The Modern Household* (1912). With Edith Abbott, also a former University of Chicago graduate student, Breckinridge coauthored a series in household administration, including *The Delinquent Child and the Home* (1912); *Truancy and*

Non-attendance in the Chicago Public Schools (1917); and *New Homes for Old* (1921). Eventually the School of Social Service Administration took over the concerns of the Department of Household Administration, which did not survive Talbot's retirement.

Like other applied or professional fields such as education or engineering, sanitary science could be taught theoretically or as a series of how-to courses. While Talbot and Breckinridge stressed the intellectual and social reform aspects of their field, the Department of Home Economics in the School of Education emphasized technical skills. Chaired by Alice Peloubet Norton, a Phi Beta Kappa graduate of Smith College and, like Talbot, a student of Ellen Richards's, the department reflected the "learning by doing" approach of progressive educational theory. An undistinguished faculty, educated at normal schools and manual training institutes, offered courses in cooking, sewing, and crafts. Yet even this narrowly conceived program provided women with career opportunities. Departmental literature listed job possibilities for home economics students: teaching or supervision of home economics in the public schools; providing extension services in rural areas; nutritional guidance for children; research positions; work for the Federal Bureau of Home Economics; managing industrial lunchrooms for businesses, schools, and colleges; journalism; and consultants for banks and other businesses. In fact, the Department of Home Economics took the initiative in discussing women's careers on campus; and no other department followed its lead. The University of Chicago became a center for home economics education, sending its students to head departments in colleges and universities across the country. Proposed careers utilized women's traditional interests in children, food, and family life but also widened their job options beyond teaching.[43]

Talbot called attention to the achievements and status of university women each year in the *President's Report* through a detailed essay, "The Women of the University." She published statistics on the attendance, grades, and degrees of women students, listed their home states, subjects studied, honors received, and the titles of their graduate theses. She also noted the number, ranks, and promotions of women faculty and commented on women's extracurricular life. She made few comments, however, about students' family backgrounds, race, religions, career plans, motives for college attendance, or male-female relationships at the university. The overriding concern of her academic generation was the demonstration and development of women's intellectual competence and leadership abilities.[44]

The city's reform atmosphere, and the presence of strong female faculty committed to women's advancement, encouraged positive attitudes toward women on campus. Some of the most prominent male faculty, especially John Dewey, Thorstein Veblen, W. I. Thomas, James R. Angell, and George Herbert Mead, supported their women graduate students and sponsored exciting research on sex differences. The University of Chicago became a laboratory for the discoveries that similarities between men and women far outweighed their differences, thus challenging the scientific basis for the ideology of separate spheres.[45]

Inspired by the new university's opportunities, Alice Freeman Palmer and Marion Talbot planned women's campus life in imitation of the eastern women's colleges. The university's urban location, contacts with prominent women in the city, and faculty participation in social reform showed students interesting options for their futures. Women students liked and respected Talbot, and generally followed her lead. As at other schools, however, this second generation of college women had its own agenda. Social class and ethnicity split the women's community, while coeducation led to questions and sometimes problems in the romantic domain.

UNDERGRADUATE LIFE

Founded at the beginning of the Progressive Era, the University of Chicago never adopted the customs of rushes, class traditions, and pranks that existed before 1890. "Service," "reform," and "self-government," ideals emphasized by the university's connections with the city, quickly took hold on campus. So did the commitment to research, although some undergraduates regretted the resulting tedium of college life. The *University Weekly* satirized the lad who

> . . . came from Wisconsin, Madison,
> Where work was light and he'd lots of fun
> To the U of C which all men know
> Is the very best place for him to go,
> Who for social doings cares not a fig
> But prefers to stagnate and become a dig.[46]

Students also complained that their organizations had to be approved by the Board of Student Organizations and the dean of women. More control in student hands would, they said, lead to a spontaneous social life. At the same time, however, the Senior Council faulted the faculty and administration for not being close enough to the undergraduates.[47]

Commuting students made it difficult to develop an active extracurricular life on campus, said the *University Weekly* in its editorials:

> Murmurings can be heard almost at any time on the campus that our students lack interest and do not properly support the various college activities. . . . No one will doubt for a moment the correctness of such a charge. . . . Why should such a condition be possible when there are six hundred or more undergraduates? It is no trick to observe the vast majority of this number file upon the campus in a long satcheled procession each morning, and each afternoon fold their lunch boxes and silently steal away. . . . The remedy will be found in showing this large class of students that outside interests are incompatible with true college life and should be dropped.[48]

Undergraduates tried to establish customs and traditions connected with class rivalries. They set aside special benches for seniors and for athletes; senior men grew moustaches; freshmen wore caps and beanies. On the whole, however, these measures proved unsuccessful. For one thing, summer students paid no attention to them, to the consternation of the student newspaper. "While elderly school ma'ams occupy the historic seats, let us have more benches so that we will not lose our embryo college customs."[49] Even regular undergraduates in this cosmopolitan, urban environment displayed little interest in such matters. Wistfully the newspaper noted that Princeton students needed a booklet describing their customs, so many did they have.[50]

Harper and the faculty showed no sympathy for class customs and outbreaks of school spirit. After a November 1899 football victory over Brown University, male students neglected to study on the weekend. Monday morning they "smashed" their classes, singing and giving college yells, claiming that President Harper had promised them a holiday for winning the game. An angry Harper arrived at Cobb Hall, told the crowd he had made no such promise, and dispersed the students, warning against a repetition of the incident.[51] When the freshmen and sophomore men battled each other over the raising of a freshman flag, Dean of Students George Vincent disciplined those involved, commenting: "Some students . . . have an idea that things done fifty years ago should be done to-day, notwithstanding the fact that they may be acts which, though innocent and harmless in themselves, lead to things neither one nor the other. I put before you this question: Will it be possible for us to continue our life here with as few rules as we had in the past?"[52]

The active discouragement of hazing, rushing, and other class contests worked to the advantage of women students. In contrast to the grudging acceptance accorded them at the University of California, Chicago's student newspaper announced: "A university without women would be a misnomer."[53] Editors asked students not to use the term *coed*.

> There is a custom prevalent in western colleges where co-education exists, of calling the young ladies attending such institutions "co-eds." Aside from the barbarity of this expression, it is discourteous and vulgar. As a joke, it is even too cheap for the average college wit. It is consoling to think that "co-ed" has not yet received a place at the University. . . . The whole weight of the best public opinion at the University should be unfalteringly arrayed against any attempt at introducing this relic of the medieval way of looking at the position of women into the conversation and writings of the students.[54]

The *University News* (1892–93) and its successors, the *University Weekly* (1893–1902) and the *Daily Maroon* (1895–96 and 1902–present), pointed with pride to the achievements of women students:

> The unusual advantages for graduate work offered to women in the University of Chicago have attracted women who are already making their influence widely felt in education and literature. How true this is, the following list will show: Elizabeth Wallace, Dean of Knox College; Emily James Smith, Dean of Barnard College; Agnes M. Lathe, professor of English, Woman's College of Baltimore; Myra Reynolds, instructor of English, University of Chicago; Madeleine Wallin, instructor, Smith College; Marion E. Hubbard and Sarah McLean Hardy, Wellesley College.[55]

Progressive Era undergraduates also spent time on philanthropy and social reform. At Chicago, student publications often discussed the University Settlement and similar organizations; women joined such activities. Furthermore, during the university's first ten years the newspapers gave a great deal of attention to social life at the women's residence halls.

When male students patronized them, Chicago women fought back. After a condescending series on the benefits of coeducation appeared in the *University News,* undergraduate Maude L. Radford wrote a sarcastic rejoinder: "We would like to say how much it pleases us that the men are allowed to study with us. It rejoices us to see how nicely they keep up with us in our common studies; we think higher education is a very good thing for them and are delighted to see them make such good use of their advantages as they do. . . . In general, we have very much admired the way in which the University men have comported themselves, and hope the coming generations will be worthy of these predecessors."[56]

Although Chicago's male and female undergraduates had a relatively smooth relationship, social class, religion, and race divided the student community. According to an alumni survey, most undergraduates between 1893 and 1930 came from business (43.5 percent) and professional (25.8 percent) families. An additional 10 percent had fathers who were farmers; the rest were in clerical, civil service, or working class occupations. The survey did not differentiate between men and women, but some evidence suggests that more women than men had upper-middle-class origins. Slightly less than half of all students' families lived within twenty-five miles of the university. The central states, including Illinois, accounted for seven-eighths of all undergraduates. Half of the families resided in urban communities of 100,000 or more; only one-third in towns of under 10,000.[57]

Whether commuting from home or living on campus, the wealthier urban students dominated the less affluent, nonurban one-third of the student body. Short stories in the *University Weekly* and the *Cap and Gown* revealed that women allowed social class to interfere with Marion Talbot's emphasis on community. Martha Lavinia Gray, a farmer's daughter who lived in the halls but was ignored by the other women, led a very lonely life at the university. Almost absentmindedly, popular Polly Sewell asked how she liked college life. Martha Gray replied, "Like it? I hate it, I hate it, I hate it! I've been here three months and no one has spoken to me, no one has looked at me, they avoid me as if I were a leper!" When Martha fell ill, her countrified mother came to the university to nurse her. Polly visited her, only to realize that Martha had lied about her "gay good times" at the university to avoid upsetting her parents. As the mother said to Polly: "Lavy has sed so much about you, an' told us how chummy you two wuz, thet I've been mighty anxious to see you. . . . Yes, she writ me how you two went to parties, and theayters and the opery together, an' what fun you wuz havin'!" Polly and the other women in the hall helped Martha deceive her mother until the sick girl was strong enough to go home. Martha's parting words: "You only pity me, you could never take me in as one of you, I'm not your kind. I'm not wanted here—there's no place for me, and I'm glad to go back home where everybody knows me, and it doesn't make any difference about your clothes."[58]

The deans of women worried that the formation of national sorority chapters at the University of Chicago would exacerbate social-class divisions among women students. Although Harper conceded to faculty-student pressure and permitted fraternities to organize on campus, he allowed Palmer and Talbot to make the decision for the women. Fearing the social exclusivity of sorority life, they banned the "nationals" from the university. Like many other issues at the controversial new university, the sorority

question became a subject for national debate and the deans received con-
flicting advice from the off-campus women's community. Florence Kelley
and Isabel Howland of the New York State Woman Suffrage Association
wrote in support of the deans' stand, pointing out sororities' cliquishness
and the suffering they caused women not invited to join. On the other hand,
Stanford sociologist Mary Roberts Smith and Jane Bancroft Robinson,
former dean of women at the Woman's College of Evanston (later absorbed
into Northwestern University), stressed the close friendships, association
with alumnae, and the "happiness and romance of college life" found in
sorority membership.[59]

Rejecting the happiness and romance argument, Talbot and Palmer
banned sororities, although Talbot admitted, in a letter to her mother:
"Under the present rules of the University, men's fraternities are allowed
. . . and there is really no reason why the sororities should not come, except
the feeling that they are undesirable. You see I have no weapon except moral
suasion, and I don't know how long I can keep up the conflict."[60]

Talbot's statement proved prophetic. Outflanking the deans, students
organized local "secret clubs" with all the trappings of sororities—rushing,
pledging, colors and pins, exclusive parties, and monopolization of campus
offices. The clubs—Quadranglers, Mortarboard, Wyvern, Sigma, Esoteric,
and others with shorter life spans—never had their own houses because of
Talbot's continuing opposition.

According to the alumni survey, 41 percent of the students never took
part in campus life. The poorer, older, nonurban segment of the student
body, more likely to be working while attending school, had less time for
social life. The urban upper-middle-class students controlled the fraternities
and clubs, which, in turn, ran the other organizations. Sons of fathers in
business or the professions earned athletic C's twice or three times as often
as sons from other occupational groups. The *Cap and Gown* listed activities
next to senior pictures, demonstrating the predominance of fraternities and
women's secret clubs. Unlike the situation at Berkeley, men's and women's
pictures intermingled in the *Cap and Gown*. In 1897, the senior class consisted of seventy-four men and forty-seven women. Eighteen of the men and
seven of the women were prominent in activities, and all belonged to fraternities or secret clubs. In 1898, a class of eighty-nine men and fifty-one
women produced eighteen outstanding men and four outstanding women;
all were fraternity and club members. In 1910 a similar pattern existed:
there were ninety-one women and ninety-four men in the class, with eighteen outstanding men, thirteen of whom belonged to fraternities, and nine

prominent women, five of whom had joined a secret club. Without exception, the four class officers in any year belonged to fraternities and secret clubs. Those with scholastic honors rarely belonged to the Greek letter societies.[61]

Marion Talbot's attempts to widen women's participation in university social life by prohibiting national sororities had not met with unqualified success. In fact, by limiting the number of women's clubs, she might have made matters worse. In 1900, the men had twelve fraternities and four honor societies; the women had six clubs and one honor society. In 1900–01, 614 men and 581 women registered as undergraduates. The women's clubs thus had nearly as many potential members as the fraternities, with far fewer places for them. Several observers reported on the resulting competitiveness and pettiness among the women. In his *Personal History* journalist Vincent Sheean '19 commented on the women's clubs and their influence during his student days:

> The men were grouped in Greek-letter fraternities with houses for residence. Half a dozen of these were "good" and the rest "bad" but their goodness and badness were not quite so irremediable as the similar qualifications among women's clubs. The fraternities were national organizations, and it was well known that the same fraternity might be "good" at the University of California and "bad" at Yale. The salutary effect of this consideration was supported by the fact that the men did not seem to have the same degree of social cruelty as the women. Men often joined a fraternity because their brothers or fathers had belonged to it, because they had friends in it, because they liked some one person in it, or even because its house or its food or its heating system appealed to them. Such homely, sensible reasons weighed little with the women. All of them, true to the great tradition of American womanhood, took the very "best" club to which they could possibly be elected, and the logic of their behavior kept their club system rigid throughout my four years at the University.[62]

If social snobbery drove wedges into the student community, so did race and religion. Sheean's disgust with the women's clubs stemmed from an incident in which a club member told him he had inadvertently joined a Jewish fraternity and urged him to quit before he ruined his campus reputation. By 1920, 12.5 percent of Chicago's student body was Jewish, representing "a very embarrassing social problem." Jews and Christians seldom mixed; eventually, Jews established their own fraternities. A campus social survey also noted: "The negro problem is one of growing importance." Without knowing the exact number of black students, the researchers stated that there were "more negro women than ever before" on campus in 1920.

The YWCA, more progressive at Chicago than at Berkeley, tried unsuccessfully to arrange interrracial picnics and lunches. "The social taboo is
almost complete and the negroes have no social intercourse with the whites
except for an occasional Settlement Dance couple." In 1907 fraternity and
club students humiliated a young black woman, Cecilia Johnson, by telling
the *Chicago Tribune* that she had passed for white and joined a secret club.
On behalf of the faculty, sociologist Albion Small apologized to Johnson
and urged her to remain at the university to finish her master's degree. Small
also told President Judson that Johnson had made no secret of her race,
brought her mother to campus for visits, and associated with other black
students. The student survey praised the unobtrusiveness and separate social life of Chinese and Japanese students. "The unfailing courtesy, the small
numbers, and the high scholastic ability of the Oriental students have combined to place them high in the respect of the American students. They offer
at present no particularly pressing problem."[63]

In spite of positive campus attitudes toward coeducation, men and wom-
en experienced student life differently. Chicago's alumni survey reported
that men had participated more frequently than women in extracurricular
activities. In the *Cap and Gown* of 1900, twenty-eight male and forty-five
female seniors listed no activities at all next to their graduation pictures; in
1910, the figure fell for men but remained constant for women. Whatever
the other reasons, men had greater opportunities, such as the recognition
and honors earned from intercollegiate athletics and intramural sports. The
Women's Athletic Association sponsored campus contests between classes,
but the administration did not consider it proper for Chicago's female
athletes to compete against other college teams. Until the opening of Ida
Noyes Hall in 1915, women had inadequate athletic facilities: only a small
gymnasium in Lexington Hall after 1900 and occasional use of the Bartlett
Hall pool.[64]

No formal restraints prevented joint participation of men and women in
the bewildering variety of clubs granted charters by the Board of Student
Organizations. A student could choose from two or three publications, five
dramatic groups, five musical, six political, nine religious and philanthropic
organizations, and student government, not to speak of the Pen Club,
Investigators' Club, Richard Wagner Society, Pre-Legal Club, Short Story
Club, International Club, Commercial Club, and five debating squads. But
many clubs *were* sexually segregated, and separatism did not favor women.
Even student government and publications, open to both sexes, prescribed
the offices women held and the jobs they did. They wrote for the *University*

Weekly but never served on its editorial board. Once a year, a female staff produced the *Women's Weekly,* thereby dramatizing their disproportionately small role on the paper. Some women's organizations excluded men, but their clubs played a less impressive role in university life and never represented Chicago in contests with other schools.[65]

Unlike the writing produced at other institutions, the fiction of men and women at Chicago did not discuss conflicts between women's higher education and femininity. On the whole, Chicago's men did not expect female classmates to minimize their intelligence for social acceptability. With few exceptions, the short stories praised intelligent women. In one such account, Katharine introduced her university friends Ralph and Dorothy, telling Ralph proudly that Dorothy had won a gold medal for scholarship and been elected to Phi Beta Kappa. Duly impressed, Ralph fell in love with Dorothy. In another story, Ada Spencewell was embarrassed to return to her small-town country home, because she had not won academic honors at the university. Her failure so disappointed her friends that they did not come to the train station to celebrate her arrival. In "Mercedes or Dora?" handsome, dashing Ralph proposed marriage to Dora Barnard, attracted by her interest in John Stuart Mill and her success in publishing scholarly articles. Dora, however, with total self-possession, refused Ralph: "I do not wish to marry. I like my own independence—and my own income."[66]

Coeducation, however, plagued romantic relationships because it led to role confusion. Men complained that women whom they knew from classes "cut" them on campus, that is, refused to speak to them. Women were unsure of the proper conduct toward men when not formally introduced. Were they simply classmates, in which case informal association made sense, or did the potential for more intimate relationships make traditional courting behavior more appropriate? In "One Recitation in the Spring Elective," a short story from the *Cap and Gown* of 1900, freshman Mary Waite defended herself to her roommate, Kitty, for speaking to "Mr. Bellingwood" in her anthropology class without an introduction: "What's the good of being a college girl if you're going to be all tied up with forms? I've seen him fifty times in class, and once I had to pass in front of him and I asked him to excuse me and he answered so prettily I knew he was nice; and he looks sort of lonely and aristocratic—as though he needed somebody to cheer him up and could appreciate the right person." In spite of her bravado, Miss Waite lacked confidence in the propriety of her actions. She cried to Kitty: "But—do—you—think—he—he'll—despise me?" Far from despising her, Bellingwood watched for her to appear so they could walk to class together, but fearful of public opinion, she avoided him. "Finally, he encountered her unexpectedly in the quadrangles. He bowed, half-stopping expectantly, but she gave him so small and cold a nod that it reminded him of the tip of an icicle." Hurt by her rudeness, Bellingwood stopped trying to be friendly. Finally, the thwarted lovers found a way to speak to each other, and Mary Waite confessed, "Mr. Bellingwood, . . . I want to tell you something. One day I spoke to you on campus. Truly, I did it because you looked . . . lonely. Afterwards, I didn't recognize you, I cut you. That was because I was afraid—do you see?" He replied: "I'm awfully glad we got to know each other some way."[67]

The *University Weekly* encouraged students to exercise common sense and regard classroom contacts as sufficient introduction, yet coeducation did not make it easier for young people to dispense with the long period of calling each other "Mr." and "Miss" before using first names.

> Why didn't they greet each other?
> Because they think they don't know each other.
> But do they?
> They have been in the same classes half a year.
> Then why do they think they are not acquainted?
> Because they have never been introduced.
> Oh, what is an introduction?
> The naming of each to the other by a mutual acquaintance.
> Does this knowledge of each other's names entitle them to speak together?
> Yes.
> And half a year's acquaintance with each other's character, opinions, and feelings as exhibited in class does not?
> Exactly.
> What is to blame for this state of things?
> Custom.
> And they, liking and admiring each other, have not the courage to disregard custom?
> No.
> Then do they deserve to enjoy each other's companionship?
> No.[68]

After becoming acquainted, male and female students faced other problems. Off campus, men and women did not associate closely unless they had marriage in mind. At college, however, men and women went to classes and dances together and saw each other every day. The situation required a different kind of etiquette and a casualness about male-female relationships. In "Points of View" Lois, a senior, invited her younger friend Dorothy to visit her at the university. The women attended a dance and received attention and compliments from the fraternity men. Lois, noted Dorothy, seemed close to one man in particular—Grant Lorimer. Later, Lois admitted her fondness for Grant but explained to Dorothy the ephemeral nature of college romance.

> Why, Dorry, it would mean years of waiting—years—and I don't trust myself or him. . . . We are awfully fond of each other right now, and it will be mighty hard to call things off in June; but call them off we must, and then I'll go abroad with Aunt Alice, have a gay time and forget everything. He'll forget too—first. . . . I have past experience to draw from. You asked me if I knew Fletcher Holward. Yes, I used to go with him in pretty much the same way— and there was someone before him, and that's all long ago, so I ought to know. . . . Does it seem hard to you, this new philosophy?[69]

Other stories reinforced the warning that courting between students was problematic. Young people away from home knew little about one another's pasts and often misinterpreted relationships. When a university couple fell in love, one of them sometimes had a previous attachment—as in Arthur Sears Henning's short story, "The Game of Tennis." While Jack and Alice, who had been courting, were playing tennis one afternoon, he asked if he could call on her that night at the women's residence halls. She told him she was busy, and when he asked why: "She reached a dainty finger down her collar and drew forth a ribbon. Something on it sparkled. 'I don't wear it now because I don't want the girls to know until the end of the quarter. The man is Mr. Raymond, a lawyer down town. I know you'll like him.'" And from "The Awakening": "There was the usual 'girl in east' whose picture he had shown her, a bright, pretty face with no power in it. That he would someday marry that little tawny-haired girl they both understood and it disturbed their summer not one whit." In Fanny Burling's "Once Again," Jack Carleton and Grace Ransome walked home together from a campus dance. He told her he loved her, and then: "A smiling pictured face rose before his excited eyes and Jack stopped. . . . 'I have no right to say this to you. Forgive me. I am engaged to be married to another girl. You can't hate me as much as I hate myself! How could I help loving you! Don't ever let me see you again.'"[70]

Male students at Chicago seemed far more comfortable with coeducation than their counterparts at California and elsewhere. As the *University News* put it: "We students at Chicago shall all our lives be better for constant association with those who may be now our sweethearts, someday our wives." But the gender equilibrium was delicate, and the faculty increasingly disturbed over women's campus strength, as the controversy in 1902 over sexual segregation revealed.[71]

"CHICAGO'S ONLY CIVIL WAR"

The possibility of effeminization, that is, of women's domination of coeducational universities, seemed particularly ominous at the University of Chicago and eventually created "Chicago's Only Civil War."[72] In 1902, 268 male seniors outnumbered 242 females, yet women made up 56.3 percent of the Phi Beta Kappa membership and outnumbered men in the Junior College. Socially, the success of the residence halls and women's clubs gave women a prominent position on campus and led to fears that they would overrun the university. Between 1900 and 1902 faculty, administrators, and trustees debated the advisability of segregated instruction and separate quadrangles for Junior College men and women. Discussion of the scheme led to a national controversy, not only because other schools had similar problems but because Chicago had offered so much to female students and faculty. Women all over the country wrote to Harper and the trustees, opposing segregation.[73]

At Chicago the move toward gender segregation came from the administration but was eagerly supported by many male professors, who had long felt uneasy with the presence of women on campus. Robert Herrick discussed the faculty's feelings about female students in *Chimes*. His protagonist, Professor Clavercin,

> could not easily get over his dislike of seeing women chatting familiarly with the men in the corners of the halls, or sitting in the empty classrooms, flirting. . . . It offended something romantic in him. . . . In his morning class the women took by prescriptive right all the front benches in the room, while the minority of men slunk into the rear, as if ashamed of exposing their cruder mentality before women in mass. . . . They seemed obsessed by a mental difference before the other sex. . . . The women were not as a rule pretty or even attractive . . . plain and not always tidy. . . . He believed in sex equality and all that but something romantic in him was offended by the evidence of coeducation. He liked to think of women as apart from the commonplace of life—as decorative, provocative, mysterious, and how could one when they stuck pencils through their hair and stood on one leg gossiping with fellow students or bent nearsightedly over a grimy classroom bench.[74]

According to Clavercin, intellectual women unsexed themselves. His affair with the brilliant scholar Jessica Stowe ended because her academic competence made her unwomanly—cold and unfeeling. Although fictional, Clavercin's statement accurately reflected faculty attitudes. When students interviewed professors about segregation, the campus newspaper reported: "(1) Instructors find it impossible to use sufficient severity with girls in class to produce the best results. (2) Tendency toward more crowding and too much physical contact in the halls of Cobb. (3) Coarsening social effect of present co-educational system. (4) Monopolizing of corridors, stairs, and grounds by girls."[75]

According to short stories in student publications, faculty discomfort with women students may have stemmed from their attraction to them. Male faculty educated in single-sex institutions, and accustomed to teaching men, had difficulty seeing women as students rather than as simply objects of romance. In "A Co-educational Episode" biology professor Dr. Dow confessed his love to student Margaret Edgerton, who made fun of him to her friends and told him not to approach her again. Later, she learned that Dow was a married man with a young child. In another story, a freshman approached a man from her German class, asking for assistance. She wanted to make a good impression on her professor, but had missed the first class and needed to know the assignment. She also told the young man of her desire to meet the professor outside class, to impress him with her studious attitude. The young man did not reply, but: "As they reached the dressing room door, he showed her the lesson, and said, as he tipped his hat: 'As far as it lies in my power, you shall certainly meet him outside of class—again.' 'Again?' she staggered against the door. 'Who is that man?' she exclaimed excitedly, clutching the girl nearest at hand. 'Who? O, that's the German Prof,' and the Freshman sat down and sobbed." Occasionally student newspapers announced the engagement or marriage of a professor to a student, as when famed physicist Albert Michelson, who favored segregation, married undergraduate Edna Stanton.[76]

In their official statements about segregation, Harper and his faculty spoke on a loftier plane, pointing out the dangers coeducation posed to inherent sexual distinctiveness. Segregation, they said, would "improve" coeducation by helping each sex develop "manly" or "womanly" ideals. Harper noted that coeducation had thus far produced "too many cases of young women who have lost some of the fine attractiveness which somewhat closer reserve would have attained. Thoughtful men and women are not unanimous that the type of comradeship which co-education has pro-

113

moted between men and women is altogether an improvement . . . [It is] a pedagogical and social mistake to assume that men and women should be trained to be just as nearly alike as possible."[77] Many faculty agreed, stressing that separation benefited both sexes. Professor Nathaniel Butler told Harper that parents kept their daughters away from the University of Chicago because "they feel that the road that leads to gracious womanhood is not throughout its extent, identical with that which leads to fully established manhood." Professor Edward Capps argued that segregation was part of the natural order: "If left to themselves the young men and women tend to separation. . . . They develop social institutions each class for itself. . . . They form separate clubs and societies representing every variety of student interest and meet together, of their own free will, only in the occasional social functions in which sex is the controlling element."[78]

Others believed coeducation most disadvantageous to men and saw segregation as a necessary measure to restore male prerogatives: "It is unquestionably true that the great advance made within twenty years in the education of women has been at the expense of men's education. The same principle has been at work as in ordinary spheres of life: Woman is being advanced, but the advancement is resulting in dragging down men. The proposed plan obviates this difficulty by permitting the natural development of both."[79] In the same vein, Harry Pratt Judson wanted men students to have a more traditionally collegiate campus life and blamed women students for inhibiting their plans: "In the old-fashioned men's colleges there is a sense of unity, a feeling of social solidarity which is notably lacking in co-educational institutions, and which is in itself a powerful educational agency. . . . Is it necessary to lose it? May it not in great part be attained, without losing the good results of co-education, if co-education is adapted in judicious form?"[80] Albion Small represented a group that claimed coeducation distracted men from their studies: "In a word, the life of our Junior College students, both in and out of the class-room adopts relatively too much of the tone of a leisure-class social function, and too little of the character of a strenuous intellectual exercise."[81]

Objections to segregation came from other university faculty, alumnae, and representatives of women's organizations. They argued that segregation circumvented the spirit if not the letter of the university's charter, cast doubts on the intellectual competence and morality of women students, was uneconomical, and would give women short shrift educationally. Behind their statements lay the fear that segregation in the Junior College would lead, eventually, to women's exclusion from the university.

Marion Talbot led the opposition. Separate instruction threatened her lifelong crusade to establish the intellectual equality of the sexes, and the expense of dual classrooms meant women might receive less qualified teachers. Furthermore, whatever the university said, the public would view segregation as a response to some failure by women students. She protested to Harper: "The atmosphere of intellectual freedom enjoyed by our students, through which they have exercised their mental powers as human beings without reference to the fact that they are either men or women has been appreciated by them and admired by the world. Separate instruction would introduce an element which would affect this condition unfavorably. If the trustees could know how eager girls and women are to study as thinking beings and not as females, they would hesitate in justice to women to adopt this measure."[82]

Dissident faculty expressed their views in "A Memorial to President Harper and the Board of Trustees," a petition signed by all the women faculty, most of whom had been graduate students at the university, and fifty male professors. John Dewey offered the most eloquent protest against segregation, disagreeing that intellectual separatism would promote healthier relationships between the sexes.

> The argument implies that the proper basis of the relation of the sexes is the life of amusement and recreation, instead of that of serious pursuit of truth in mutual competition and co-operation. The proposed measure thus takes away the chief safeguard of co-education and leaves all its weak points exposed and multiplied. Quadrangles contiguous to each other for social purposes and absolutely remote for intellectual purposes are a standing invitation to silliness, flirtations, and even scandal. When such results come, as they surely will, will they be attributed to their original cause, or used as arguments for going further along the path of separation.[83]

Latin professor William G. Hale warned that segregation would attract more frivolous women students to the university: "It is not sure that there would be fewer young women under the proposed system. There would indeed be likely to be a less serious class of young women, since those who plan serious work might well avoid a plan which openly discriminated against them. . . . I am by no means sure that the throwing open of Harvard College would not result, through the greater natural conscientiousness of women, in rousing young men to the exercise of their faculties."[84]

Led by Angeline Loesch '98 and Theresa Hirschl '00, the Chicago Alumnae Club polled its members about segregation. Of 191 replies received, 172 alumnae opposed separate classes, and 19 were in favor. Accordingly,

Loesch and Hirschl issued a leaflet denouncing the plan and mailed it to faculty, students, and women's groups at Chicago. The Alumnae Club argued that even limitations on women's enrollment, as instituted by Stanford University, were preferable to segregation: "It is a violation of good faith with the public, who have understood this to be a distinctly co-educational institution and not one of the annex type. . . . It will be interpreted everywhere . . . as a blow against co-education and as evidence of its partial failure where it had been tried under favorable auspices. . . . It is an unjustified reflection upon the conduct of the young men and women in the colleges."[85] And Harper's argument that he was improving coeducation through segregation did not impress former graduate student Madeleine Wallin: "These arguments do greater justice to Dr. Harper's ingenuity than to his candor. . . . The issue here is not between co-education and separate education but between bona fide co-education and a so-called 'higher form of co-education' which belies its nature by omitting the essential element of the union of the sexes: classroom work."[86]

Disapproving letters reached Harper and the trustees from the Minnesota Woman Suffrage Association, the Chicago branch of the Association of Collegiate Alumnae, the Sioux County Equal Suffrage Association of Des Moines, the Toledo Woman Suffrage Association, the National Committee to Promote the Establishment of the University of the United States, the Utah State Council of Women, the Wisconsin Woman's Suffrage Association, and the wives and daughters of prominent men. A typical letter, from a judge's wife, Mineola Graham Sexton, commented: "Thousands of club women all over the United States are watching with grave anxiety for the decision of the University of Chicago upon co-education. Women have worked so hard and so long for the privilege they now enjoy of securing a college education, and so many women are looking forward to entering your University, that the possibility of being excluded in the future means far more to womanhood than you perhaps realize."[87]

Judging by the paucity of articles on the subject in their newspapers, Chicago's undergraduates paid less attention to the controversy than their elders. When they did discuss segregation, student publications either opposed it or, reserving judgment, gave all views on the subject. The *University Weekly* found coeducation responsible for a lack of chivalry among male students but did not recommend segregation as a remedy. Men should be careful, they said, not to transfer informal classroom attitudes to social situations. The *Weekly* polled students on segregation, finding all the women and most of the men students opposed to it. As undergraduate Charles

W. Collins said, "If it is a masked attack upon the fundamental principle of co-education, I am absolutely opposed." The *Daily Maroon,* beginning publication in autumn 1902, recorded faculty and student opinion on both sides of the issue, noting that women students uniformly opposed segregation. The paper took no editorial stand on segregation, deciding to reserve judgment until the plan's defeat or implementation.[88]

During the summer of 1902, the Faculty Senate voted nineteen to twelve to recommend separate instruction to the Board of Trustees, which approved the plan thirteen to three in October. During the winter quarter of 1903, the administration set up separate sections of required courses in the Junior College, planning to expand the practice to electives when economically feasible. By the autumn quarter of 1904, 80 percent of Junior College students had at least one segregated course, although 21.4 percent of the women and 28 percent of the men had none. Only 19.8 percent of the men and 27.1 percent of the women had segregated sections for all their courses. In the winter and spring quarters of 1903–04, when students included more electives in their programs, 62.7 percent of the men (34 percent in winter) and 40 percent of the women (28 percent in the winter) had no separate instruction at all. In the spring quarter, 1.8 percent of the men and 4.2 percent of the women had completely segregated courses.

The dean of the Junior Colleges praised the plan, saying it had "quickly become a recognized institution" and met the objections of some faculty to throwing young men and women together too often and too quickly. Yet by 1906–07 only 50 percent of Junior College students were affected by the plan at all. After 1907 there is no information on the functioning of separate instruction and no indication of when it ceased to exist. Neither the *President's Report* nor the *Annual Register* mentioned separate sections of courses for men and women. In 1916 Marion Talbot wrote to Cornell University president Jacob Gould Schurman that only nine of fifty-four Junior College courses had segregated sections. Segregation became a pro forma policy, with minimal effects on campus life.[89]

Discussions of coeducation also disappeared from the university records after 1902. Harper, subsequent presidents, and faculty wishing to limit the influence of women students did nothing further, possibly because other faculty and off-campus opinion would permit no more tampering with coeducation. Yet the controversy revealed considerable faculty resentment over women's success at the University of Chicago. And shortly thereafter, the balance of campus power, already in male hands, tipped heavily in their favor.

CHICAGO AFTER SEGREGATION:

1 9 0 2 – 1 9 2 0

After 1902 male enrollments increased, as the university opened a law school, established business courses, and built a men's clubhouse. This trend appeared nationwide because of the growing utility of a college degree in the business and professional worlds. Articles on football, debate, and other intercollegiate contests in the new campus newspaper, the *Daily Maroon,* reflected growing male enrollments and the rise of collegiate spirit. The newspaper dropped the literary, religious, and intellectual pieces characteristic of its predecessor, the *University Weekly.* The names of women reporters showed up less frequently on the masthead, and women restricted their contributions to "women's news," printed on the back pages. The *Maroon* also referred to men as "the students." In 1907, celebrating the beginning of the fall quarter, an editorial commented: "*The Daily Maroon* . . . is also glad to see the old men come back. . . . The greatest part of coming back in the fall is to greet the men with whom we have worked and whose friendship we have come to prize."[90]

The *Daily Maroon* displayed a new attitude toward women students, claiming that they detracted from college spirit unless they stayed in their place. "Men should not take girls to football games was a resolution lately brought up in Council. . . . They say that it interferes with the cheering— that the men cannot mass themselves together and show the football team that they can cheer." The paper acknowledged that "sometimes the support of the girls has put more heart into a team than the rooting of a thousand men," and recommended that the women continue their singing apart from the men. And like the men at Berkeley, Chicago's male students complained that women voted unwisely in campus elections: "It is useless to deny that men have been chosen over better men because they are good society 'stars,' 'fussers,' in the parlance of the campus, because they wear good clothes, talk well, dance well, or have entertained some members of a particular coterie, or are members of a mutual political and social alliance."[91]

In other ways, too, women's campus position weakened after 1902. Between 1893 and 1900 women's scholastic averages at Chicago had been significantly higher than the men's; after 1900 the men did better than the women. Although the university greatly expanded its faculty in the 1910s and 1920s, women professors remained few in number and concentrated in the lower ranks. In 1908–09, sixteen years after Harper's original seven female appointments, women faculty held only eleven positions: one full professorship, one associate professorship, two assistant professorships, five instructorships, and two assistantships. The university sometimes hired its female doctoral students as instructors, but they advanced no further through the ranks.[92]

In 1924, just before her retirement, Marion Talbot joined Elizabeth Wallace and English professor Edith Foster Flint in a communication to President E. D. Burton and the Board of Trustees. They pointed out that women did not sit on the Board of Trustees, were inadequately represented on the faculties of arts, literature, and science, and did not get promotions or salary increases at the same rate as men. At a time when women made up 40 percent of the university's graduate students, they received only 20 percent of the fellowships. The university neither permitted women to join the faculty club nor asked them to speak at convocations and dinners. Beyond the promotion of Sophonisba Breckinridge to full professor, the petition received no response from the trustees.[93]

Even after 1902, however, connections between the university and progressivism in the city gave women students at Chicago richer campus experiences than their counterparts at other coeducational schools. The *Daily Maroon* gave extensive coverage to the university's chapter of the College Equal Suffrage League, founded in 1907 by Professor Breckinridge and undergraduate Harriet Grim after their return from a national suffrage convention. The *Maroon* also reported professors' opinions on suffrage, campus speeches by suffragists from the city, prizes offered for suffrage essays, and plays given by the league. The paper urged students to attend Jane Addams's suffrage lecture, scolding the university community for its indifference to the issue:

> The comparatively small membership of the University Equal Suffrage Association is an arraignment. For the various amenities of undergraduate life, all of them well in proportion, we find or make time, but for the interests of millions of earnest young women, we protest that we are too busy, or that it is a good cause and go our ways, or repeat that dead excuse that "woman's place is in the home" and we wish no part in taking her out of it. We have no right to lend so little thoughtful consideration or personal activity to the problem. . . . We owe a hearing to Miss Addams and her sex.[94]

The male editorial "we" expressed none of the hostility found in the *Daily Californian*. Somewhat apprehensively, the *Daily Maroon* supported the selection of Harriet Grim '08 as the university's first female debater, and Hazel Stillman '11 as the first woman president of Undergraduate Council.[95]

Like women at Berkeley, female faculty and students at the University of Chicago expected that intellectual integration and social separatism would lead to an equality of complementary spheres. At Chicago, however, women fared far better with this ideology, especially before 1902, developing communal and extracurricular activities, participating in reform movements, and setting the tone of campus life. At Chicago, male students did not demonstrate the hostility toward educated women that was so common elsewhere. The location of the university in a center of urban reform, its commitment to graduate education, connections among women faculty, social reformers, and feminists, and the determination of Marion Talbot made possible women's achievements.

Harper and the faculty disliked the growing influence of women's culture in higher education, viewing it as an encroachment on men's sphere, and their fears of effeminization led to the establishment of separate classes. Academic segregation proved ineffective, but male enrollments and influence gradually increased across the nation, as men began to view college attendance as a necessary prerequisite to a professional career. Female students and faculty at Chicago never regained the status they enjoyed in the first ten years of the university's history.

When Marion Talbot retired in 1925, the university divided her duties among several committees instead of appointing a successor. Except for the secret clubs, separate women's organizations also disappeared in the 1920s. Many regarded these changes as positive. The evidence does not show why Talbot was not replaced, but possibly the university no longer considered a dean of women necessary to guide and protect female students. Emancipated by the Nineteenth Amendment, women had become men's equals and should be treated as such. Yet women students of the mid-twentieth century still found themselves excluded from much of campus life, and the lack of a separate power base made matters worse. An exception for a time, the University of Chicago came to follow common patterns for coeducational schools.

CHAPTER FOUR

Vassar College, 1865–1920:
Women with Missions

Matthew Vassar, the Poughkeepsie brewer who founded the college bearing his name, clearly stated the institution's purpose as intellectual equality: "It occurred to me that woman, having received from her Creator the same intellectual constitution as man, has the same right as man to intellectual culture and development." The first president, John Howard Raymond (1865–78), carefully distinguished between intellectual and political egalitarianism:

> When Vassar College as represented by its seniors and alumnæ becomes popular with the vulgar and extreme "women's rights" people and disgusts the wise, we must confess our error. . . . So long as the young women . . . command a universal admiration for the breadth and clearness of their intelligence, for the sobriety and soundness of their judgments, for the simplicity and delicacy of their manners and for the dignity, purity, and symmetry of their character, we feel that we may fairly ask for a little longer trial.

Written by Raymond, the *Prospectus* of the college underplayed themes of educational equality, pledging to preserve sex roles with a curriculum "specially appropriate to woman." The plan acknowledged male-female differences and stated the college's aim "to maintain a just appreciation of the dignity of women's home-sphere; to foster a womanly interest in its affairs; to teach a correct *theory* at least, of the household and its management, and to give some practical training in such domestic duties as admit of illustration in college life."[1]

Caught between the contradictory objectives of offering intellectual equality with men and special education for domesticity, Vassar College resolved the dilemma in favor of the former. Like men's colleges of the day, Vassar balanced traditional liberal arts courses with offerings in the natural and social sciences, modern languages and literature, and fine arts. During its first twenty-five years, the college prescribed two-thirds of the students' courses. The nine departments included the standard subjects of philosophy, ancient and modern languages, mathematics and astronomy, and newer studies, such as English language and literature, design, music, natural history, physics, physiology and hygiene.[2]

If the curriculum was uncompromisingly masculine, the students' social world followed Raymond's prescriptions and imitated more traditional forms. To reassure parents and readers of Dr. Clarke that higher education would not endanger students' health, the college strictly regulated each hour of the day. Raymond and Lady Principal Hannah Lyman laid down rules to be enforced by "corridor teachers," female faculty sharing the students' quarters. Students rose at 6 A.M., said morning prayers at 6:45, breakfasted at 7:00, then arranged their rooms and observed a twenty-minute "silent time"; had morning study hours and recitations from 9:00 to 12:40; dinner at 1:00; recreation from 2:00 to 2:40; afternoon study from 2:45 to 5:45; supper at 6:00, evening prayers and another "silent time"; then evening study hour from 8:00 to 9:00, and required lights out at 10:00 P.M. Sunday's routine included two church services and a Bible study group. Students also had to take one hour of daily exercise.

The administration adopted additional policies to make women's higher education respectable and to ensure its control over the lives of young women, some of whom in the preparatory department were as young as sixteen. Lyman insisted that students change their dresses for dinner, submit permission letters from their parents if they wished to correspond with men, get her approval for their skirt lengths, give her a list of proposed purchases before they shopped in town, maintain strict chaperonage, and be prompt for meals and chapel services. Lyman also believed that intellectual attainments should not take precedence over good manners in Vassar's faculty; teachers should be Christian ladies. When asked her opinion about a candidate for a teaching position, Lyman inquired, "Do you think her Unitarian influence is likely in any way to be pernicious?"[3]

Some viewed Vassar's strictness as a means of accustoming women to life in the public sphere, where time and order had more meaning than in the household. While in school, schedules and bells symbolized women's liberation from the intermittent and interminable demands of domesticity and their freedom to follow a prescribed course of study, prayer, and recreation. Such regulations had, in fact, represented a bold departure in women's education when instituted at Mary Lyon's Mount Holyoke in the mid-nineteenth century.

In her memoir about the early days at Vassar, alumna Mary Harriot Norris defended the college rules as necessary to instill dignity in the students, thereby counteracting the public image of young women as silly, gossipy, flirtatious creatures. She noted the students' dismay at the discovery that their real names, rather than nicknames like "Joy" or "Posie," would appear in the catalogue: "I believe it gave them the first pull against the tide of gushing girlish exuberance, of affectionate display in public, enabling them, outside of the inner circle of their loved ones, to put aside childishness. There was less baby talk, less walking with arms around each other, more of the dignity and reticence of the modern woman."[4]

Most students and faculty, however, did not agree with Mary Norris. Finding the rules and regulations insulting, they constantly pressed for their modification or elimination. Women of the post–Civil War generation, they defined freedom not as the opportunity to follow a schedule but as the right to make personal choices about their use of time and space.

Thus, from the college's earliest days, faculty and students fulfilled their own needs at Vassar, often defying the authorities to do so. Instructors who found the institution restrictive had an ally in astronomy professor Maria Mitchell. Unlike other female "teachers," who lived in the residence halls with students, Professor Mitchell and her father made their home in the Observatory, where, to Raymond's dismay, she did not "observe" Sunday. While students and faculty went to church and Bible classes, Mitchell sat at her window, in full view, and did her mending. Mitchell rejected the view that deportment came before scholarship. She scolded students who interrupted a lecture to remark on her unfastened collar; took a group to Denver, Colorado, to view an eclipse; and encouraged students to break the 10:00 P.M. lights-out rule to gaze through the Observatory's telescope. Involved in off-campus organizations, such as the Women's Educational Association of Boston, Mitchell also worked for women's advancement at Vassar. She demanded salaries equal to the male faculty's for herself and other women teachers, insisted that her publications be included in the president's annual report, and invited leaders of the women's rights movement to speak at the college. As her guests, Julia Ward Howe, Mary Livermore, and Elizabeth

Cady Stanton lectured to students and mingled with them afterward at Mitchell's home.[5]

Maria Mitchell's encouragement of other faculty earned her their respect and devotion, while her international scholarly reputation impressed President Raymond. As another woman faculty member put it: "However interested you might have been in woman suffrage and all the other subjects concerning the cause, you felt that in comparison with this grand woman, you hardly knew the alphabet. She judged everything from the standpoint of 'How is this going to affect women.'" Through her prodding, Raymond came to view "woman's sphere" as extendable and supported the idea that women had the right to choose between marriage and a career. As Mitchell said of the president: "He was not broad in his ideas of women, and was made to broaden the education of women by the women around him."[6]

Like the faculty, students found ways to make their presence felt at Vassar. In 1868 they began a Students' Association, informing a startled President Raymond that they would elect a chair as soon as he left the room. Although the *Prospectus* promised that Vassar women would not learn to debate as men did but would instead practice reading aloud, students organized two debating societies—Qui Vive for the even-numbered classes and Tempus et Mores for odd-numbered classes. Philaletheis (lovers of truth) began as a lecture club and turned into a dramatics group after Matthew Vassar's will established a permanent lecture fund. Other clubs included the Floral Society, the Society of Religious Inquiry (later the Christian Association, Vassar's version of the YWCA), a student newspaper, and a yearbook. Vassar women also participated in bowling, riding, dancing, calisthenics, croquet, baseball, and chess. They held elaborate celebrations on Founders' Day (Matthew Vassar's birthday), Washington's Birthday, Valentine's Day, and for commencement. The classes gave parties for each other and gradually developed traditions. Students staged mock political campaigns and "voted" during presidential election years, a curious practice at an institution officially opposed to women's rights. Harriot Stanton '78, daughter of Elizabeth Cady Stanton, founded a Democratic Club during her student days and fined members who neglected to read the newspapers before attending meetings.[7]

In spite of the administration's conservatism, officials permitted women's rights advocates to speak to students. In addition to speakers invited as Maria Mitchell's personal guests, suffragists Caroline Dall, Anna Dickinson, and George William Curtis lectured at the college. Matthew Vassar himself heard Dickinson speak on "Idiots and Women," referring to the law denying the vote to "criminals, paupers, idiots, and women," and invited him to address the students. As the horrified founder noted in his diary: "I am surprised to find our Fair Sex in so shamefull (sic) a category. . . . I think it is full time my 300 daughters at Vassar knew it and applied the remidy (sic)." Students held their own suffrage debate in 1868. And whatever their views on women's rights, Vassar students tolerated no disrespect for their minds. They became angry at Ralph Waldo Emerson for saying he would modify his lecture because he felt they could not understand it as written. They forced Raymond to rescind his decision not to let the "radical" Wendell Phillips speak at the college and called Matthew Arnold's conservative views of women "medieval."[8]

Students circumvented Hannah Lyman's watchfulness; few women consistently observed the 10:00 P.M. curfew, staying up instead to read, study, or talk. Helen Dawes Brown '78, herself much influenced by the political activism of classmate Harriot Stanton, discussed student interaction in her novel, *Two College Girls,* published in 1886. Her heroines, Edna Howe and Rosamond Mills, entered Vassar as different "types." Edna had been raised by a poor aunt in a small town and expected her college education to help her earn a living as a teacher. Intellectually arrogant and aloof, she refused to associate with the other women, preferring to spend her time studying. In contrast, Rosamond, a frivolous society girl from a wealthy Chicago home, despised "grinds" like Edna and socialized her way through college. By the novel's end, through their friendship and the association with other students, each girl had changed markedly. Impressed by her friend's standards of scholarship and service, Rosamond decided to go to medical school, while Edna promised to marry Rosamond's brother Jack after her first few years teaching.[9]

Some women came to college with specific postgraduate plans, but others did not. Yet instruction, friendships, and influences of faculty heightened and defined expectations. Notwithstanding the aims of John Howard Raymond—that is, to educate women without changing sex roles—students, inspired by their faculty and influenced by each other, often found their way to new goals. In *Two College Girls,* Helen Dawes Brown re-created what must have been a common dormitory conversation:

> *Mary Lloyd:* I wish I did know what women were to do with themselves. I know very well what I do not believe in, but I'm not at all sure what I do believe in. The education of women is the only thing I am clear about. I confess I don't see a step further.

Edna Howe: It's a little odd that we don't talk more here about the education of women. We hardly ever mention the subject.

Mary Lloyd: Because the argument is ended. We are here: this is the conclusion.

Edna Howe: I'm not sure this is the conclusion. All the rest of our lives will have to be the conclusion.

Nora Allen: It's a rather selfish business, this trying to make ourselves so perfect, going about our own evolution in such a scientific, Darwinian way.

Mary Lloyd: I can't settle the woman question for anybody but myself. I have no doubt about my own destiny. I'm going to Germany to study chemistry, and then I am going into the dye room of my uncle's factory.

Rosamond Mills: If I ever marry—and I hope I shall—it will be to the man of all the world that believes the most in me; will help me best to be a useful woman; will put new heart and courage into everything I do.

Julia Territt: Mamma and I have our compact. I am to accept invitations for Friday and Saturday. But teaching algebra is not the final goal of my ambition. I want to found a training school for house servants. We are going to have regularly graduated servants, with certificates. Mamma has been so tormented in her housekeeping that she is interested; and all her friends are delighted with our scheme. You know my hobby is training, training, training. We must submit to it, we women, before we can do self-respecting work—work that asks no favors.

Mary Pruden: That is splendid. I wish I were going to do something. My mother is sick, and I am going to keep house and take care of her.

The discussion continued in this vein. Twins Kate and Cora Baldwin announced their parents' intention of sending them to Europe after each proved she could earn five hundred dollars a year. Cora planned to be an assistant librarian while Kate worked for their father. Josephine Weston, class valedictorian, opted for European study, and May Lovering to do missionary work in China.[10]

In their class prophecies, sibyls predicted a wide range of careers for their classmates, including astronomy (demonstrating Maria Mitchell's influence), social reform and work for women's rights, academics, medicine, archaeology, literature, journalism, and music. Vassar women also displayed ambivalence about marriage. The sibyl for 1873 prophesied that no one from her class would marry—and attributed this startling pronouncement to her classmates' educations. Progressive women all, they would not be content to pass time with volunteer work while waiting for a man to come along and provide them with a home. Instead, they would make their own homes, supporting themselves with interesting careers. Other class prophecies displayed similar sentiments, with sibyls angry that marriage tradi-tionally meant retirement from public life. The sibyls acknowledged that society expected women to choose between the two alternatives and blamed such a custom on men. Whereas 61.9 percent of the first five Vassar classes (1867–1871) eventually married, only 55.6 percent of the next five classes did so. Between 1865 and 1890, 53–60 percent of each class married.[11]

Vassar students of the first generation had high aspirations and a sense of mission—to prove, through their lives, the virtues and utility of educating women. Some earned graduate degrees at prestigious universities and be-came college professors. Scientists Christine Ladd-Franklin '69, Ellen Swal-low Richards '70, and English literature professor Myra Reynolds '80 were well known to second-generation Vassar students through their articles in student publications and lectures at the college. Alumnae faculty at Vassar included Abby Leach '85, professor of Greek; Laura J. Wylie '77, professor of English; Achsah Mt. Ely '68, mathematics; Elizabeth Hazelton Haight '94, Latin; Margaret Floy Washburn '91, philosophy and psychology; Emi-lie Wells '94, economics; Gertrude Buck '97, English; Mary Whitney '68 and Caroline Furness '91, astronomy; Adelaide Underhill '88, librarian, and Ella McCaleb '78, dean of the college.

The large number of graduates of women's colleges who went into social settlement and social reform work continued the communal life they en-joyed during their college days. Vassar's most famous representative in this group, Julia C. Lathrop '80, worked with Jane Addams at Hull House in Chicago before becoming the first chief of the U.S. Children's Bureau in 1916. Some Vassar women did not live up to their ideals and hopes in the postgraduate years. In class reunion books they apologized for their failure to achieve great things, for letting the college and their classmates down. Even they, however, often undertook a wide range of volunteer activities, including an active role in alumnae affairs.

As faculty and alumnae, the first generation of Vassar women became a compelling campus presence during the 1890s and continued to be so throughout the Progressive Era. The Associate Alumnae of Vassar College, founded in 1871, pressured the administration and the trustees to close the preparatory department, appoint alumnae representatives to the board, and relax social regulations. When Matthew Vassar's nephews left endowed professorships "for men only" to the college, the Alumnae Association supported Maria Mitchell in a successful protest to the trustees. The associa-tion raised money for scholarships, fellowships, buildings, and graduate studies. With other women's college graduates, they participated in the

College Settlement Association and encouraged students to give their time to settlement work.

Alumnae also provided vocational information for students and recent graduates. In the student newspaper and alumnae magazines they discussed openings for women in different occupations. Sample articles included: "The Scope of Domestic Science" by Katharine Bement Davis '92; "The College Settlement Movement" by Elsie Nichols '99; "Housekeeping from the College Woman's Standpoint" by Ellen S. Richards '70; "Women and the World of Newspapers" by Ella S. Leonard '85; "The Best Preparation for a Woman Physician" by Dr. Emma B. Culbertson '78; "The Parlor Lecturer" by Helen Dawes Brown '78; "Work for Trained Women in Reformatories for Women" by Katharine Bement Davis '92; "The Work of Vassar Graduates in Psychology" by Margaret Floy Washburn '91; "The Outlook for Women in the Field of Scholarship" by Myra Reynolds '80; "Opportunities for College Women in Civil Service" by Ruth Child '08; "Women in Law" by Mabel E. Witte '08; and "Vassar Students as Wage-Earners" by Amy Reed '92.[12]

Although they did not contest the value of a liberal arts education, alumnae wanted the college to acknowledge women's need for postgraduate work. Ellen Richards, Julia Lathrop, and Katharine Bement Davis led the drive to add domestic science and child study courses to the college's curriculum. They saw these studies as necessary to inform and encourage college women to work for child welfare legislation, improved family and community life. New careers in government, science laboratories, and universities could open up to women trained in this way. Others, like Margaret Floy Washburn, denounced this "dilution" of women's liberal arts education, seeing such courses as leading the way back to the female seminary and the kitchen. Both sides fought the battle with a passionate concern for women's intellectual and professional development; each accused the other of halting progress in women's higher education.

Finally, alumnae passed on to the second generation their pride in Vassar's traditions. Elizabeth Hazelton Haight '94, the college's unofficial historian, edited the life and letters of President Taylor and with him wrote *Before Vassar Opened* and *Vassar*. Other works about the college by alumnae include Agnes Rogers, *Vassar Women: An Informal Study;* Elizabeth Woodbridge Morris, *Miss Wylie of Vassar;* Dorothy Plum, *The Magnificent Enterprise: A Chronicle of Vassar College;* Mary Harriot Norris, *The Golden Age of Vassar;* and Marion Bacon, *Life at Vassar: Seventy-Five Years in Pictures.* The Vassar Alumnae Historical Association held elaborate celebrations on the twenty-fifth (in 1890) and fiftieth (1915) anniversaries of the college and in 1905 opened Alumnae House on campus, making it easy for alumnae to visit and participate in college life.

Students knew of alumnae achievements and admired prominent individuals. They requested articles from alumnae on careers, politics, and social issues for their own publications. In 1896 the *Vassarion,* the college yearbook, published a list of representative alumnae, all well-known career women, intended as models for students. Besides Vassar's alumnae faculty, the list included Association of Collegiate Alumnae presidents Annie Howes Barnes '74 and Helen Hiscock Backus '73, also a Vassar trustee; Dr. Emma Culbertson, vice president and the first woman in the American Academy of Medicine; Margaret Sherwood '86, professor of English at Wellesley; Edwina Hersey '76, professor of English at Smith; author Elizabeth Knight Tompkins '89; Mary L. Avery '68, head of the English Department, State Normal School at Whitewater, Wisconsin; artist Elizabeth R. Coffin '70; Susie Forrest Swift '83 of the Salvation Army; Katharine Bement Davis '92, head worker, Philadelphia Settlement, lecturer in household economy; and several other physicians.

The Vassar faculty also helped students develop self-confidence for the postcollege years. In the early days, with few exceptions, women on the Vassar faculty were referred to as teachers rather than as professors. As the first college women earned graduate degrees in the 1880s and 1890s, the college hired them, fulfilling Matthew Vassar's wish for a female professoriat. The Vassar faculty sometimes fought over its students. Helen Lockwood '12, later an English professor at Wellesley and Vassar, told an amusing story from her college days that illustrated this aspect of faculty-student relationships. In a letter to her family she described an encounter with Greek professor Abby Leach:

> The first thing she said to me was, "You're going on with your Greek, aren't you, Helen?" Now of course I have been intending to tell her, but I was going to do it gracefully. . . . However, I said as nicely as I could that I was afraid not. . . . She raked me over in great style. "Do you see what you are doing? You will go on with this broadening plan of yours, and when you get through there won't be a single thing you can teach." . . . I suppose I will have to have a real time with her before I get through.[13]

Vassar's most popular teacher, Laura J. Wylie, came to the college as a freshman in 1873, with a poor academic background. Family responsibilities, including the care of a tubercular sister, kept her from receiving a thorough secondary education. At Vassar she studied English with Truman

Backus, also a favorite professor of Harriot Stanton's, and graduated as class valedictorian. After commencement, she taught at the Packer Collegiate Institute in Brooklyn under Backus, its new director. During her years at Packer, Wylie also worked at the Rivington Street Settlement, founded by Vassar, Smith, and Wellesley graduates, and debated whether to make college teaching or social work her career. Deciding on teaching, Wylie took her Ph.D. at Yale University. Her dissertation, "Studies in the Evolution of English Criticism," was the first woman's thesis published by Yale.

As an English professor at Vassar, Wylie combined teaching with community volunteer work and a commitment to suffrage and social reform. She used her academic specialty, the social implications of literature, to help students think critically about social issues. As one of her students put it: "In the somewhat stodgy atmosphere of our then College authorities, she moved carefully for the sake of the things she thought valuable, restraining her ready sarcasm, selecting the moment for plain speech. And to us she never gave the authorities away. By no direct statement did she expose to us their obviousness. But she cleared cobwebs from the young minds that came to her, and prepared them, if they had it in them, to think."[14] Confirming Wylie's influence on students, Joan Shelley Rubin has identified historian Constance Rourke's student days at Vassar, and in particular the association with Laura Wylie as the source of Rourke's progressive social attitudes and methods for studying American culture. One of Rourke's graduation gifts in 1907 was a volume by Jane Addams, containing a clear call for college women's social activism. Through her studies and attendance at Vassar, Rourke began to feel herself part of a nationwide movement of women in social reform.[15]

Like other academic women of her generation, Wylie did not marry. She and Gertrude Buck, also on the English faculty, lived together for years in devotion and friendship. Through Wylie's social criticism and Buck's experimental theatre, they made Vassar's English department innovative. They also opened their home to students for teas, dinners, lively conversation, and debates over college life and politics.

Another popular and inspiring Vassar teacher, Lucy Maynard Salmon, began her career as an undergraduate at the University of Michigan, class of 1876. There she found the social life, consisting of class rushes and competitions, restricted to men. She became a leader among the women students, who formed eating clubs and societies for discussion and mutual support. Refusing proposals of marriage, Salmon spent a few years teaching in secondary and normal schools before returning to Michigan for graduate study in history. Her work with Charles Kendall Adams on territorial Michigan history, and her activities in the western branch of the ACA, led to an invitation from President Alice Freeman Palmer to teach at Wellesley. Salmon refused, desiring more graduate work, and went to Bryn Mawr College to study with Woodrow Wilson.

She helped Wilson with the research for his books and learned to deal with his distaste for female academics. To Adams, who told her she knew more history than Wilson did, Salmon commented:

> I am quite sure that he [Wilson] never wholeheartedly believed in college education for women. He once said to me that a woman who had married an intellectual, educated man was often better educated than a woman who had had college training. All of this used to amuse me, and I never presented any other side of the subject to him, or stated my own views—it would have been useless to do so. I felt that his opinions were simply derived from a limited educational and social experience and hoped he would sometime learn better.[16]

At Bryn Mawr, Salmon also established women's groups, organizing some graduate students into the "L.S." (Learned Six) and counseling undergraduates like Emily Greene Balch, a future Wellesley professor and peace activist. Through round robin letters she kept in touch with L.S. members for the rest of her life.

Dr. Eliza Mosher, a friend from her Michigan women's groups and college physician at Vassar, recommended Salmon to President Taylor for the newly created position of history professor. Salmon came to the college in 1887, remaining there, except for European sabbaticals, until her death in 1927. A shy woman, sensitive and somewhat retiring, despite many friends, Salmon initially throve on Vassar's built-in social life. She wrote one friend, "All that is necessary when you feel like seeing anyone, is to take the engaged sign from your door and your room will be swarming with lovely and charming people." She enjoyed having students call upon her, bringing their friends, inviting her to their parties, and sending her flowers.[17]

As time passed, Salmon felt more keenly the restrictions and lack of privacy at turn-of-the-century Vassar. Resenting the social regulations, both for herself and the students, she urged President Taylor to abolish them. Upon her arrival at Vassar, in 1887, the Lady Principal handed her a list of students' names with times noted beside each one. When Salmon asked the purpose of the list, the Lady Principal informed her of the corridor teachers' duty to supervise students' baths. Salmon refused: such chores infuriated her. She insisted, too, that faculty and administrators speak of students as "women," not "girls." When Taylor objected to her wearing culottes to bicycle around the campus in 1891, she attacked Vassar's preoccupation with propriety: "Over and over again I feel that I must advise able young women in whom I am interested to go to a co-educational college rather than to come here because of the greater opportunities and the fewer educational restrictions. . . . We spend our time and energy in seeing that students do not do various things while neglecting the positive and constructive side."[18]

Adelaide Underhill '88, later Vassar's librarian, became her closest friend and companion. When Salmon left the dormitories, she and Underhill bought a house in Poughkeepsie. As Salmon's biographer and colleague in the history department, Louise Fargo Brown, said: "Between the two shy women there developed a perfect understanding. . . . Between them there always existed a delicate reserve, which was bridged by deep affection on both sides." Salmon called Underhill "sister." Like Wylie and Buck, Salmon and Underhill frequently entertained students at their home.[19]

Campaigning for the relaxation of social rules was part of Salmon's larger effort to create a self-governing community of equals. Salmon wanted students to have a greater voice in their course selection. Most important, she believed Vassar women should practice democracy and cooperation. A suffragist, she expected women voters to reform the electorate and the country. As future citizens and potential voters, students should avoid competitiveness and shun distinctions. She urged Vassar women to work for self-government and an honor system and asked the college to stop using the word *servant* to describe Vassar's maids. Salmon set an example of democracy by returning, unopened, letters addressed to her as anything but "Miss Salmon" and by objecting to the seating of faculty by rank at college dinners. In the student newspapers she denounced the awarding of commencement honors to seniors with high grades and opposed the establishment of a Phi Beta Kappa chapter. When the University of Michigan wanted to elect her, retroactively, to its new PBK chapter, she declined. During the gap between President Taylor's resignation in 1914 and the inauguration of Henry Noble MacCracken in 1915, Salmon organized the faculty to demand more power in setting college policies.

These crusades did not come easily to the shy Lucy Salmon, and she often found her actions resented or misinterpreted. Taylor's pride in her scholarship did not keep him from wishing she would take some matters less seriously, as when she complained to him that the college laundry kept losing her stockings. Her feud with economics professor Herbert Mills also created problems. Mills came to Vassar as a history professor in 1891, and Salmon protested the creation of a separate economics department under his leadership in 1893.[20]

Students, too, sometimes thought her strange, silent, or standoffish. Margaret Shipp '05 found Salmon's parties an ordeal, as she explained in a letter to her sister:

> I wish I could do justice to Miss S. and yet tell her lack of tact at the same time, but I'm afraid I can't. . . . She cannot converse, but she talks delightfully . . . to a group! She seems to have no power at all to respond to what you say to her individually. . . . Fanny Bell asked her: "Miss Salmon, may I ask you a *very* personal question?"
>
> Miss S. said yes, with a rising inflection. Fanny: "Do you use the *Century Cookbook?*" Well, that nearly finished Peggy! But really, any question whatever would have seemed a personal one to be asking Miss S. that night.[21]

Ruth Adams '04, daughter of a historian, told her family about Salmon's awkward attempt at career counseling:

> I had a conference with Miss Salmon yesterday and certainly she is a peculiar specimen. One of the questions she asked me was whether I was going to follow my father's profession, or your mother's, shall we say, Miss Adams? I wanted to tell her that I would follow my mother's if I could get a man, and my father's if I had to, but I didn't. Then she told me that by heredity and by early training and influence I should be the leader and shining light for the others.[22]

A progressive educator and excellent teacher, Salmon stressed the use of original research and primary sources in her teaching of history, rather than the customary memorization and recitation. Henry Morse Stephens, professor of history at the University of California, said that his best graduate students came from Lucy Salmon's classes. Her interest in women's careers originated in her dismay at seeing so many students go into teaching because they could think of nothing else to do. A gifted teacher herself, she was horrified by such a notion. Salmon served on committees for the American Historical Association; wrote history questions for the College Entrance Examination Board; published books and articles on domestic service, the history of newspapers, and constitutional issues; lectured on teacher training at Teachers College, Columbia University; and worked for women's suffrage.[23]

Herbert Mills's popularity was second only to Lucy Salmon's and Laura Wylie's. Mills came to Vassar as a history professor in 1891 and headed his own Department of Economics from 1893 until his retirement in 1934. Mills's work established the social sciences at Vassar. Future social workers took his course on charities and corrections; his students hotly debated socialism and labor problems. Mills felt his courses instilled a measure of social consciousness in an important segment of the American upper middle class. Students flocked to his department. Between 1890 and 1900, 81.2 percent of Vassar seniors took at least one economics course; between 1900 and 1910, the figure was 72.5 percent, and between 1910 and 1920, 78 percent.[24]

Mills set a personal example of social concern and activism through his own community work as president of the Poughkeepsie Family Welfare Association; manager of the House of Refuge in Hudson, New York, a reformatory for young women; president of the Dutchess County Board of Child Welfare; almshouse commissioner of the city of Poughkeepsie; and dean of the Training Camp for Nurses, held at Vassar during World War I. Honoring him at his retirement, the alumnae published a book of essays describing Mills's influence on their careers in social service. In the introduction to the volume, President MacCracken commented on Mills's effect on students: "He not only participated in social movements of his time, but his passionate partisanship of the right inspired his pupils to share in the social movements of the day. The writer can recall a mass meeting at Vassar at a time when the suffrage seemed nearly won when his own counsel of conciliation and moderation was vehemently opposed by Professor Mills who urged the undergraduates to fight passionately for the cause."[25]

In contrast to the liberal views of many alumnae and faculty, James Monroe Taylor, fifth president of the college (1886–1914), had a more conventional outlook. In 1908, he forbade an on-campus suffrage meeting, enraging alumnae speakers Harriot Stanton Blatch and Helen Hoy, attorney for the Equality League of Self-Supporting Women, who were accompanied by the feminist-socialist writer Charlotte Perkins Gilman and labor leader Rose Schneiderman. Inez Milholland '09, a student activist and founder of a secret campus suffrage club, led forty students over the college walls to hear the speeches in a nearby cemetery. Newspapers, students, and the speakers themselves never forgot the event and gave it wide publicity. For some, then and now, it exemplified Vassar's conservatism at the turn of the century.[26]

Yet the graveyard suffrage incident does not tell the whole story of Taylor's attitudes toward women and his efforts on their behalf. His fund-raising ability, diplomacy with trustees, alumnae, and faculty, and popularity with the students made his administration a successful one. And in spite of his refusal to connect women's rights with women's higher education, Taylor's actions as president showed considerable respect for women and their talents. Taylor believed Vassar College should remain dedicated to women's liberal arts education. He had little use for the sanitary science movement and resisted alumnae pressure to add such courses to the curriculum. Contemporary critics, including his successor Henry Noble MacCracken, considered him hopelessly stodgy on this issue. Taylor, however, believed that domestic science education, although intended to widen vocational possibilities, would in fact limit young women's options. "The demand to put Domestic Science into such an institution gains fascination, especially for men, from the totally erroneous idea that every woman is to manage a house."[27]

Although he certainly misunderstood the type of domestic science proposed by Richards, Davis and others, Taylor viewed himself as defending women's intellectual rights. Replying to G. Stanley Hall's attacks on educated women, Taylor wrote:

> The college girl as she really is in our women's colleges is normal, healthy, heartily womanly, and almost universally without fads and peculiarities. If she is not always married, it is not because a few years of study, well-seasoned with recreation and broken by months at home, have warped heart and mind from nature's deepest feelings and holiest relations. No figures so far have produced any scientific value, nor can they have until we can compare college girls in large numbers with those of her own class, friends and relatives who do not go to college. . . . This leaves unanswered her claim to decide for herself as to the using of her mental faculties.[28]

Taylor had a more progressive view of women's lives than John Howard Raymond, encouraging them to choose satisfying work. Like Lucy Salmon he believed women should seek careers of service rather than personal glory, but he defined such fields more narrowly than she did. When Helen Lockwood '12 was debating her career choice, Taylor helped her decide on teaching.

> "What are you going to do after graduation?" asked the President. "I think I am going to teach." "That's splendid," said Prexy, "how wise you are not to be swept off your feet by the faculty who are talking about business and law. Teaching is the most beneficial and socially useful profession a girl can go into. A good many women nowadays don't realize the tremendous influence a teacher has but look more to something startling which will resound to their personal glory."[29]

Taylor accepted ideals of service for himself as well. He emphasized his devotion to women's higher education and his belief in their abilities by refusing to leave the presidency of Vassar for more prestigious opportunities. As a member of the American Baptist Education Society and a friend of John D. Rockefeller, Taylor served on the committee to plan a new

University of Chicago. William Rainey Harper, first president of the University of Chicago, asked Taylor to come with him as a professor and his special assistant. Taylor refused. Had he gone to Chicago in 1892, he might well have succeeded Harper when the latter died in 1906. In 1899 Taylor declined an offer to become president of Brown University, to the delight of the Vassar community. "The joy of Vassar women at his refusal was unbounded. At last! Here was a man who believed a woman's college was a more rewarding place for a life work than one of the best colleges for men."[30]

An indefatigable fund-raiser, Taylor added $500,000 to the college's endowment. During his administration the college built six dormitories, a recitation hall, biology and chemistry laboratories, a library, chapel, infirmary, and students' hall; and increased the library's holdings from twelve thousand to eighty thousand volumes. In the 1870s, faced with competition from Wellesley, Smith, and Cornell in attracting students, Vassar's enrollment had suffered, but by 1905 the college could accommodate no more, and the trustees voted to limit the size of the student body to one thousand students. Parents registered their infants for Vassar. Although Ella McCaleb '78, dean of the college, accepted twice as many registrations as the class had places, in September of any given year, approximately the right number of freshmen showed up. Even with a limited enrollment and increased dormitory space, the college could no longer house all its students and reluctantly allowed some women to live off campus.

Taylor fostered a good relationship with the alumnae. During his first year as president, he granted their two long-standing demands by closing the preparatory department and appointing two alumnae representatives to the Board of Trustees. He sought qualified alumnae to teach at the college, complaining about the loss of so many to the new profession of social work. Sharing their pride in the college, he coauthored, with Elizabeth Hazelton Haight, a two-volume history of Vassar, establishing its claim to be the first legitimate women's college.

Henry Noble MacCracken, his successor, felt Taylor's greatest achievement lay in building an outstanding faculty. "I was amazed to find the quality of teaching at Vassar definitely better than that I had known at either Harvard or Yale." In addition to adding twelve new positions in history, biology, economics, psychology, Biblical literature, and political science, twice during his presidency Taylor persuaded the trustees to permit more electives, thus giving faculty incentive to create new courses. Whatever his feelings about suffrage meetings on campus, he never halted the freewheeling debates in Mills's and Salmon's classes, or Laura Wylie's "social criticism."[31]

Taylor offered most available faculty positions to women, believing that the college had a responsibility to provide opportunities unavailable at coeducational institutions. In 1905, he appointed two professors, eight instructors, and six assistants; of the sixteen positions, only one went to a man. By 1911–12, Vassar had a faculty of 108, including 17 men. Sixteen of the women had professorial rank; 75 were instructors and assistants. Of the 44 Vassar alumnae on the faculty, 8 were professors, and the other 36 instructors. Furthermore, Taylor, perhaps influenced by Lucy Salmon, understood the emotional strain that living in the dormitories placed on single women faculty and raised funds for off-campus faculty housing.[32]

Taylor's sense of humor frequently carried him through sticky situations. Dealing with suffrage militant Inez Milholland, for example, could not have been easy. For a final examination in his senior ethics class, she wrote two papers, "The World as Prexy Thinks It Is" and "The World As it Really Is," earning an "A" from Taylor.

Taylor dealt less successfully with the male-female polarization of the faculty. In spite of his efforts to offer equal opportunity to women professors, nearly all the male faculty headed departments. These men formed a conservative bloc, resistant to change, while the women's majority in the junior faculty ranks outvoted them on most issues. As might be predicted, departments with female heads sought to keep men from any posts in their field, and the men preferred to add only males to their staff. Faculty active in reform, such as Salmon or psychologist Margaret Floy Washburn '91, whom MacCracken called "a dangerous woman," antagonized the shyer teachers. Divisions and arguments notwithstanding, Vassar's older generation—alumnae, faculty, and president—offered students encouragement, support to fulfill their goals, and models for successful postgraduate lives.[33]

Vassar students generally embraced their mentors' goals of campus democracy and social missions for educated women. Yet the second generation brought its own plans to turn-of-the-century Vassar, including expanded recreational activities (reflecting the easing of social regulations in the 1890s) and the students' desire for more contacts with men.

SECOND-GENERATION VASSAR

No longer prisoners of Hannah Lyman's lists and schedules, Vassar students of the Progressive Era traveled to New York City for opera, shopping, theater, and museums. They hiked twenty miles to the ferry at New Paltz and to Lake Mohonk for picnics, "bacon-bats," and the enjoyment of nature. Defensiveness about college women's health and the required exercising of earlier days gave way to an active athletic life, with students forming basketball, field hockey, and golf teams. In 1889 mathematics professor Achsah Mt. Ely '68 spearheaded an alumnae drive for a new gymnasium, and in 1895 the Athletic Association organized the first Field Day ever held by American women.

Students added clubs representing a wide variety of cultural, civic, and literary interests to the few societies developed by the pioneers. Organizations listed in the yearbook of 1902 included the Contemporary Club, Civitas, Current Topics Club, Teachers' Club, Southern Club, Chicago Club, Rochester Club, Wake Robin Club, Kemper Hall Club, Greek Club, Floral Society, Marshall Club, Dickens Club, Shakespeare Club, Club Francais, Der Deutsche Verein, Daughters of the American Revolution, the New England Club, and the Grand-daughters of Vassar. Music lovers could choose from the Vassar Symphony Orchestra, the Glee Club, the College Mandolin, Guitar, and Banjo Club, the Choir, and Thekla. Philaletheis gave several plays each year. In 1893, Greek professor Abby Leach directed a production of *Antigone* in the original Attic Greek, attracting New York City critics, who were astonished to see a women's college hold such an event. Professor Gertrude Buck's experimental theatre, later run by Professor Hallie Flannigan, also gave Vassar a reputation for having an innovative dramatics program.[34]

Dormitories became stages for dress-up parties, informal plays, and singing sessions. One Saturday night, Adelaide Claflin '97 and her friends acted out the society wedding of Consuelo Vanderbilt to the Duke of Marlborough. Dressed appropriately, they held a ceremony: "We are assembled to join this title and this filthy lucre in the bonds of matrimony." On Valentine's Day the students decorated the dining room, wore paper arrows on their blouses, and sent valentines to each other. A student wrote her parents about the elaborate party given by the juniors for their sister class, the freshmen:

> The freshmen wore bathing suits, the juniors sailor suits and either trousers or skirts. I was taken to the party by a junior. To get to it, we had to climb up a fire escape with the top fixed like a ship's deck. Girls dressed as sailor boys were handing out programs. On the other side of the "ship" we went down into the "sea" and saw Scylla, Charybdis, the old man of the sea, and a girl dressed as a diver. They did take-offs on the faculty and some students, and "mermaids"

danced. The refreshments were French cakes and ice in pale green. Then the juniors gave a "Neptune Play." Neptune is President Taylor and Mrs. Kendrick queen of the mermaids. Then the two classes sang to each other.[35]

Other dormitory activities included parties to enjoy the contents of boxes of food sent from home. The college provided nourishing but boring food, leading students to nightly feasting in their rooms. They bought crackers, jam, and fruit from a campus store, replenishing their cupboards with supplies from town. Food from home, however, was the biggest treat, and students' letters frequently thanked their mothers for providing the "spreads." Adelaide Claflin '97 told her parents about her birthday party and her friends' provision of fried oysters, chocolate, and charlotte russe. Students formed informal eating clubs like the Nine Nimble Nibblers, and some complained that college life made them fat. As Dorothy Hawley ex-'14 remarked: "What a lot of gay young butterflies my friends are becoming. But you have to be thin to be a butterfly. My 150 pounds would look more like a lemon. Yes, on the whole, I think Vassar is the best place for me."[36]

The attention second-generation Vassar students gave to their friends, games, and extracurricular activities seems to confirm observations, both contemporary and modern, that they attended college primarily to participate in student life. Having a good time does not preclude additional educational objectives, and, in fact, college life had long-range goals as well as short-term pleasures. In campus activities, Vassar students practiced their future social roles as educated women. They learned public, communal, and political obligations through such traditionally masculine pursuits as competition, self-government, and career planning. At the same time, campus society celebrated aspects of Victorian women's culture, as Vassar women modified competition, envisioned service-oriented vocations for themselves, and fostered intimate friendships with each other.

Like their own faculty, and like male students elsewhere, Vassar women of the Progressive Era made "college as community" the most significant theme of campus life. At coeducational schools and the eastern men's colleges, however, socioeconomic and religious distinctions turned democracy into an imperfectly realized ideal. Vassar and the other private women's colleges had from their beginnings a far more homogeneous student body, allowing them to practice democracy more easily and effectively. Vassar students of that era probably represented the most demographically cohesive group in the school's history. The pioneers had included both very young women in the preparatory department and older ones who taught school for a number of years before saving the money necessary to attend Vassar. The *Ladies' Home Journal* offered a scholarship to Vassar as first prize in a subscription contest, the winner of which was a teacher, for whom higher education was a lifelong ambition. Between 1900 and 1920, however, the age range narrowed, and most students were between eighteen and twenty-one years old.[37]

Vassar students from the 1870s through the 1920s came almost exclusively from upper-middle-class families; their fathers were merchants, manufacturers, bankers, or lawyers. The fee for tuition, room, and board rose steadily from $350 in 1865 to $550 in 1917. Students also needed yearly allowances of $100 to $250 plus money for clothing and transportation. Vassar offered few scholarships; as late as 1925 only 9 percent of students received financial aid. The administration discouraged students from working, saying they would find it difficult to keep up with their studies. Because the college required most students to live on campus, few could save money by boarding more cheaply in town.[38]

Admissions policies also narrowly defined the composition of the student body. Badly needing students in its early years, the college accepted anyone who passed the entrance examinations. Even women who failed these entered with "conditions" or as members of the preparatory department, until its abolition in 1888. By 1905, when the trustees limited the student body to one thousand, attendance at Vassar became a social custom in some circles, and the college started a Grand-daughters Club for students whose mothers or aunts were alumnae. Prospective freshmen still had to pass entrance examinations or arrive with a certificate from an approved secondary school, but the college reserved only a few places in each class for competitive entry based on intellectual merit.[39]

Regional and religious similarities reinforced the closeness of Vassar students. Women from New York, Pennsylvania, and New Jersey made up half of the student body between 1865 and 1925, while New England contributed 15 to 20 percent, the South 3 to 10 percent, and the North Central states 15 to 28 percent. Each year a few students, probably daughters of missionaries or diplomats, listed foreign countries as their homes. In 1914–15, with a total of 1,120 students, the Dean's Report listed 274 Episcopalians, 256 Presbyterians, 180 Congregationalists, 78 Baptists, 84 Methodists, 56 Unitarians, and 120 women from other Protestant denominations. Only 28 Roman Catholics and 35 Jews attended Vassar that year. Required daily attendance at chapel, with Protestant preachers, reiterated common religious ideals.[40]

Not only did Vassar students have common backgrounds, but family ties continued to be felt on campus, as revealed in letters to parents from second-generation students. When women confronted new situations at college, they turned to parents for support. Only mildly impatient at parental overprotectiveness, students sought guidance in dealing with courses, politics, communal living, social conduct, clothing, and relationships with men.

I am far away from the bathrooms and the drinking water is fine. . . . There's a resident physician in the building. It would not be exactly the thing for me to call on a member of the faculty as you suggested and ask if the drinking water is all right.

I took your advice about not writing to boys and told that boy in New York that I would not write to him.

I think it will be all right to take the labor economics course—not to decide what's right or wrong, but as an historical approach. Father, I don't wish to impose my views on other people, just to sound sensible if people ask me things.

Mama, I am hurt and grieved that you should think I would be in love and not tell you.

We made Bryan and McKinley banners. It was great fun. I wish papa would tell me my politics.

Rollin Eldridge asked me to a dance in New York given by Purdue alumni, but I talked to Dad over the phone, and he said I shouldn't come to New York again so soon.

As to the suit you spoke of, the short waist scares me. Is it awfully broad shouldered and big? . . . What is the hat like? Seems to me I need a dress hat more than a street hat. . . . I might have my pale yellow class day gown made now, except it might not be in style by next June, and of course it's customary not to wear that dress before the day appointed.[41]

Proud of their commitment to a democratic community based on shared backgrounds and values, students boasted that they needed no sororities to promote social life. Every student was a Vassar girl, and that was distinction enough. The *Vassarion,* the college yearbook, described the students' "democratic" social life:

Despite the long waiting list, due to the number limit of one thousand, the conditions of life and the customs at Vassar, are ill-adapted to cultivate any spirit of snobbishness. No one can have better accommodations or service by paying a higher price. . . . This means that room-mates are chosen purely for congeniality not for equality of income. No private maids or motors are permitted at Vassar. No select number, moreover, can retreat to a luxurious club. There are no sororities, secret societies, or their equivalent. Nor is their lack felt. The only social club house is one for the employees of the college. . . . The duties cannot all devolve upon a few because Vassar enforces a point system, rating each non-academic activity and allowing no one girl to carry more than ten points. These conditions of democracy, both planned and voluntary, are fostered by Vassar's more or less isolated situation in the country near but a small city. The girls are thrown upon their own resources largely for amusement. . . . So it has been possible to preserve a natural camaraderie and a close-knit community spirit.[42]

The self-selection of Vassar students made it easy for them to deal with each other according to democratic principles. Undoubtedly some students had less money to spend than others, but college literature treated differences among students largely as matters of personality or character. Julia Schwartz's novel, *Elinor's College Career* (1906), illustrates how college life drew the "right sort" of students together and focused their loyalty on Vassar. Elinor Offit, sent to college by a proud alumna mother, took no joy in her status as a Vassar granddaughter, wishing she might travel and amuse herself instead. Her three roommates also brought their idiosyncrasies to Vassar. Myra Dickinson, a playful scatterbrain, could not discipline herself to study and flunked her freshman courses. Lovely regal Lydia Howard came to the college to help run it as class president. Ruth Allee, a serious and intense scholarship girl with considerable literary talent, developed a crush on Elinor, to the latter's disgust.

As the novel took the four women through their college years, each submerged her selfishness in the good of the community. Lydia's "politicking" became less self-centered; she worried, instead, about how she could best serve the college. Myra learned to be responsible about her work, to present a better image of the Vassar girl to the world. Ruth, whose unpopularity stemmed from her attitude rather than from a lack of money, focused her feelings on her writing rather than on Elinor. And on graduation day, Elinor rebuked two outsiders for describing Vassar as "namby-pamby" and "provincial." In her first act as a loyal alumna, she donated her "Europe money" to the college's scholarship fund.[43]

Although more successful than other college "democracies," Vassar's campus life excluded those who did not really belong. Students' letters to their parents show disparaging, or at best condescending, attitudes toward Jews, Judaism, and Jewish Vassar students. As Adelaide Claflin '97 said to her mother: "There are two Jewesses here who room on the floor above us—They will never eat ham, and we have it quite often, and they never study on Saturday, but always on Sunday. They are lovely girls though— nicer than any Jews I ever saw before." And unlike Wellesley, with its evangelical tradition of treating black women as part of the community, James Taylor's Vassar did not admit nonwhite students.[44]

Male students of the Progressive Era also emphasized collegiate community and the welfare of the group, but they continued to compete with each other and with the students from other colleges in class events, school elections, debate, and athletics. But because competitiveness, and its accompanying assertiveness, belonged to the world of men, coeducated women competed only occasionally, for offices in their own organizations or in intramural athletics. At women's colleges, however, competition became an important focus of campus life. Since the Vassar community believed its graduates would be active in the public sphere, competitiveness, normally thought of as a manly attribute, played an important role in student activities. The absence of male students made it possible for women to incorporate aspects of manliness, such as competition, into their social education.

While endorsing competition, Vassar students and faculty worried about its divisive effects on the community. Students set boundaries on competitions inside the college, while faculty regulated extramural games and debates. If honors came naturally to well-liked or respected individuals, students accepted them as tributes reflecting glory on the team or the class. They did not approve of women who sought prominence for individual gratification. In class and club elections the nominating committee frequently agreed on one candidate to avoid a divisive campaign. Students denied interest in holding office, expressing relief if they were not chosen.

> I am not secretary, which makes me happy. You have no idea how scared I got when they were balloting. Oh! Just suppose I had been elected.
>
> •
>
> I was almost chosen president of Christian Association, but I am glad I wasn't nominated, for she has more responsibility than any college president.
>
> •
>
> My vanity has been quite enough flattered by two other people saying they thought I should have made the Daisy Chain. But I know I'm too fat and my eyes are too small.[45]

Such letters to parents minimized disappointments yet also indicated socially acceptable attitudes toward distinction. In another Julia Schwartz story, freshman Lois Exeter decided that she would be president of the Students' Association in her senior year. Lois spent her four years at Vassar building a loyal coterie to vote for her when the time came. Students saw through her scheme, however, and the designing Miss Exeter lost the presidency.[46]

The college underplayed intellectual distinctions as well, by not revealing students' grades, except for failures, until graduation. Even then, no one knew which grade came from a specific course, but only how many A's, B's, C's and D's she had earned throughout her four years. The twenty students with the highest marks received honors, were elected to Phi Beta Kappa, and won graduate fellowships. The *Vassar Miscellany*, the student newspaper, shared Lucy Salmon's disapproval of honors and discussed doing away with them. Letters to families often complained about so-called grinds: "There were 16 honors and 7 honorable mentions which is a good many for a class. They are very proud. But there aren't many of the girls who are most prominent in college life among them. A good many are freaks who have just spent all their time grinding." While jealousy probably entered into such complaints, the woman writing the above letter made Phi Beta Kappa herself. Undoubtedly, too, cliques formed, electioneering took place, and some women craved and won offices and prizes. Yet Vassar women thought it good form to deny or downplay wishes for individual success or distinctions.[47]

Even interclass competition did not replace the college as the primary focus for loyalty. As rivals, freshmen and sophomores played jokes on each other throughout the school year. Traditionally, the sophomores played a Halloween joke on the freshmen, emphasizing their greenness and the need for upperclasswomen to subdue the newcomers until they learned their place. One fall the sophomores placed a tiny diploma tied with green ribbon and labeled "A.B." for "Artless Baby" at each freshman's dinner plate. The sophomores also mocked freshmen in the Trig Ceremonies, skits held every spring to celebrate the sophomores' completion of required math courses. In turn, the freshmen tried to discover and halt the sophomores' secret Tree Ceremonies.

Vassar had a tradition of "sister classes"—made up of the seniors and the sophomores, the juniors and the freshmen. Although men's colleges also had brother classes, upperclassmen used the custom mainly to set freshmen and sophomores against each other. At Vassar, however, the custom further softened the edge of rivalries and competitions. Seniors chose the twenty prettiest sophomores to carry the famous Daisy Chain at commencement.

Sophomores also ushered at the ceremony and gave graduation parties for the seniors. Each senior invited a sophomore to the fall opening of senior parlor, a special lounge decorated by the senior class and reserved for its use. Throughout the year, juniors and seniors held sings, teas, and plays for their younger sisters. And against tradition, the classes of 1903 and 1904 became so close that they held a "wedding ceremony" to commemorate their relationship. Students representing the two classes acted out their "love" for each other, one dressed as a bride, and the other as a groom, while "Precedent" tried to break up the wedding. She failed and the two classes were united before the "throne of Vassar."[48]

Through her short story, "In the Course of A Year," Maude Louise Ray '00 cautioned Vassar students that class loyalties should not take precedence over friendships and ideals. Contrary to custom, junior Gertrude Van Arsdale and freshman Sally McKenzie enjoyed each other's company, but because the relationship annoyed Sally's classmates, she lost the election for class president. Gertrude then broke off the friendship, on the advice of other juniors, who told her she was harming Sally's standing with the freshmen. Hurt by Gertrude's sudden indifference, Sally turned to her classmates and became a recognized leader. When she ran for president of the sophomore class, her friends worked openly for her election instead of quietly awaiting the vote. Only Gertrude knew how much Sally detested electioneering and how betrayed she would feel by winning the presidency that way. She told Sally about the situation, proving that she was Sally's true friend, even if not her classmate, because she understood her ideals. Sally responded nobly. Although she won the election, she refused the office and scolded her supporters for campaigning for her. Impressed with her integrity, the class reelected her by popular acclaim. Sally became class president, but not before she, Gertrude, and the other Vassar students learned that principles and friendship should override class spirit.[49]

Vassar students' ambivalence about campus competition contrasts with their eagerness to take on the rest of the collegiate world. Students worried far less about the negative effects of intermural competitions, because such contests focused and integrated the loyalties of the Vassar community rather than divided them. Students suggested, and faculty approved, a limited program of intercollegiate matches for the two debating societies, Qui Vive and Tempus et Mores. College women did not normally debate, because at most institutions they had to join men's teams to do so. Debate drew women's attention to public issues and fostered aggressive, critical behavior; thus many did not think it a suitably feminine activity. When Vassar not only debated on its own campus but also competed with Wellesley, it represented a significant departure in women's collegiate activities. In April 1902, the Vassar team defeated Wellesley, arguing the negative side of "Resolved: That the United States should subsidize a merchant marine." A year later, at Vassar, when the home team won, the students lit bonfires and marched around the campus singing and cheering. After the Wellesley-Vassar matches, the Students' Association hoped to join an Inter-Collegiate Debating Society, made up of teams from women's colleges. The faculty refused permission, however, saying that the excitement interfered with academic work. In 1914 regular intercollegiate debating resumed, in a three-cornered match with Wellesley and Mt. Holyoke.[50]

Debating led Vassar students into a spirited defense of women's right to compete with men. In 1907 Columbia University debaters refused to debate against a Cornell team member, law student Elizabeth Cook. The *Vassar Miscellany* reprinted Columbia's statement and added a scathing comment:

> *Columbia:* We do not wish to see women participating in contests that were intended for men. You would have to apologize before you could even attempt to answer her arguments. A girl would have the advantage every time because she could immediately prejudice the judges in her favor.
>
> *Vassar:* We refrain from any comments.[51]

A few years later, when Cornell women declined an invitation to debate a Vassar team, the *Miscellany* complained:

> "We leave debating to the men," writes the feminine half of Cornell in reply to our challenge for an intercollegiate debate with them. Whether from charity they yield up one of the most interesting and productive college activities, or whether, secure in the fact that they as women "have the last word anyway" they think debating unnecessary, we do not know. Here we have no one to hand T & M and Qui Vive over to, but it is doubtful if we would, given the opportunity. We protest against "leaving debating to the men" with the demand that women themselves are . . . to be allowed to think for themselves, to disprove that women "cannot think in a straight line" and that "there is no use arguing with a woman. . . ." Perhaps if at the beginning Eve had been a good debater, her last word might have been more efficacious, so that we would be believing that it was Adam and not Eve who listened to the Fallacies of the serpent.[52]

In 1916, Vassar challenged Princeton to a debate, but the *Daily Princetonian,* insulted by the invitation, ridiculed the notion of competing with women:

The proposal to cross words with the petticoated representatives of this bitter rival is too much. . . . Our vocabulary of invectives is utterly inadequate. Why not debate Vassar? . . . Why not a knitting or sewing tilt with Bryn Mawr? Why not a ping-pong match with Barnard, or a spelling bee with Wellesley, or a tea-pouring contest with Miss So-and-So's finishing school . . . Think how a verbal victory over this dangerous rival would influence prospective freshmen. . . . And if they (the team) must go . . . then *The Princetonian* urges them to beware of the wisdom concealed behind the horn-rimmed glasses of America's future schoolmarms and stateswomen.

Some "Letters to the Editor" in the *Daily Princetonian* indicated that not all students shared the editor's views, but that did not mollify the *Vassar Miscellany,* whose editors replied in kind:

The manly position taken in *The Princetonian's* recent editorials reminds us of the protest against the higher education of women, as expressed by a Harvard reporter in a recent interview. . . . May we hope for a contribution from Yale to complete the three-ringed circus.

> If Princeton comes to Vassar,
> To debate the dangerous "shes"
> What can Vassar do to make them
> Feel more happy and at ease?

> If they take such awful chances
> Don't you think to save the males
> From succumbing to our glances
> Vassar ought to take to veils?

> *The Lady and the Tiger*

> He thought he saw a worthy foe the shafts of logic hurl,
> He looked again and saw it was a silly college girl.
> Pray, don't debate with me! he said
> I must not waste a pearl.[53]

Vassar women practiced additional political activity as they sought self-government and the abolition of social regulations. In 1889, the Students' Association won a great victory when the faculty allowed an honor system for chapel attendance, the daily exercise rule, and the regulation of lights out at 10:00 P.M., making each student responsible for reporting her own transgressions. In 1899, amid much student rejoicing, the faculty suspended the 10:00 P.M. rule for one year. When no one observed an accompanying decline in student health, the college permanently abandoned lights-out regulations.

Self-reporting, however, did not work, and student proctors replaced the honor system in 1902. The Students' Association continued to press for fewer rules and greater student responsibility. Vassar women participated in conferences with representatives from other women's colleges, comparing and discussing their progress in self-government, and returned with new ideas to try out at Vassar. In 1910, delegates went to Cornell, in 1914 to Radcliffe; and in 1915, in honor of its fiftieth anniversary, Vassar hosted its own student government conference. The Students' Association made fewer gains in self-government after 1900, although it persuaded the faculty to adopt a modified "cut" system in 1904. Under the new system a student presented a written excuse for her absence to the instructor, who then decided whether or not to accept it. After 1913 a Board of Wardens replaced the student proctors and the Lady Principal, but not until Henry Mac-Cracken's administration (1915–45) did students get further significant liberalization of college rules. Discussing, proposing, and negotiating for reforms, however, provided them with atypical political experiences for young women.[54]

Some college organizations connected students to progressive social reform groups outside the college gates. The Vassar chapters of the College Settlement Association (1891), the Consumers' League (1900), the Good Fellowship Club (1908), and the Christian Association (1863) expressed social consciousness, reform goals, and service ideals through their work on and off campus. The Settlement Association, begun by women's college graduates, operated settlement houses in New York City, Boston, and Philadelphia. Students collected money, volunteered for short-term projects, and sometimes spent their vacations living and working at the settlements. The Consumers' League promoted awareness of labor problems. League members urged other students to shop early in the season for Christmas but never on Saturday afternoons, not to accept packages delivered after 6:00 P.M., and to buy underwear with the league label. In 1890, Lucy Salmon started a Steadfast Club for college employees, providing them with a lending library, meeting rooms, and job counseling. Students modeled their Good Fellowship Club for maids after Salmon's earlier effort. They collected money to build a clubhouse and tutored maids who sought formal education. Reform organizations proved very popular on campus. In 1902, one-third of the students joined the College Settlement Association, although we do not know the extent of each individual's participation. These groups and the social problems courses taught by Herbert Mills gave Vassar a reputation as a center of social reform activity. The *Vassar Miscellany* explained students' enthusiasm for social work—it provided missions for educated women: "This college is renowned for its enthusiasm on the subject of social work. We all talk about it a great deal. Some of us take it up in the nature of a fad— 'the things one ought to be interested in.' Others are working earnestly and diligently to prepare themselves for some feature of it which they hope to give the very best that is in them. . . . It surely shows that it is possible for a woman without specialized knowledge to accomplish things in the world's progress, if she is but possessed of eyes to see and a will to do."[55]

Although social work and social reform gave educated women a sense of purpose, some undertook these activities with an elitist attitude. The *Vassar Miscellany* accused such students of insincerity:

> We have heard, spell-bound, Professor Mills' exposition of our present in-dustrial system, and the horrible hardships of the great unknown working classes. . . . We have enthusiastically preached the doctrine of Socialism. . . . We have talked of the unearned increment and the exploitation of the pro-letariat. . . . We have denounced mythical Capitalism, the oppressor of the mythical working classes. . . . We also have sat at a foot-ball game with steamer rugs and fur coats and young men . . . and hardly noticed the little black-eyed boy, selling peanuts, in a worn gray sweater. . . . Let us look at the plain life around us with open eyes, at the girl in the red mackinaw hurrying across campus with shirt-waists over her arm . . . at the pretty little elevator-maid with the wan smile.[56]

In a short story, "The Social Status," Katharine Krom Merritt '08 poked fun at the student social reformer. Her heroine, Alicia Lane, left college with many theories, much zeal, and a red-hot desire for reform. Her first effort at making friends among the working classes came at a church reception in her home town of Bradford. On this occasion, the pewholders, including Al-icia's family, entertained less distinguished church members with cake and ice cream. Dressed in her simplest suit and eager to test her democratic ideals, Alicia arrived at the party with great excitement. A working girl of her acquaintance introduced Alicia to a young man who wished to meet her, and the conversation quickly took an unfortunate turn:

> "Now that's funny," he laughed noisily in her ear, "I've seen you lots o' times in church, and on the street, and I was telling Susie here how I thought you looked haughty like, but you ain't." Dead silence and a pause during which Alicia looked desperately around, seeking for a loophole of escape from the all-too-personal conversation. . . . She became suddenly, vividly, aware of the purple necktie and of the fact that she must say something. All her social instinct seemed to leave her suddenly, and left her staring at him blankly.

"Do you—do you like Bradford?" she asked wildly, and quickly changed her patronizing smile for one of perfect equality.

"Seems pretty good to me," he said and winked.

Alicia started involuntarily, and seeing her mother's rotund form across the room, said hastily, "I must speak to my mother," and vanished. "Are you going home?" she asked breathlessly.

"I hadn't thought of it, dear, but of course—why, Alicia, aren't you well? You look so flushed." "I am a snob," said Alicia.

"A snob?" said Mrs. Lane vaguely. "You're not well, dear."[57]

Not every student enjoyed the obligations of the Good Fellowship Club, although most experienced enough social pressure to feel uncomfortable about their lack of enthusiasm. When a maid asked Muriel Tilden (Eldridge) '14 for music lessons, she refused, explaining to her mother: "I feel mean. . . . I was unwilling to share my gift, which isn't in reality my own at all, but that of the world's. I have been trying to justify myself by saying that after all it isn't real music that she wants but merely knowledge of how to bang out rag-time, and I can't spare the time out of my own life to pound that into the head of a stupid Norwegian. . . . But it feels unChristian and selfish."[58]

Wartime activities also reflected students' commitment to communal and social service. Aside from Red Cross work, knitting for soldiers, and selling Liberty bonds, students and alumnae raised money to send a Vassar relief unit overseas, in cooperation with the Red Cross and the YMCA. Three unit members—Ruth Cutler '12, Annabel Roberts '13, and Dorothea Gray '11—died in France. Economics professor Herbert Mills organized a summer training camp for nurses and urged college women to become nursing administrators. Students gave up extracurricular activities and their prom to provide funds for preparedness courses in farming, auto repair, modern languages, home economics, and office skills. Over half the students reported doing war work during the summer vacation of 1918. Some stayed on campus to run the Vassar farm and raise food for the college community to eat during the school year, thereby freeing money for the war effort.[59]

Whether deeply felt or superficial, their social concerns often caused Vassar students to advocate women's rights. Like Lucy Salmon and other suffragists of the Progressive Era, they expected women to bring compassion and morality to the electorate and to promote social reform. Students discussed and debated women's rights in the pages of the *Vassar Miscellany*, which printed long, thoughtful articles such as "What Feminism Means to

Me" by Crystal Eastman Benedict '03; "The Socialist Movement and College Women" by Elizabeth Dutcher '01; and "Militant Suffrage in New York City" by Violet L. Pike '07. Vassar and Barnard students attended demonstrations and meetings in New York City and ushered for a lecture by Mrs. Emmeline Pankhurst, the famous British suffragist.[60]

In letters to their families students express opinions on suffrage ranging from indifference to hostility:

> I did not especially fancy her mother because she is Woman's Suffrage. She talked quite long and seriously on the subject at the table, and I believe she was really trying to convert us to believe in it, because none of us did. I wanted to laugh so badly.
>
> •
>
> I did not go to hear Sylvia Pankhurst speak. I prefer a dance to a ranting suffragist's spiel. Some girls thought she was good, and some didn't. I'm just as glad I didn't go.
>
> •
>
> As I have never been to a suffrage meeting I guess I will go and improve my education. One of the speakers is Miss Milholland, a graduate of Vassar.[61]

Education, however, and Vassar's intensely political atmosphere favored the growth of prosuffrage sentiments. A campus poll in 1911 showed 27 percent of the freshmen, 33 percent of the sophomores, but 57 percent of the seniors favoring women's rights.[62]

Life at Vassar fostered the close relationships between women that characterized Victorian culture. Some college associations produced emotionally intense friendships known as crushes or smashes. Usually younger students developed crushes on upperclasswomen who affected not to notice or to despise the idea. Sometimes upperclasswomen, in turn, had crushes on their teachers. Margaret Shipp '05 wrote to her sister, with amusement, about freshmen who had crushes on her. One woman, invited to tea, told her: "Miss Shipp, I wish I were a man . . . a Harvard graduate. . . . I'd like to make love to you. . . . Only if I were a man, I couldn't be here and see you serve tea so charmingly." Shipp commented: "Wasn't it funny! And anything more perfectly naive and composed than the child's manner I never saw." Shipp herself developed a close and sentimental relationship with her German teacher, Kristine Mann. She sent her sister a copy of a poem written in Mann's honor:

> Butterfly never gleamed so blue
> In fluttering flight through sunlit air
> So brightly blue as My Lady's eyes,

Nor, perfume-laden, did arise.
From flower more yellow than her hair
And soft as are they velvet wings,
O Butterfly My Lady's voice:
Which full of rich repose, together
With the warmth of summer weather
Who can hear and not rejoice.[63]

As in the case of faculty women who lived together, some of these relationships were erotic; others not so. However, the intensity of living close together led to stronger emotional bonds between students at a women's college than at coeducational institutions where men were present and dormitory life nonexistent.

The second generation of Vassar students showed some unease about emotional relationships between women, greater interest in men, yet ambivalence about the consequences of heterosociality. In her short story, "Heroic Treatment," Julia Schwartz described the reaction of an annoyed senior, the recipient of seven valentines from a smitten freshman. Moving away from women's culture and accepting male norms for friendship, the senior wanted the freshmen to treat her as men dealt with their same-sex friends: "Hero worship is good for boys—a shoulder-to-shoulder healthy admiration, and it need not hurt the normal girl who keeps her nerves steady with bicycle and basketball. But this child is the dreamy kind; she is wasting her energies thinking of me. . . . She cannot think of anything else when I am in sight . . . at least that is what she says. She blushes when I speak to her, and mopes when I forget to smile."[64]

Unlike the students of Hannah Lyman's era, Vassar women in the 1890s and afterward had opportunities, although limited, to meet and entertain young men. Couples were permitted chaperoned visits either in the college parlors or in the students' rooms. On Sundays, women might leave the campus with brothers, fiancés, or close relatives. Some restrictions remained. To the students' great annoyance, fathers had to be chaperoned in dormitory rooms, and mothers were not considered adequate chaperones. And while Vassar women invited men to their twice-yearly college dances, they could not, until 1896, actually dance with them. Instead each male visitor had a card filled with the names of his hostess and her friends. He "promenaded" or walked with his partners up and down a specially decorated corridor.

Despite their new privileges, Vassar women often showed little enthusiasm for male guests.

I am sick of the nuisance of having a man already and won't ever again if I can help it. They are coming up this afternoon rather early, much to our disgust.

•

How much you must have thought I had changed. I still consider that men or boys for a steady diet would be insufferably stupid.

•

I was pretty tired, and didn't feel like entertaining young men any more. You know I never could stand much of them at a time, and though the dance was altogether *delightful* and *adorable,* I think enough is enough.

•

You see, there being no gentlemen here, the girls have to act in that capacity, both with other girls and with teachers. . . . I consoled myself very well with the company of girls.[65]

Students also doubted that men were attracted to intelligent, educated, purposeful women. The difficulty of getting men to attend Vassar dances became a standard college joke.

Prom: A Question of Marginal Utility

Overheard on campus: "Yes, it costs five dollars to go to the prom. Of course you have to get a dress—and there are a few incidentals."

Incidentals

Stationery and stamps to Ted	.77
Stationery and stamps to Jim	.89
Stationery and stamps to John	.95
Stationery and stamps to Walter	1.00
Telegram to Ned	1.50
Telegram to Fred	2.00
Telegram to Phil	2.26
Two telephones to New York	1.00
Two telephones to Philadelphia	2.00
Two telephones to Albany	1.50
Telegram home for 16 year old brother	.50
Brother's railroad fare both ways	30.00
His board	10.00
His meals	20.00
Bribe to induce him to come	30.00

Total: Year's Allowance[66]

More seriously and sadly, short stories in the *Vassar Miscellany* showed talented and principled women losing their men. In "The Critic and the Criticised" a young man in love with his co-worker at a publishing house asked her to read and comment on his first novel. She did so, telling him in no uncertain terms that the work was shabby and unworthy of him. Furthermore, if he insisted on publishing it, she would write a scathing review. The young woman expected, in true nineteenth-century fashion, to be a good influence over her beloved, but

> he went straight to the house of A Girl He Knew, and when she came down-stairs with pink cheeks and starry eyes, without much ado he seized her hand and asked her to be his wife. His arguments proved effective, and the bitter look around his mouth began to soften. She looked up. "I'd like to ask you some-thing." "What, dear?" She buried her head in his coat. "I want to help you write your stories. I know I'm rather stupid—I always spill the ink—" She dimpled radiantly. "But couldn't I criticize?" "That's awfully sweet of you, dearest," he said, and he kissed her again. "But I've just about decided that I can do better without criticism."[67]

Similarly, in "A Girl I Have Known," a Vassar freshman in the midst of a hectic first year thought fondly of James Carter, the young man she had left behind to attend college. She reminisced about their summer together and their plans for the future. The mail brought a wedding invitation; he planned to marry her best friend, "frivolous" Louana. Louana's letter rubbed salt in the wound: "Recalling an old promise . . . that Elizabeth should be her maid of honor, she went on to say that she knew Elizabeth was, of course, entirely too busy with her college duties, so she had asked Eloise White instead. She wished she could be there to see Elizabeth's face when she got the letter. She remembered how fond of James Elizabeth had always been, and she almost felt as if she were taking him away from her, but that they were so happy, and so on."[68]

Sometimes the woman chose love, sacrificing her career to do so. In "A Woman's Point of View," the city editor sent young Maud Stanway to investigate a case of industrial corruption. Unsafe equipment had caused a terrible railway accident, and the editor suspected the companies involved of collusion to provide faulty equipment. He wanted Stanway to cover the story—since women had high moral standards, her viewpoint on such deals would make interesting reading. Stanway eagerly accepted the assignment. One of the accused men, Howard Cantrell, had proposed marriage to her, and she wished to prove his innocence. Cantrell, however, told her that he had been involved in an arrangement to purchase substandard equipment and pocket the extra cash. He begged Stanway not to print the truth, so that by morning when the other newspapers got the story, he could be far away.

> "Oh, how can I tell what is right to do?" she said aloud, though knowing he would not help her. She sat quiet for a moment, the tears raining unheeded down her white cheeks.

"You said I would never be sorry if I gave you this chance. Do you believe it, Howard?" she said at last to the man waiting with his life in balance.

"Yes, I do," he answered simply.

She rose. "Very well," she said gravely. "Please do not thank me. I have betrayed my paper and stained my honor, but it was for you, and you will show me some day that it was not in vain. Good-by dear. God keep you." And she was gone.[69]

Louise Elizabeth Dutton '05 won a prize from the *Vassar Miscellany* for "Miss Carter, Critic." Elizabeth Carter, a thirty-one-year-old journalist, agreed to mind a cousin's baby, normally her sister Ruth's charge, while Ruth went for a drive with Jim, Elizabeth's former beau. After they left, the baby awoke and needed attention. She managed, with great difficulty, to quiet the infant and sat for a long time with him on her lap, regretting what she had missed in life by having a career. The sight of the intellectual Miss Carter enjoying her temporary motherhood pleasantly surprised Jim, who renewed his proposal, and she accepted immediately, without a thought for her past interests.[70]

The class of 1911 satirized the dilemma of modern womanhood in their skit honoring the graduation of the class of 1910. Marjorie McCoy '11 described the play to her parents:

"Victoria Vassar, Or After College, What?"

It was the story of Victoria, who was determined to have a career after college, and not get married to Reggie Yaleston who didn't agree with her on that subject. So first she tried Biology—enter the Frog Chorus, which was killingly funny. But Reggie pursued her. So she decided to go into social work and interviewed an Italian woman in a tenement—many hits on Economics and House Sanitation. But the suffragettes came in and tried to persuade her to join them—they of course were take-offs on some of 1910's suffrage-ites: "Sahara Slinckes" (Sarah Hinckes) and "Witsneva Fayles" (Katharine Taylor). After them came in four shirtwaist strikers—the worst looking toughs you've ever seen. She was so shocked at these she decided not to—and that's just the way it went on, till finally she decided to give up a career for Reggie![71]

In their activities, organizations, games, and friendships, Vassar students of the second generation used their curriculum and collegiate activities to explore the problem of the educated woman. With guidance and support from faculty and alumnae, they looked toward a postgraduate future bright with promise. Their expectations of social usefulness, reform, and having their talents welcomed reflected the optimism of the era and the hard work of their predecessors. The underlying wistfulness about men and marriage, and the ambivalence about choices, came to a head in the 1910s. During this decade the aims of women faculty and students diverged. They continued to share political and reform objectives, but the younger women moved in the direction of greater male-female sociability, creating a crisis in campus relations and ultimately a split between the two generations of college women.

VASSAR COLLEGE: A DAWN THAT PROMISES THE MODERN AGE

In June 1921, Vice President Calvin Coolidge asked, "Are the Reds Stalking Our College Women?" Writing in the *Delineator,* Coolidge discussed women's moral influence as mothers, teachers, and voters, complaining that a "new element" at the women's colleges created an atmosphere hostile to the American form of government. He found little subversive activity at Bryn Mawr and Mt. Holyoke, and Smith was "sane," but Wellesley, Barnard, Radcliffe, and Vassar harbored dangerous "study clubs" under the auspices of the Intercollegiate Socialist Society. The "Vassar spirit" especially disturbed Coolidge, who quoted a Vassar student as saying in her campus newspaper: "I know what I am. I'm not pessimistic. I'm not optimistic. I'm just antagonistic."[72] Helen Bennett, director of the Chicago branch of the Intercollegiate Bureau of Occupations, agreed with Coolidge's estimate of Vassar as radical but pronounced it admirable: "But perhaps your girl will go to Vassar. Then, indeed, you must pin your hat solidly to your head when she returns, for from Vassar come the young adventurers, the pioneers in curious fields, the radicals. The Vassar girls check interest in social conditions, woman suffrage, a combination which indicated pioneer or radical tendencies.[73]

This spirit, evident at Vassar before 1910, grew stronger in the next decade as students participated in the Intercollegiate Socialist Society and the College Equal Suffrage League. Vassar faculty and students overwhelmingly supported the League of Nations and joined their counterparts from Barnard, Bryn Mawr, the Woman's College of Brown, Goucher, Mt. Holyoke, Radcliffe, Smith, and Wellesley in pledging support to Woodrow Wilson. They formed an intercollegiate organization with Harvard, the University of Pennsylvania, and Wellesley to help college students obtain permission for radical speakers on their campuses. In 1917, the college started a debating league with Barnard, Radcliffe, Holyoke, Wellesley, and Smith. Not content to wait for the "revolution," Vassar socialists cooperated with Poughkeepsie citizens in civic improvement projects. The *Vassar*

Miscellany estimated that every third student did some form of social service work under the auspices of the Christian Association.[74]

As in earlier years, however, the privileged background of Vassar students conditioned their responses and limited their understanding of social problems. Discussing the race riots of 1918 in East St. Louis, Socialist Society members concluded: "Though the negro is biologically and intellectually inferior, his condition may be greatly improved by an industrial education, and the establishment of the proper attitude between negro and white. The East St. Louis riots at least served to call attention to the fact that the South cannot handle the problem alone, that it is the problem of the nation as a whole." When students from the Hampton Institute, sponsored by their teacher, Ida Alice Tourtellot '00, visited the college, they ate separately in the Vassar dining room. Even under those segregated conditions, white southern Vassar students left their tables.[75]

Students expressed more interest in suffrage after 1910. Although President Taylor continued to oppose suffrage clubs and speakers, the *Vassar Miscellany* printed numerous articles, letters, and editorials on the subject, several times polling students on their views. Taylor allowed a campus suffrage meeting in 1912, and students discovered, to their dismay, that they were not sufficiently in touch with the issues to put on a good program. Following this event, letters in the *Miscellany* chided students for lacking interest in current affairs and complained bitterly about the administration's refusal to permit an official suffrage club. A suffrage poll taken in 1914 revealed that 476 students (or 64 percent, up from 43 percent in 1911) favored suffrage, 154 were against, and 114 were neutral.

James Taylor resigned in 1914 amid rumors that the trustees had encouraged his early retirement in favor of a more progressive president. The faculty-trustee committee governing the college until the inauguration of MacCracken in 1915 permitted the Suffrage Club, operating clandestinely since the graveyard incident of 1908, to declare itself a division of the College Equal Suffrage League (a national organization founded in 1906 and affiliated with the National American Woman Suffrage Association [NAWSA]) and to recruit members openly. The Vassar chapter became the first to establish a suffrage school, training debaters and speakers. Students were particularly active in the successful campaign for suffrage in New York State in 1917, attending parades, canvassing, and speaking. Mary Culver Pollock '17, who joined the Suffrage Club and canvassed for women's enfranchisement in Poughkeepsie, wrote to her parents: "I asked the man in the bank today if he was in favor of suffrage, and he said that women were next to angels—and of course angels couldn't vote—so how could women vote?" Undaunted by the banker, she went to New York City in October 1915 to march in a suffrage parade.[76]

Clearly the prosuffrage wing at Vassar represented majority opinion and controlled the student publications. Antisuffragists had no public forum at the college, although the *Vassar Miscellany's* writers often argued that students should hear all viewpoints. Even apolitical women began to take the suffrage issue seriously in the intense atmosphere of the 1910s. Concerning a new style of corset, Marion Willard Everett '13 told her mother: "All I wear every day now is one with two stays in front and two behind. . . . It's lots more comfortable. . . . Don't tell the girls at home. . . . They'll think I'm becoming a suffragette." Yet when Mrs. Willard visited the campus, her daughter took her to hear a prosuffrage address in Poughkeepsie.[77]

As in the past, students drew inspiration from alumnae and faculty achievements. Lucy Salmon, who had attended the NAWSA convention where the College Equal Suffrage League was formed, became the league's honorary vice president in 1911. At a prosuffrage rally in Poughkeepsie in 1916, ten male faculty from the college were enrolled as vice chairmen of the event. MacCracken himself served on the executive committee of the Men's League for Woman Suffrage and spoke at many suffrage rallies. Students knew of Julia Lathrop's address of 1912, "Woman Suffrage and Child Welfare," the classic statement linking women's enfranchisement to social reform.

Even the liberal MacCracken would not accede to the Suffrage Club's request to invite Inez Milholland Boissevain '09 to campus, but the *Vassar Miscellany* frequently discussed her views and activities. Student writers also praised other alumnae, most of them recent graduates, who had become members of the radical Congressional Union, (later the National Woman's Party), including Lucy Burns '02, Elsie Hill '06, Elizabeth McShane Hilles '13, Mary Fisher de Kruif '12, Mary Gavin '13, Edith Hilles Dewees '14, Crystal Eastman '03, and others. One alumna wrote to the *Miscellany* about suffrage radicalism:

> Whether you believe it is a thing to boast of or to conceal, the fact is that Vassar is more prominently and numerously represented in the National Woman's Party . . . than any other college. . . . It has occurred to me that it might be of interest to Vassar to know the policy behind the picket, to know why various of its alumnae insist, in the face of public vilification, upon holding banners at the gates of the White House, and serving sentences of sixty days to six months in the work house, rather than agree not to do it. . . . The radical

suffrage movement has kept suffrage alive, and proclaimed to the world that women will no longer wait patiently for their enfranchisement.[78]

Aside from the suffrage issue, alumnae inspired students. The college's fiftieth anniversary celebration in October 1915 brought many graduates back to campus and greatly impressed Dorothy Danforth Compton '17, who wrote to her parents:

> I think these last few days I have gotten a broader view of the college woman than ever before and the opportunity that she has in her community after she leaves college. As the speakers at the banquet tonight emphasized, it is the college woman who does things. She is fitted for the fullest life. She has gotten the vision. . . . It is interesting to look at all the old graduates. As a whole they are the most splendid worthwhile looking women I have ever seen. Their faces are so strong. They look as if they stood for something in the world and had contributed much towards improving it. It's great to feel that you belong to such a body.[79]

Students' interest in careers other than teaching reached new heights during the 1910s. As before, they were aided by alumnae, who chided families and friends for expecting the graduate to return home unchanged by her education:

> The trouble is not so much that the college graduate does not conform sufficiently to the standards of the world as that the world makes no effort to approximate his [sic] ideal of it, thereby losing a mighty opportunity.
>
> Here came these two ideals face to face at commencement. Inspire the college girl to lead a full life. Compel the college girl to live the life planned by her parents. Isn't it true that we college women earn the right of freedom by our college training, just as surely as college men?[80]

Alumnae also wrote about careers in their own and student publications and supported the college's new vocational director and employment bureau. In 1912 Alice Barrows '00 cofounded the Intercollegiate Bureau of Occupations in New York City. Yearly campus vocational conferences included lectures on department store education, social service, psychology in business, business opportunities, psychological testing, and teaching. At the conference held in 1920, 906 of the 1,100 Vassar students filled out forms listing their preferred vocations. Most wanted a career in business; others listed social service, secretarial work, psychology, teaching, medicine, chemistry, mathematics, library work, nursing, physics, and law, in that order.[81]

After 1910, the literature on careers suggested that Vassar women go into wage earning rather than into volunteer work. Violet Pike told readers of the *Vassar Alumnae Monthly:*

> I don't mean to underrate the value of the splendid volunteer work of Vassar women all over the country. But most of us will work better and with greater satisfaction to ourselves when held to an economic standard. And when the world's work is so wide and interesting and the opportunities for women increasing every day, it seems a pity that college women should often have to waste so much time in their efforts to find their places in the scheme of things when they are most eager and ready to start.[82]

The new emphasis on business careers reflected Vassar women's desires for a greater role in the "man's world" and their growing emphasis on individual achievement. And although shared activities and goals continued to link Vassar faculty and students, in the 1910s the younger women took a greater interest in men and in personal freedoms, thereby creating a gulf between the generations. We can see these issues taking shape in letters to parents, which reflected a more rebellious and less deferential tone. Sample remarks from suffragist Mary Culver Pollock '17 illustrate the shift:

> If you write me any more letters telling me to study, I shall return them unopened.

> So you see what too much study does for one. Lalitha M. Folks '15 studying at Wisconsin for her Ph.D. had overworked, gotten melancholy, and committed suicide.

> Well, Mother, I'll have enough to keep myself in stamps anyway, and maybe by scrimping I can go to a nickel show once in six weeks. I have every sensation of the youth who has been cut off without a shilling. . . . You're cutting me down from about four dollars a week to a dollar and a quarter. . . . I don't see how you can hate the thought of my enjoying myself so, when you look back on your own good times.

> Nobody understands why I don't go away for all my weekends, and I can't tell them it's because my family is so stingy. Why do you write on that expensive theme paper? Don't you know it costs 12 cents a pad? Why don't you be more economical like me?[83]

A similar style of language and argument pervaded letters denouncing Vassar's social regulations. Because the students had never liked these rules, the college liberalized them in the 1890s. In the 1910s, however, students demanded much greater freedom to enjoy male company. Their letters emphasized the joys of off-campus social life. Dorothy Danforth Compton told her parents indignantly that prom rules allowed dancing only at the prom itself. Additionally, men had to stay in "approved" residences, could not escort Vassar students to and from their dormitories, and were not permitted on campus the Sunday after the dance. Mary Culver Pollock wrote happily of her fraternity "weekend," which included a "sing," a tea, a dinner, and a dance. Marion Willard Everett '13 described her trip to West Point:

> Tom and I have loads of fun. There are heaps of things I don't approve of in him and he thinks I am a stick in lots of ways, but we do have a grand time laughin'. I don't think you should go around with a man with the intention of marrying him anyway. Tom has done me the honor of saying that he'd never think of asking another girl down now, and told me to write him anytime I wanted to come, and it would be all right. I nearly fell over, but remarked that was rather awkward, and he'd better ask me every month and let me take my pick. We are allowed four times a year there. We had an adorable chaperone this time . . . a French instructor.[84]

Muriel Tilden Eldridge '14 told her mother: "I met the nicest men and had the best dances ever. . . . Saturday morning we spent skating. . . . Met a Cornell man who was a dandy skater. . . . He is very musical. Oh! I never go anywhere that I don't thank you for making me musical. It's *such* a help."[85]

In 1913, the "tango crisis" highlighted growing differences between faculty and students. Should students dance the tango and the one-step, both requiring close bodily contact with male partners, at college functions? After a student-faculty committee attempted a compromise, the faculty banned all but the two-step, waltz, and Boston from the prom. According to one student, however, "Nearly everyone danced everything. I feel very proud to be able to say that I kept the law except for one half of one dance when it was so everlastingly jammed that we couldn't do a thing but one-step. We didn't dare risk going to dinner with the boys because of the everlasting college rules."[86]

Alumnae response to the tango crisis illustrated the growing generation gap at Vassar. Even very recent graduates did not approve of the new styles in social behavior. Louisa Brooks '07, adviser of women at the University of Oklahoma, wrote to the *Vassar Miscellany:* "When one has grown accustomed to think of Vassar as a tower of strength in conservative social usage, it is grievous to be obliged to view with alarm where one has been wont to point with pride." Social worker Margaret Culkin Banning '12 reminded students of their responsibility to set an example for less privileged women: "The girls in the public dance halls ought to be kept from dancing the tango because its results are apt to be morally bad since there girls are comparatively unprotected. We, of the Vassar College dance, sure of our own protection . . . put our sociology and interest in human welfare into practice by setting our stamp of approval on the tango and giving an impulse to the ruin of girls not necessarily worse, but necessarily less protected than ourselves." Students replied that they meant no "Boston Tea Party" but had only been enjoying themselves. Dorothy Phillips '14, contributor to the *Vassar Miscellany* of articles on socialism, told readers that students did not see the tango as vicious and did not understand objections to it. "Honi soit qui mal y pense," she concluded.[87]

Vassar students of the 1910s viewed their college years as a transition to an exciting and challenging future, combining personal and professional fulfillment. In December 1919, the editors of the *Vassar Miscellany* described their expectations, calling their own era "The Present Middle Age":

> When a man on campus can be passed with equanimity and the escorted girl be not marked for a week . . . when girl and faculty conceive a democracy in which they converse with frankness and freedom and pleasure . . . when the rational attitude is applied to our now "sacred" undisturbed questions, and a girl can be a theist or an atheist or a psycho-analyst or believe in New Thought or her own thought without raising the eyebrows of her friends; when we smoke or do not smoke, or go to the city or remain here as an increased capacity for judgment determines; when we are brave enough to confess that we frequently go to the Libe for pleasure; when any girl on campus might tell you the prospects of the Peace Treaty at the moment . . . then may the old order change to the new, and light strengthen to a dawn that promises a Modern Age.[88]

Once again, uneasiness about present and future trends emerged in campus short stories. Authors descried the frenetic social life based on weekends at men's colleges. In "The Prom," Helen visited Rob at his college for a weekend of fun and dances. Disgusted with the frivolity and glitter, she happily returned to her own campus, grateful for the opportunity to see the emptiness in such gaieties.[89]

Other students questioned the compatibility of political idealism with new styles of sociosexual behavior. In her short story "The Wall of Dominoes," Edna St. Vincent Millay '17 depicted heroine Sydney Murray abandoning college ideals to become a "man's" woman, one who smoked, drank, and flirted. She played ragtime music for her suitors instead of her muchloved classical pieces. Unable to feel passion, Sydney decided that an affair with a married man, Brander Leighton, would complete her transformation into a modern woman. On her way out the door with Leighton, he handed her a hat with feathers. Murray's last remaining ideal from her student days was her refusal to wear anything made from dead animals. She hesitated; then, finding the price of modernity too high, she pushed away both the hat and Leighton.[90]

Some writers recognized the difficulty of planning their own lives. Women, they said, had little control over what happened to them. Whatever careers they wanted, most would marry or teach school:

After Vassar—What?

A dippy double alley-way
    A very polyglot
An open forum held one day,
    On "After Vassar—What?"
And each blew up, sans any trouble,
    A rainbow "After Vassar" Bubble.

"A suffrage leader, I will be,
    And save our sex," A cried.
Said B, "I'm in for charity,
    Uplifting the East Side."
"And I'll for labor agitate."
    Said C, "And found the perfect state."
And D remarked with nonchalance—
    "Well, as for me I guess,
Across the ocean I'll advance
    And stop the war's distress."
"Dear me," said E, "I think I'd rather
    Of thirteen be the model mother."

The feminist is peeling now
    The priceless pale potater
And with a frown upon her brow,
    The labor agitator
Is cramming in the school child's bun
    Old "Put down three and carry one."
The Red Cross peace at any price
    Sews for the Ladies' Aid
And Model Ma still finds it nice
    To be a single maid.
While she who'd save the world from want
    Has made a charming debutante.

> Was there no F? you cry,
>   And now I'm in a pretty fix,
> For F, you see, was I
>   The little Shakespeare-still-to-be
> Throughout the coming century—
>   Unless *my* bubble bursts on me!

In the above limerick, students' dreams did not come true partly because they had made such grandiose plans. The same yearbook, however, accused seniors of hypocrisy:

> You've spent a year in talk about "vocation,"
>   Career or "line of business" just for you,
> About a future after graduation,
>   And philanthropic work that you will do.
> Your plans we know are only for convention
>   Your minds are settled irretrievably,
> The left hand of the class shows one intention,
>   And all your fuss is idle mockery.[91]

The "sceptical junior" who wrote the above limerick said that seniors made career plans "for convention." Only in a college, and especially a women's college, would women making career plans in the 1910s be considered conventional. Although the earliest Vassar students differed from their successors during the Progressive Era, both generations believed that access to higher education gave women a mission to make the world a better place.

CHAPTER FIVE

Sophie Newcomb and Agnes Scott Colleges, 1887–1920: From Dutiful Daughters to New Women

PRECARIOUS BEGINNINGS: 1886–1906

Sophie Newcomb and Agnes Scott Colleges, both southern, white women's schools funded in the 1880s and located, respectively, in New Orleans and Decatur, Georgia, had different objectives in educating women. Founded by those interested in women's need for vocational training, Newcomb students and alumnae associated themselves (although far less strongly than Vassar women) with social housekeeping and urban progressivism. Newcomb women became particularly active in advancing southern women's educational opportunities. In contrast, Agnes Scott announced its purpose more narrowly as the education of future Christian mothers. Students lived on a self-contained, religiously oriented campus, where their extracurricular activities had few connections to the outside world.

At both schools, however, administrators and faculty initially experienced difficulty separating students from family concerns. Creating time and space for young women to study and participate in the college community proved more difficult at Newcomb, because most students lived at home, but it was a problem at residential Agnes Scott as well. Judging by students' short stories portraying the suffering of parents and siblings when daughters went off to school, southern college women worried about the selfishness involved in pursuing their own interests.

Gradually, both the institutions and the students matured. Growth in numbers, higher academic standards for students and faculty, and financial stability brought regional and national accreditation and recognition to Sophie Newcomb and Agnes Scott. Students on both campuses developed an absorbing collegiate culture resembling that at the eastern women's colleges. Newcomb continued to be more secular and reform-oriented, but Agnes Scott students also demonstrated their interest in careers and civic activism. Although both colleges employed women faculty whose qualifications, longevity in their positions, devotion to their students, and interest in causes matched the professoriat at the eastern women's colleges, southern students preferred to make alumnae their models. In the first two decades of the twentieth century, Newcomb and Agnes Scott alumnae provided a variety of activities and achievements as examples for students of the Progressive Era.

The Civil War and Reconstruction virtually destroyed New Orleans's economy, and even the upper classes became accustomed to genteel poverty. Silt partially blocked the mouth of the river, and mercantile prosperity vanished. Open drains caused a nauseating stench in the streets; yellow fever, smallpox, and leprosy menaced the citizens. White residents found it difficult to adjust to the verdict of the war. Leaders reacted angrily to any criticism of the South and to suggestions that New Orleans emulate enterprising northern cities. In 1884, Paul Tulane, a wealthy Franco-American merchant, donated money for an elite university in New Orleans, so that southerners would not have to send their children to college in the North. To gain tax-exempt status and eligibility for state revenues, the new institution took over the existing University of Louisiana, consisting mostly of a law school and a medical school. Paul Tulane's will specified only "white youth," not "white males," as students for the school he funded. Pointing to the gender ambiguity of the term *youth,* New Orleans women sought access to the new university.[1]

In the 1880s, New Orleans women participated in social reform and educational projects, founded civic organizations, and used the Cotton Exposition of 1884 as a showcase for their talents and achievements. Suffragists Susan B. Anthony and Julia Ward Howe attended the exposition and lectured on women's rights. During her stay in the city, Howe also promoted art education, urging women to produce native American handicrafts as an alternative to the standardized ugliness of machine-made objects. Through her influence, Tulane professors William and Ellsworth Woodward, graduates of the Rhode Island School of Design, began women's art and architecture classes at the exposition. White southern women looked to these activities as possibilities for self-support. After the fair closed, women wanting to continue this work founded the Ladies' Decorative Art League in 1885 and the New Orleans Pottery in 1886, hoping all the while for admission to the university as art students. These organizations formed the link between the exposition and the founding of Newcomb College in 1886.[2]

Aware of the university's reluctance to coeducate, Ida Richardson, wife of a Tulane trustee, suggested to her friend, the widowed philanthropist Josephine LeMonnier Newcomb, that she endow a women's college to be associated with Tulane. Richardson emphasized the practical value of the exposition's art education classes to women needing training for respectable work. Colonel William Preston Johnston, president of Tulane, also called on Mrs. Newcomb to assure her of the university's interest in women's higher education. He committed Tulane's trustees to writing a yearly budget for the women's college, supervising its endowment, and setting long-range goals, although the new institution would have its own administration, faculty, and campus. The project appealed to Josephine Newcomb as an appropriate memorial to her intellectually gifted daughter, Harriott Sophie, who had died of diphtheria in 1870 at the age of fifteen. In 1886, Mrs. Newcomb gave $100,000, the first of many gifts, for the founding of the H. Sophie Newcomb Memorial College of the Tulane University of Louisiana, the first women's coordinate college in the country. Although a devout Episcopalian, she asked that the college admit young white women on a nonsectarian basis, operate "in harmony with the fundamental principles of the Christian religion," and provide a practical as well as a cultural and intellectual education.

Josephine Newcomb's money, Johnston's cooperation, and the support of the city's women launched the enterprise, but it was President Brandt Van Blarcom Dixon (1887–1919), a St. Louis high school principal, who made Newcomb a true college. At the request of Tulane trustees, Dixon came to New Orleans for an interview. A supporter of the South's cause during the Civil War, Dixon liked New Orleans and its people but thought a women's college ill advised, given the city's poverty and the lack of adequate secondary education. He suggested that Mrs. Newcomb's donation go to Tulane for opening university classes to women, but neither she nor the university would consider coeducation. Instead, they pressured Dixon to accept the presidency, offering him an appointment to the Tulane faculty and promising him a free hand with the new college.

Dixon agreed to take the position if the trustees would allow him to admit only those students prepared for college work and not assign him responsibility for the institution's financial standing. They accepted his conditions, but ironically money and academic standards became Dixon's chief concerns in the first twenty-two years of the college's existence. Like other educators in the postwar South, he had to establish his school on a firm financial footing. And like the Southern Association of College Women (SACW) in later years, Dixon worked to make Newcomb a first-rate college, comparable to the eastern women's schools.[3]

Housed in a large brownstone at Camp and Howard Streets, Newcomb College opened its doors in October 1887. Thirty young women registered, and Dixon quickly learned that although parents in New Orleans wanted their daughters to attend Newcomb, they regarded it as a finishing school or a teacher training institute, with a prestigious connection to Tulane. They expected women to complete the course at seventeen, whereas Dixon wanted his students to be between the ages of seventeen and twenty-one. Of the thirty original students, only four had training in Latin, considered an essential prerequisite to a college education, and only ten had studied algebra.

Thus, in the same year that Vassar College closed its preparatory department, Dixon reluctantly turned the top floor of the Newcomb College building into Newcomb High School. In 1887–88 fifty-nine academic students registered, mostly in the high school; Newcomb also had ninety-one special and art students. His faculty was somewhat unusual, including married women, inexperienced teachers, and few degree-holders. Of the six women and three men (Mrs. Jane Nixon, English and speech; Mrs. Evelyn Ordway, chemistry; William and Ellsworth Woodward, art; Florian Cajori, mathematics; Mrs. I. J. Gomez, Spanish; Florian Schaffter, director of vocal music; Miss Marie Augustin, French; Miss Elizabeth Edwards, Latin; and Mrs. Gertrude Roberts Smith, art), only Cajori and Ordway were college graduates.[4]

In spite of this modest and unpromising beginning, Dixon decided on a bold step to ensure the college's future. Her persuaded Josephine Newcomb to purchase a property at 1220 Washington Avenue in the city's Garden District, large enough to hold an academic building, an art building, a chapel, a pottery, and three dormitories. With more space, Dixon hoped to raise enrollments, attract better students, hire additional faculty, expand and upgrade the curriculum, provide physical education classes, clubs and other activities. In January 1891, 174 students (63 academic, 55 preparatory, 31 art, and 25 special) moved to their new home.

Dixon and Josephine Newcomb developed a close relationship that bene-fited the college. In 1892 the founder began spending winters in New Orleans at the Josephine Louise House, one of the new dormitories. She supervised the decoration of the chapel, with its stained glass windows depicting events in her daughter's life, and gave numerous smaller gifts for other college needs. She died in 1901, while visiting New York City, and left her entire estate to the college. Her relatives contested the will, and for seven years the courts held up distribution of the money. When the college finally received the funds, her bequest totaled $3.6 million. This financial security enabled Newcomb College to keep its tuition low, at $100 yearly for the academic course, and to continue expanding.

By 1900 Dixon had increased his staff from fifteen to thirty, 47 percent of whom had at least one degree. Alumnae faculty included Myra Clare Rogers '96, Ph.D. Chicago, professor of Latin; Caroline Francis Richardson '95, Ph.D. Columbia, professor of English; Lydia Elizabeth Frotscher '04, Ph.D. Chicago, professor of German; Anna Estelle Many '07, instructor of mathematics and Dean of Women; Amelie and Desiree Roman, graduates of the art school and instructors in design. Dixon also appointed faculty from eastern schools, such as Susan Dinsmore Tew, A. B. Smith, Ph.D. Yale, professor of Greek; Mary Leal Harkness, president of the SACW and pro-fessor of Latin; Imogen Stone, Ph.D. Cornell, professor of English; Mar-garet Elsie Cross, A. B. Barnard, Ph.D. Columbia, professor of physical education.[5]

Dixon raised entrance standards in 1902–03, requiring examinations in mathematics, languages, history, and English, and estimated that the grade of work had advanced two to three years between 1887 and 1902. The city's success in halting yellow fever epidemics after 1905 resulted in more health-ful conditions, attracting young women from outside of New Orleans to Newcomb College. Dixon encouraged this, touring Louisiana and other Gulf Coast states to recruit southern students. He hoped that increased numbers, an expanded curriculum, and the physical advantages of a larger campus would create a college atmosphere like Vassar's or Wellesley's. By 1906, then, when the U.S. Commissioner of Education gave Newcomb an A rating, the college had overcome initial obstacles to become a leading institution for the higher education of southern white women. Still, enroll-ment in the collegiate liberal arts program increased slowly; in 1907, New-comb had 433 students, of whom only 135 registered for the four-year bachelor's course.[6]

Like Newcomb, Agnes Scott College in Decatur, Georgia, began as a seminary and high school established by a philanthropist, and evolved into a college. Although located only three miles from Atlanta, its origins and educational philosophy drew on traditional Christian values rather than more modern urban concerns about women's needs for self-support. Founded in 1889, through the efforts of Dr. Frank Henry Gaines, pastor of the Decatur Presbyterian Church, the school offered a primary education that year to sixty-three young women and six small boys under the age of twelve. In 1890, Colonel George Washington Scott gave $40,000 to the Decatur Female Seminary, the first of many such donations eventually totaling $112,500. To express their gratitude for Scott's gifts, the trustees renamed the school the Agnes Scott Institute, honoring the colonel's mother. Intending from the first that the institute should grow to be a college, the trustees named Dr. Gaines president; he served in this position until his death in 1923.[7]

The mother of seven children and stepmother to another five, Agnes Irvine Scott symbolized, to her son and the school's trustees, the ideal Christian wife and mother. Devoted to Shakespeare and the poetry of Robert Burns, she taught intellectual and spiritual values to her children. As her son John put it in the ceremony dedicating Agnes Scott Institute to his mother: "She met the duties of her sphere with the sublimest faith and trust in the goodness of God. . . . She was a Presbyterian and loved her church. . . . She . . . saw to it that no child of hers should go out into the world ignorant of the Shorter Catechism."[8]

The founders and trustees of the institute adopted the Agnes Scott Ideal, thereby proclaiming their desire to educate young women who would follow in the footsteps of Colonel Scott's mother. Printed each year in the institute's catalogue, the school's goals were: "1) A liberal curriculum, fully abreast of the best institutions of this country. 2) The Bible a textbook. 3) Thoroughly qualified and consecrated teachers. 4) A high standard of scholarship. 5) All the influences of the College conducive to the formation and development of Christian character. 6) The glory of God the chief end of all." Additionally, early leaders of the school formed a covenant, agreeing to offer daily prayers for the school, its unconverted students, and the glory of God.

The president and trustees of the institute were all required, by the terms of the charter, to be Presbyterians (by the 1920s the board had eleven trustees representing the synods of Alabama, Georgia, and Florida); and teachers, practicing Christians. No rules limited the student body to Presbyterians, or even to Christians, but required Bible study, chapel services,

Sabbath observance, and vesper services were all part of the Agnes Scott experience. On Sundays, students rose at half past seven, breakfasted at eight, had Sunday School at nine, church at eleven, a special Sunday dinner, meditation time, supper, Christian Band meetings, evening services and hymn singings. For many years faculty gave no assignments for Mondays, so that classwork would not tempt students from their prayers.[9]

Between 1889 and 1906, when the institute officially became Agnes Scott College, the trustees struggled to raise both money and academic standards. Although the college elected to remain independent of direct church control, southern Presbyterian churches contributed heavily to Agnes Scott's support, helping the institution match funds donated by the General Education Board. When Gaines died in 1923, the college owned twenty acres and eighteen buildings. To achieve collegiate academic status, the trustees gradually eliminated the lowest grades and added higher ones. This made it difficult for some students, who, for example, might spend four years as seniors without graduating. As James Ross McCain, second president of the college, noted in his history of Agnes Scott: "It is a small wonder that of the 1663 students who attended Agnes Scott Institute, only 68 received diplomas."[10]

In 1906 the institution officially renamed itself Agnes Scott College and conferred its first bachelor's degrees. Like Newcomb, the new college continued to offer preparatory work; the Agnes Scott Academy remained open until 1913. The number of residential students reached 130 for the year 1906–07, with an additional 31 non-resident students (figures refer only to the college, not the academy); by 1918–19, 335 college students lived on campus; an additional 53 were day pupils. In 1898–99, resident students paid $127.50 per term; by 1910–11 the college charged $325 to $350 a year for tuition, room, and board. The college assured parents that: "Every effort is made to give . . . the character of a Christian home. Teachers and students constitute one household. Care is taken to render the home life of the student not only attractive, but conducive to the cultivation of those graces which mark refined women. . . . Instruction in manners and etiquette is given by the Lady Principal."[11]

The Student Government Association (SGA) of Agnes Scott printed the social regulations at the beginning of each school year for the benefit of freshmen, and as a reminder to upperclasswomen. In the handbook of 1912–13, the SGA cautioned students to observe the 10 P.M. lights out rule, register for a chaperone when leaving Decatur, avoid soda fountains, moving pictures, and talking on the street when in the company of young men, obtain the dean's permission for any campus visitors, and of course, to maintain silence and decorum on Sundays. When visiting friends, the handbook cautioned: "Follow the rules of the lady of the house, but receive no permissions from her not in accordance with college rules."[12]

The number and quality of faculty grew with the college. In 1913–14, the faculty roster listed four men, all with Ph.D.'s, fourteen women with undergraduate and graduate degrees from prominent colleges and universities, and three women who did not have bachelor's degrees but had studied at normal schools, colleges, and universities. The faculty also included two Agnes Scott alumnae: Alice Lucile Alexander, B.A. Agnes Scott, A.M. Columbia University, adjunct professor of French; and Margaret Ellen McCallie, B.A. Agnes Scott, Ph.B. Chicago, and graduate student at the universities of Berlin, Heidelberg, and Paris, adjunct professor of German. Gaines and the trustees took great pride in the school's rapid acceptance into the Southern Association of Colleges and Secondary Schools in 1907.[13]

While administrators, trustees, and faculty sought to make Newcomb and Agnes Scott the academic equivalents of Vassar and Wellesley, students at these institutions carefully considered the nature, meaning, and effects of their college years. Like college women in the North, they found that higher education, even when designed to preserve tradition, conflicted with family claims and created new imperatives. As southerners, however, they defined those imperatives somewhat differently and more conservatively.

THE NEWCOMB SPIRIT AND THE MEANING OF WOMEN'S HIGHER EDUCATION

Newcomb's success brought public acclaim. New Orleans newspapers praised both the college and the women who attended it, assuring readers that higher education did not destroy the charm of southern ladies: "*The Picayune* hails the fair bachelors of Sophie Newcomb. Bachelors of science and of arts they are withal girls, gay, bright, tender, and sweet. And what if their pretty little heads be stuffed with philosophic theses and parallelopipedons and Greek prepositions. There is just as much room as ever for thoughts of flounces, frills, and furbelows and all the charming frivolities of girl life." Although Newcomb designed its art program to prepare women for careers, the *Picayune* ignored this promotion of female independence, commenting: "Art design and decorative work are fully in the reach of the gentler sex and well adapted to the strength and condition of females."[14]

Newcomb's commencement speakers, usually ministers, disapproved of "the charming frivolities of girl life." They stressed instead the connections between higher education and domesticity and assured seniors and their parents that men found educated women attractive and marriageable.

> No man likes a fool for a mate; a bright clever intellect counts for much in moral training. . . . Good intelligent men believe in sensible intelligent women. . . . Sentimental slenderness and delicacy have gone out of style. . . . Men like a girl who can eat a good hearty dinner and enjoy it.
>
> •
>
> The college for the higher education of women is the pride and glory of New Orleans and in fact of the whole South, for it is the only one in the South that ranks with Vassar and Wellesley. . . . It has been proven conclusively that a woman's mind is as capable of taking as high an education as man's and to this noble end the college is doing a lion's share.
>
> •
>
> If you prefer to pass what you call domestic life with a woman who is distinctly ignorant so be it. You have the right, and may God have mercy on your soul.[15]

Tulane president Edwin Alderman agreed that college women should concentrate their efforts on domestic matters: "The old time woman had a charm, a definite charm. . . . Like the woman of today, the old time woman wanted to do great things, but did not trouble herself much about reform in the world without; she tried, first, to get things right around her, in her own home . . . [to] hold fast to that essential charm, homemaking genius."[16]

The bankers, professionals, and government workers who sent daughters to Newcomb were pleased to educate them under Tulane's auspices, thereby ensuring their capacities for self-support. Despite the middle-class status of Newcomb parents and the relatively low tuition, 25 percent of the students went to college on scholarships. Besides the traditional bachelor's course, the college offered degrees in art, music, education and domestic science. Although each department or school had a four-year course combining liberal arts work with professional training, most students stayed two years, received a certificate of proficiency, and went on to teaching jobs in elementary and secondary schools. The prestigious Newcomb art school produced graduates able to support themselves as independent craftswomen. The school offered instruction in embroidery, brasswork, jewelry, and bookbinding but was best known for its pottery. Using the blue and brown college colors and depicting southern flora and fauna, the pottery won prizes at the Paris Exposition of 1900 and at similar exhibitions in the United States. Orders poured in, and art school students filled them. Graduates who set up their own shops and kilns earned forty to fifty dollars a month.[17]

Relationships with Tulane men reinforced views of Newcomb students as charming, marriageable girls. Until 1918, when the college moved to the university campus, three miles separated the institutions, and poor public transportation prevented informal social contacts. Fearing distractions or worse, Newcomb faculty and administrators strictly controlled access to their campus, discouraging males from strolling around the grounds or waiting for women in the halls. Thus, in contrast to the situation on coeducational campuses, Tulane men did not have to deal with the constant presence of women. They invited Newcomb students to their campus for plays, lectures, and dances, but as guests; women did not threaten masculine prerogatives. In 1896, a writer in the *Jambalaya*, Tulane's yearbook, celebrated the charms of college women with a limerick:

> *My Pearl Is A Newcomb Girl*
>
> I've met all the girls in the city,
>   Some wild, some gay, and some free,
> Though mine won't be out till next winter,
>   I tell you she's in it with me,
> She's bone-ing her studies at Newcomb,
>   And learning whatever she shall;
> She's the best-looking girl in the College,
>   Is my little Newcomb gal.[18]

Newcomb students reached out to young men. Perhaps because they had little interest in independent professional careers, student authors found no incompatibility between romance and a college degree. Short stories published in the *Arcade*, Newcomb's journal, had a standard boy-meets-and-wins-girl format. In one example, "According to Cable," a Newcomb freshman fooled and charmed an arrogant northern college man into thinking that she was a young Creole girl fresh out of the "convent on the Rue Royale." The young man discovered her ruse but did not hold it, or her college education, against her. They planned a wedding and a home in the South, where "college girls" were more feminine than those the bridegroom had seen back home. The Newcomb student had no qualms about quitting college for marriage. In another story, a Newcomb student en route to visit a college friend arranged to meet the friend's brother on the train. They agreed to wear blue ribbon bows to recognize each other. A series of mishaps followed because other passengers had adopted similar schemes.

Toward the end of the trip, the student met a handsome Cornell man who asked to see her again.[19]

This widespread social acceptance of Newcomb College, and public approval of higher education for southern women, actually masked serious familial tensions. Parents expected that their daughters' lives would continue as before, even though they were going to college. Although he won the battle to restrict entrance to women seventeen and over, President Dixon had to assert the college's claim to students' time and efforts. In a letter to parents he noted:

> The College and Faculty solicits the cooperation of the parents and guardians in securing for the students the fullest opportunities for uninterrupted study. It is not possible for the young ladies to devote themselves to social entertainments and at the same time perform their college duties in a satisfactory manner. . . . The standing of many of our students has been seriously affected by the social distractions of the past quarter, their energies impaired, their interest and faithfulness in their work greatly lessened. It is therefore urgently requested that such disturbing influences be more carefully avoided in the future.[20]

On another occasion the president resorted to sarcasm: "Your letter is received asking that your daughter be excused from gymnastic exercises on the ground that she has sufficient during her summer vacation for the demands of the whole year. Permit me to ask the following: I presume that she has a hearty Thanksgiving dinner; is she excluded from later dinners on that account?"[21] As Dixon and his faculty contended with the family claim on students' attention, he blamed the difficulties on traditional southern attitudes toward women:

> The Southern girl has been accustomed to the most solicitous care, and has learned to expect every attention and courtesy from her associates and others; in consequence she is inclined to be self-willed and exacting, but not self-reliant; alert and quick-witted, but not persistent and steady, eager for novelty and possessing a fine initiative, but changeable and dependent upon others for results. She lacks the discipline which comes from interest in that which requires hard work. . . . She has not been required to fend for herself, is guarded and supervised continually.[22]

Students may have entered Newcomb with the habits and attitudes Dixon described, but they came to share his concerns. The 80 percent of Newcomb women who lived at home had difficulty combining family and college responsibilities, as students' short stories demonstrate. In "The Gospel of Work," Jessica's family continually interrupted her attempts to finish an essay. With her father away on business and mother feeling her rheumatism, Jessica had to help her sister Marion perform household chores and look after the younger siblings. Domestic life became particularly hectic when Uncle Daniel dropped by, and her mother wanted to prepare a special meal. Frustrated and angry, Jessica exploded: "What was work? Wasn't her essay a noble work? Wasn't it greater work than beating eggs, or setting the table, or putting tin soldiers into a rickety pasteboard box, or putting a dolly with a broken head to bed? Wasn't the paper she had written a month ago, pleading for children's playgrounds, of value? Had it not helped a good cause? Wasn't that work and service? Really, it seemed a very much greater, far-reaching service."

Jessica became reconciled to her situation only when Marion explained their mother's gospel of work: "She said that when we helped her about the house, whenever we straightened things up, or mended our clothes, or swept, or did anything like that, no matter how little it seemed, it helped her, and then she could help father all the more, and he could get more done, and would be doing his part better, and then we'd all be doing something to help the world along, and then . . . we'd all be happier." A reformed Jessica rose at six to prepare the family's breakfast, so that she would have time to write her essay on the value of different kinds of work.[23]

In another story, when senior class president Eliza Rotfield went home for the holidays, she found her younger sister Barbara ill with pneumonia. Mrs. Rotfield asked Eliza to remain at home, but the latter refused, explaining the honor and importance of being senior class president. After graduation, Eliza said, she would return home, get a job, and devote herself to helping her family. With assurances from Mrs. Rotfield that no immediate danger existed, Eliza kissed Barbara good-by and returned to college. Once back in school, she became involved in defending an innocent student from a charge of cheating on a French examination. Just before Eliza's turn to present her case to the Student Council, she received a telegram from home and grimly decided not to open it: "She had worked up for this great moment and she felt that she had to do her part, her duty at once. She went to the meeting. . . . She conquered." After the successful conclusion of the case, Eliza read the telegram, which told her of Barbara's death that morning. In both stories, the student authors presented sympathetically the claims of college life. Yet in these two cases at least, protagonists found it impossible to combine family responsibilities and the demands of higher education.[24]

Like parents who wanted their daughters educated but not involved with college life, Tulane men also expressed ambivalence about women's higher education. They admired Newcomb women from a distance but had difficulty dealing with them as fellow students. Newcomb and Tulane occasionally shared activities; when they did so, men assumed leadership, just as male students did on other, fully coeducational, campuses. The *Arcade* contained some serious writing, but women contributed only gossip columns to the university's papers, the *Olive and Blue* and the *College Spirit*. Newcomb women entered and won the annual Carnot debate competition in 1911 and again in 1912. Tulane men thereafter refused to compete, saying they were "too much taken up with their daily work." Clearly, Newcomb's status as a coordinate women's college won its students autonomy they could not have received as coeds. And so long as they did not work or compete with men, Tulane students continued to regard Newcomb women as suitable recipients of their romantic attentions.[25]

Eventually, Newcomb women established some distance from their families and participated more freely in college life. After the move to Washington Avenue and the establishment of a real campus, students founded chapters of national sororities, class and self-government associations, a dramatics club, a debating society (the Agonistic Club), and basketball teams. These activities and work on student publications kept nonresidents at the college afternoons and evenings, fostering friendships and institutional loyalties. Excited by the change in students' attitudes, Dixon revised his views of southern womanhood: "I was obliged to recognize in them a responsiveness to ideals, a growing persistency of purpose, and an initiative which I had not at first suspected." Through these activities, Newcomb students developed new identities as college women and self-consciously sought the meaning of their education.[26]

New Orleans of the Progressive Era had a social reform-settlement-suffrage network working through women's clubs. At Kingsley House, head resident Eleanor Laura McMain, a student of Jane Addams and Graham Taylor, spearheaded programs for public health, education, and labor law reform. Nationally known reformers Kate and Jean Gordon founded the Era Club, a women's suffrage group. They urged passage of child labor laws, reorganized community welfare activities, and Jean Gordon became Louisiana's first state factory inspector. These women all had connections with Newcomb College: they spoke on campus; Jean Gordon judged student debates; and in 1913, Eleanor McMain offered a course in social settlement work.[27]

Just as southern progressivism was more conservative, less widespread, and less successful than the northern variety, so Newcomb students responded differently to reform imperatives than their counterparts at Vassar. Writings in the *Arcade* did not deal with social reform or politics and denied any student interest in suffrage. When the college offered its first economics course in 1911, the journal reassured the community that the study of political economy would not produce suffragists:

> This course in Political Economy was offered at the special request of the girls themselves. Certainly this is a sign that Southern women, too, are becoming interested in those things that were once thought of as strictly "men's affairs." Woman's Suffrage has had very little support or encouragement among Southern women—the majority of us knew little and cared less about it. The fact that at Newcomb Political Economy is studied does not mean, however, that Newcomb girls are to become suffragettes—or even suffragists. Far from it! I can see mothers and grandmothers holding up their hands in holy horror and letters from dear old aunts and god-mothers advising the parents not to send their precious children to college to be demoralized. No, but a course in Economics and Sociology does mean that the girls at Newcomb are taking an intelligent interest in, not politics in the narrower sense of the word, but in political economy.[28]

Although conservative in their political beliefs, Newcomb students felt themselves to be different from their "dear old aunts and god-mothers." The public continued to see them as "southern belles," but they fashioned new self-images, asserting their intellectual capabilities. When Agnes Scott students came to an intercollegiate debate on compulsory military training dressed in formal evening clothes, Newcomb women, who lost the match, accused their opponents of using feminine wiles on the judges.

In a satiric skit, printed in the *Arcade,* Newcomb debaters wore military costumes, while Agnes Scott wore "Mary Pickford curls, a fluffy frock with a large sash, and carried some knitting." The Newcomb student took her task seriously: "Ladies and gentlemen, in this world crisis when America finds herself plunged into dangers on every hand, does not every condition, every situation point to the absolute necessity of military training for every man and boy in America?" The Agnes Scott debater looked up from her knitting and responded: "Well, I think nothing could be worse than compulsory military training. In the first place, the poor boys would be bored to death, you know they would. Then, they'd have to do their training in summer, mostly, and can you imagine a vacation without any boys?" In the skit, as in reality, the negative won, and the *Arcade* writer added a speech in which judges proclaimed the "superior womanly intuition" of Agnes Scott.[29]

As college women, Newcomb students accepted public social and educational responsibilities. Southern women's college faculty did not become role models for their students, as female professors did in the North. Instead, alumnae maintained contacts with the college and current students and set an example of civic activism. The Newcomb Alumnae Association, founded in 1893, allied itself with other New Orleans women's clubs to run a night school for working people. Graduates wrote a section entitled "Of Alumnae Interest" in each issue of the *Arcade,* using it as a forum to reach students and to keep in touch with each other. They frequently discussed the question of appropriate postcollege activities. Old-fashioned mothers, they warned, could no longer serve as guides for their daughters' lives. Yet the family claim continued to be strong after graduation. In the following skit an alumna author made fun of her classmates but also expressed the conflicts between the intellectual, professional, and reform interests fostered by college attendance, and customs confining unmarried daughters to home duties.

> Yes, I'm going to stay home next year. I did want to go up north—I know I could *easily* get a position on *The Atlantic* or *The Century* or one of those magazines; Miss Stone and Mr. Butler always gave me "A" on my essays—but mother and father won't hear of it. Yes, after all, a woman's sphere is the home. No, I won't do the actual housekeeping. Mother will do that, but I'll attend to the rest. And, Jane, we *must* keep up our French and German and read together for a couple of hours a day. And then our settlement work—I intend to devote *all* my time to that. And I expect I can write something.[30]

As a cure for the postgraduate blues, the Newcomb Alumnae Association recommended continuing involvement with college affairs. In two skits, "Newcomb News at Home" and "More Newcomb News at Home," Jane's comments about her daughter Mary's student activities showed her own inability to comprehend college life. Mary's letter said: "As soon as we all get our bloomers, we will play basketball out on the court, but now we only play in the gym." Jane turned to her sister Susan, a Newcomb alumna, complaining: "That is the most improper thing I have ever heard. I shall talk seriously to Mary's father . . . about sending for her immediately. To appear outside her room in such a costume. . ." In another letter, Mary mentioned the college chapter of Phi Beta Kappa. At first her horrified mother thought it was a "colored society." Then she decided it was a plan for all the students to wear latchkeys around their necks, to let themselves into the dormitories late at night. Finally, upon learning that it was a scholastic honor society, she sent a dollar for dues so her daughter could "sign up." Aunt Susan could not offer much help, because she had never joined the Alumnae Association, kept up with college activities, or set foot on campus in twenty years. Her remarks were more laughable and inappropriate than her confused sister's.[31]

The Alumnae Association found its niche in fighting for white women's educational opportunities. Newcomb graduates became officers of the Louisiana chapter of the Southern Association of College Women and published the proceedings of each meeting in the *Arcade,* along with frequent discussions of how to raise southern academic standards. They sponsored "college days" in local high schools to interest women in attending Newcomb. Most important, perhaps, they challenged Tulane's policies on women's higher education and sought expanded privileges for Newcomb women within the university.

A campus quip accused Tulane of "marrying Newcomb for her money." In part, this joke referred to the battle between Tulane and Louisiana State University (LSU) for Morrill Act funds. Tulane's admission of women, although separately, through Newcomb College, qualified the university to receive state revenues. Responding to this pressure, LSU slowly coeducated; in 1906, it had twenty-one women students. During the legislative session of 1906, however, New Orleans women's groups argued that Tulane's greater commitment to women justified its sole possession of public funds.

After supporting Tulane in this fight, women demanded access to the university's medical school. For the next seven years, Jean Gordon and the Era Club joined the Newcomb Alumnae Association in placing their case before Tulane and the public. The university agreed to admit women to the first two years of laboratory work and to the pharmaceutical and dental programs. Even the hiring of two female faculty in medicine, however, did not get women students into the physicians' courses. The persistence of the women's groups finally paid off in 1914, when the trustees voted to allow females into all four years of medical school.[32]

Tulane was also interested in Newcomb's endowment. Under the terms of the original agreement between Josephine Newcomb and the trustees, Tulane administered Newcomb's funds. Although forbidden to use the college's money for other departments of the university, the trustees came up with several plans for diverting a few dollars. Dixon, for example, resisted the board's demand for a large "donation" to the graduate school when it agreed to admit Newcomb alumnae. The Alumnae Association sought representation on the Board of Trustees to prevent future "requests" and give themselves a voice in college policies. The board refused, citing a Louisiana statute barring women from public positions requiring voting, and subsequently denied petitions for nonvoting advisory alumnae committees.

The Alumnae Association, with student support, aired the controversy in the *Arcade,* coming perilously close to a defense of women's rights: "At Newcomb College, a college endowed by a woman in memory of her daughter, women professors of the same capacity and standing as the men professors are given much smaller salaries. We recognize that it is the custom of the time to underpay women for the same grade of work men perform, but an unjust commercial practice should not be carried into use in such a center of culture and uplift as a great twentieth century University."[33] Alumnae also satirized the board's fears about their presence at meetings:

A Meeting of the Tulane Board

Irby: If it were merely a question of having them on the Board, I'd say all right if it gave them any pleasure. But I don't propose to have any extravagant women dictating how to spend the fund. Newcomb spends quite enough money as it is. . . . Look at that budget. . . . Three dollars last month for repairing benches in the hall. If that isn't throwing away money.

Magruder: Of course, I'm new on the Board . . . but it seems only reasonable that they should have chairs to sit on.

Walmsley: The point is out of order.

Dymond: I don't believe in women in public life; they're just a nuisance. And their mothers don't do it. It seems to me that the Newcomb Alumnae are a very troublesome group of women.

Farrar: They're all suffragettes, that's what's the matter with them, and there is no more objectionable class on earth.[34]

Joined by Jean Gordon and the Era Club, the Alumnae Association campaigned for a bill allowing women the vote on charitable and educational boards. They won their fight in 1916, two years before the college moved to the Tulane campus. Alumnae felt their newly won representation would help them protect Newcomb's interests and retain its independent spirit.

EXPANDING CHRISTIAN SOCIAL
CONSCIOUSNESS AT AGNES SCOTT

Loyalty to the college developed more quickly at residential Agnes Scott than at Sophie Newcomb. In spite of the religious atmosphere and strict social regulations, Agnes Scott was no Presbyterian nunnery. Young women away from home organized social and extracurricular activities to develop friendships and have a good time. In her research on the early days of Agnes

Scott, Amy Friedlander found that the women faculty, who lived in the dormitories with students, initiated and encouraged college life to develop students' attachment to the institution and to weaken ties to home and family. Professor Louise McKinney, whose career at the college spanned forty-six years, described the campus atmosphere as familial, reporting that "the girls" used to ask her to kiss them good-night.[35]

In 1897, the first edition of the *Aurora* (the college's literary magazine and yearbook) listed four sororities, a Chafing Dish club, a Cotillion Club (members dressed like men for their yearbook picture), a Baby Club (nine girls dressed as babies and sucking their thumbs), a Bicycle Club, Art Club, Sewing Club, Deutsch Club, Choral Union, and Alumnae Club. In 1898 three new sororities, a Cooking Club, Hemstitching Club, Spooners Club, Early Risers Club, Kodak Club, Le Cercle Français, and others joined the list.

Twenty years later, students had developed more sophisticated organizations and activities. Active social calendars fostered close friendships between students and offered opportunities for taking part in the traditionally male activities of politics, debate, and athletics. Writing in the *Agnes Scott Bulletin* for 1917, Emma Jones '18 entitled her essay "Not In The Catalogue," intending it as a description, for freshmen, of the yearly extracurricular cycle. She promised new students that "Agnes Scott will make up to you for the good times you'll miss at home." Activities began in the fall semester, with a reception given by the YWCA and each freshman signing up to join one of the two literary societies, Propylean or Mnemosynean. After these initial encounters, as at other women's colleges, sophomores initiated freshmen into the campus community with a series of stunts and pranks. Class concerns then gave way to a series of common holiday celebrations— Halloween, Thanksgiving, Christmas, Valentine's Day—and opportunities to join the Blackfriars (dramatics society), Hoasc Club (senior service honor society), debate or athletic teams, the *Agonistic* (student newspaper), the *Aurora*, or Gamma Tau Alpha (the academic honor society). Toward the end of the year, "the young debutante is not so rushed as is Miss Senior." Concerts, plays, operettas, and, finally, commencement honored seniors and formally ushered them out of the college community.

Agnes Scott women also learned how to deal with campus regulations. In 1909–10, when they requested a holiday that the faculty refused, the students, led by the president of student government, left the campus in a body to have a picnic in the woods. Their angry instructors took points off the students' grades, but thereafter spring holidays became an annual event.[36]

Having fun did not keep Agnes Scott students from moving toward greater self-consciousness, distance from domesticity, and activity in the public sphere. As at Sophie Newcomb, home responsibilities conflicted with students' campus lives. Although Agnes Scott was residential, the catalogue of 1896–97 found it necessary to request parents "not to interfere with the studies of their daughters by withdrawing them during the session to spend a week or so at home." And in the catalogue of 1904–05, administrators urged: "It is desirable that dressmaking, dentistry and vaccination be attended to at home, that the time, strength, and thought of the student may be given to the special objects for which she has entered the Institute."[37]

Like Newcomb women, Agnes Scott students viewed the joys and duties of college life as oppositional to family responsibilities. A "Senior Sketch" from the *Aurora* of 1899 showed students disappointed because their friend Edith could not return for her senior year. As her classmates lamented, they focused on Edith's loss of the freedom to come to school rather than on her mother's illness and possible death. A telegram, however, announced the mother's recovery and Edith's imminent arrival at Agnes Scott. Similarly, in another sketch, senior Margie overheard a conversation about a college girl whose father's death was announced to her by telegram. Thinking that they were referring to her family, Margie became hysterical until the two students talking outside her door reassured her that they were discussing a short story from a magazine in the college library. And "Aunt Mabel's" stories of college life included the tale of "Bessie, our class musician. How we all loved her and expected her to distinguish our class. . . . It was truly a sad day for the class when she was called home and had to give up graduating, but she did it so bravely that nobody would have guessed that it had been a sacrifice on her part. Even though she did not get her diploma we always numbered her as one of our class."[38]

College life, although "homey" (as the catalogue asserted) and fun (as the students described it), created public, communal obligations. When a fictional sophomore class depended on Happy's basketball prowess to beat the juniors, she played with a painful ankle injury, against her doctor's orders, and won the game for her team. In "How Clara Got First Honor," Mattie L. Tilly '04 told the story of best friends, Clara McBride and May Rosan, who were tied for first place in their class. The faculty decided to determine the recipients of first and second honors on the basis of a final essay. May was the better writer of the two, and both women expected that she would win. May, however, knew that first honors would mean a great deal to Clara's widowed mother and to Clara herself, anxious to fulfill her father's dream of seeing his child in first place. She turned in a second-rate essay, and when Clara found out, May persuaded her friend not to say anything. Although Clara graduated with first honors, her conscience bothered her, and a year later she told the story to their English professor. Without revealing the circumstances, the college announced that May Rosan had actually taken first honors at the previous commencement, and Clara McBride, second place. In a more traditional Victorian story about women's friendships, Clara would not have discovered May's act of unselfish friendship and womanly sacrifice. Here, however, the student author gently rebuked May for well-intentioned but unethical behavior, while praising competition and merit, commonly associated with men's sphere.[39]

Students celebrated their achievements and sought meaningful ways to live as educated women. A writer for the *Mnemosynean* criticized Washington Irving's portrayal of women in his novels and stories. Although admitting that good wives and mothers were important, the student stated: "We who have seen what higher education will do for women cannot admire those who have only such accomplishments as are necessary to the education of a fine lady, and who never seem to reach any great mental height."[40] And in a valedictory to the class of 1894 from the Mnemosynean society, Mary Mel Neel warned her classmates:

> If we do not undertake our life-work with proper ideas of our duty to society and our responsibility to God, then our opportunities have been wasted, and will only bring reproach upon education; and the world will fold its sanctimonious hands and say: "What has she done with her coveted higher education?" . . . Women are often compelled by dire necessity to be the breadwinners. The nineteenth century has given her ampler opportunities and broader fields for her endeavors, but, I am sorry to say, not equal compensation for her labors.

Although women's employment opportunities were limited and salaries unjustly low, Neel considered the possibility of self-support an important and desirable option. Unlike their mothers and grandmothers, Agnes Scott graduates had choices to make. They need not marry unless the right man came along.[41]

Class prophecies depicted graduates as doctors, lawyers, opera singers, newspaperwomen, teachers, college professors, politicians, dentists, missionaries, and judges; rarely as housewives and mothers. Meant to be facetious by pointing out the individual quirks of seniors, the prophecies also demonstrated awareness of women's expanding roles and the knowledge that marriage interfered with the best-laid plans. Nellie Mandeville's intelligence and strength of character had clearly impressed her fellow students. In one prediction she was a successful New York City lawyer, while another prophet sent her to Havana to straighten out the Cuban crisis. On the other hand, Cora Strong '97 became a humorist on the *Atlanta Constitution,* only to be dismissed for flirting with male reporters. Florida Bethel, disappointed in love, was an engineer, who died in a terrible train wreck. Astronomer Midge McAden gave up star gazing for marriage. The class prophet of 1897 also reported that Ella Belle Emery, Susie May Wallace, Emma Wallace, Julia Dudley, Annie Council, and Florence Hildreth founded a "woman's town" in New Mexico, "where they lived in peace and happiness until Julia, who could never find a man of good enough family to suit her, eloped with an Italian peddler, who had managed to make his way within their town walls."[42]

Additional evidence from student sources shows their interest in men but some ambivalence about giving up educations, careers, or independence for marriage. In short stories, far more like Vassar writings than Newcomb fiction, women made these choices without interference from friends, families, or even the men in question, who did not actually appear on the scene. Nineteen-year-old Helen Davenport turned down a proposal from the man she loved so that she could finish college; in contrast, Marguerite gave up her singing career to marry Ted. Men were equally absent from the frequent Civil War romances in student publications. In each case they died in battle, leaving women to grieve and raise their children alone.

When student authors allowed men into their stories, they usually mocked them. Jack Manning saw a beautiful girl on an Atlanta streetcar and fell in love when she smiled at him. He followed her home, learned that she was an Agnes Scott student, and arranged to go to the college's next reception. Late at night when he finally succeeded in isolating the girl from her many admirers long enough to talk to her, he found that she had smiled at him not with admiration, but out of pity because he looked so mournful. In a similar story, Harvard student John Sawyers spotted a lovely young woman at a football game. He sent her a card with his name and college written on it: she sent one back reading "Miss Elizabeth White, Wellesley." When Sawyers went to Wellesley to call on "Miss Elizabeth White," he discovered that she was not a student, but the college's cook, and he beat a hasty retreat.[43]

Through the Alumnae Association, founded in 1895, students heard of graduates' achievements and learned how to follow in their footsteps. The *Agonistic,* the *Aurora,* and the *Agnes Scott Alumnae Quarterly* listed marriages and children but also noted the volunteer work, civic offices, graduate study, and jobs of alumnae. In a pamphlet published by the Alumnae Association, "wives and mothers" was only one of forty-three job categories filled by Agnes Scott graduates. Other occupations included advertising, banking, biology, bookkeeping, book reviewing, chemistry, church secretaries, educational management, home economics, industrial work, institutional work, journalism, law, library work, mechanical drawing, medicine, missions, nursing, pastor's assistants, physical education, public health service, Red Cross, secretarial work, social service, summer camp work, teaching, and YWCA jobs.

The writer of the pamphlet stressed that southern conservatism not only placed severe limits on the availability of education and training for women but also closed many occupations to them; thus, the achievements of Agnes Scott women were especially remarkable. She singled out six graduates for individual mention: Nan B. Stephens, playwright, musician, and vice president of the National Federation of Music Clubs; Louise Davidson, theatrical manager; India Hunt, graduate of the Woman's Medical College of Philadelphia and the first woman professor at the University of Virginia; Mildred Thomson, director of research for the schools of Arizona; Nannie Lee Winn, graduate of Johns Hopkins Medical School, and assistant superintendent of the New England Hospital for Women and Children in Boston; Mary Kirkpatrick, theatrical producer. Only Hunt lived and worked in the South; Stephens listed her residence as Atlanta, Georgia, but her career was in New York City. In the 1920s, alumnae wrote long articles about their experiences at southern, northern, and European graduate schools, offering advice to prospective applicants from Agnes Scott. And in June 1927 six missionary alumnae told the Agnes Scott community about "What Happened to Us in China" during the Chinese revolution and civil wars.[44]

President Gaines came to agree that Agnes Scott College trained women for leadership, public service, and the professions. In the *Agnes Scott Bulletin*, an administrative publication used to publicize the college and encourage donations, Gaines wrote about the advantages of women's higher education. One such article listed forty-two graduates who became teachers, including Anna I. Young '00, M.A. Columbia, and professor of mathematics at Agnes Scott; Cora Strong '97, B.A. Cornell, chair of mathematics department, Greensboro Normal, in Greensboro, North Carolina; Lucile Alexander '11, adjunct professor of French, Agnes Scott; Rusha Wesley '00, principal of the East Atlanta School; Margaret McCallie, '09, Ph.B.,

Chicago, adjunct professor of German, Agnes Scott; Rachel Young '07, teacher of Latin, Decatur High School, Decatur, Georgia; and Rose Wood '08, teacher in the Atlanta schools. In a special issue entitled "The Woman's College and Women," Gaines argued that the woman's college was necessary to maintain the advanced position of women and that women's colleges furnished and would continue to supply, leaders for all the great woman movements, such as the Women's Christian Temperance Union (WCTU), social settlement work, philanthropy and charities, the Federation of Women's Clubs, suffrage, and Christian activities. In 1918, the campus YWCA established a program to help students select careers "open to twentieth century women."[45]

Interest in reform and politics accompanied talk of careers and service. The *Agonistic* ("pertaining to sharp mental combat") first appeared in February 1916. In it, students discussed the world beyond Decatur, Georgia. A regular column, "Aggie's Jollies," contained jokes about world affairs. In March 1917 the paper reported that "all the college girls who could get off went to Atlanta to hear Taft speak." On another occasion, editors told their readers that "even if not a suffragette, you should be sorry to have missed Anna Howard Shaw's talk. The true woman is in no danger of being contaminated by society." In 1917 social feminism arrived on campus, when the college's YWCA chapter added a social service department to "educate students about the pressing needs of the present day." The *Agonistic* began discussion of industrial problems in 1921, urging students to take notice of the "industrial girls" in Atlanta department stores: "What are we going to do about the tired girl, who makes our shopping easy for us?" In 1918–19, the catalogue announced a course called "Socialism and the Social Movement," open to juniors and seniors.[46]

Agnes Scott students had no personal connections, through campus speakers, organizations (except the YWCA), or faculty, to offer information and analysis of social issues. As a result, campus opinion remained naive and displayed considerable class prejudice. In response to its question about tired industrial girls, the *Agonistic* proposed that students join these young women for a good supper at the YWCA and attend club meetings together. As friendships between the groups developed, students could participate in "recreational sociology," taking hikes and camping with the industrial girls, and learning "how the paper cups around chocolate are made, and how boxing is done" as they "tramped along the road munching apples together." In October 1921, Agnes Scott students presented a program of stunts on factory girls and college girls, "each thinking she is the only one who works hard." In reporting the program, the *Agonistic* concluded: "The need is for college women to be broad enough to catch the viewpoint of the ignorant factory girl."[47]

Comments about blacks or race relations rarely appeared in student literature before the 1920s, but the following student short story reveals that in this area, too, notions of noblesse oblige prevailed. A young teacher in "a Sabbath-school for colored people" was discouraged over her pupils' slow progress. In particular, an old family nurse, Margie, never failed to attend class but did not seem to comprehend the Bible stories and their moral lessons, especially the most recent tale of Philip and the eunuch. During a social call on Margie's "mistress," the teacher asked the name of the new baby boy in the household. "Oh," said the mother, "I must tell you about what a time we had selecting the name. It will show you one of the results of your teaching on Margie." Delighted that she had made an impression on her pupil, the teacher asked for details. "Well," said the mother, "one morning we held a family consultation about the baby's name, but no two of us could agree. Even little Philip came up and stood smiling into his little brother's face. . . . Just then old Margie came towards us and stood with arms akimbo, looking at the baby. "Is yer tryin' to git a name fur the preshus angel? Why, 'hit's jes as easy! Here's Philip and now call that un Eunik and 'hit'll jes suit fine." In the South of the Progressive Era, even women's higher education, itself a liberal reform, did not lead to a reexamination of racial ideology.[48]

By 1920, Sophie Newcomb and Agnes Scott Colleges had traveled a long way from the ideals of their founders. Students and alumnae of both schools would not have denied that higher education produced better wives and mothers, but they also expected their lives to include church work, social service, community leadership, and sometimes careers. As a group, these women were more politically conservative than female students elsewhere, particularly regarding suffrage, and had fewer doubts about marriage and traditional family life. Yet like other college women of this era, their education combined aspects of men's and women's culture, allowing them, as graduates, to move woman's sphere into the public arena.

Conclusion

Women students of the Progressive Era found no ivory towers on their campuses. At coeducational colleges and universities, many male faculty, administrators, and students viewed women's higher education as an unwelcome threat to the social order. And at women's colleges, administrators proclaimed their own and their institutions' adherence to traditional gender roles.

And yet, in spite of their conservatism, ambivalence, or outright hostility to the process and consequences, real or imagined, of educating women, colleges and universities at the turn of the century provided unique opportunities and a somewhat protected environment for intelligent and ambitious young women. In classrooms, women students encountered faculty influenced by progressive developments in research and scholarship and active in social reform movements. Such teachers promoted new and exciting courses, argued for the expansion of the elective system, encouraged discussions among their students, and brought thought-provoking speakers to campus.

The second generation of college women, with the help of female faculty and deans, created a lively student life. In dormitories, organizations, and through informal contacts with each other, college women broadened their experiences, and utilized leadership opportunities. Women at single sex-colleges engaged in a wide range of activities normally restricted to males, such as athletics, debate, politics, and career planning. On coeducational campuses, women students and their mentors won resources and recognition through the establishment of separate female communities.

The growing likeness in men's and women's extracurricular activities combined with the lessons of the classroom to produce assertiveness in the women students and resistance in the men. At the University of California, extracurricular separatism began as a response to men's exclusion of women from the privileges of student life. As the women's community at Berkeley developed, however, separatism provided the power base from which female students challenged men's control over resources and activities. Ironically, in doing so, as in the debate over the relationship between the Associated Students of the University of California and the Associated Women Students, they questioned the viability of separatism itself. At the same time, the growing numbers and influence of women students caused Berkeley men to increase their jibes against women's higher education, to struggle to maintain strict separatism, and to suggest that it be extended to classrooms.

The urban location of the University of Chicago, its connections to progressive social reform, and the presidents' desire to minimize the rowdier aspects of male undergraduate life made the institution congenial for women. Gender separatism at Chicago originated not with men's desire to exclude women, but in the determination of Alice Freeman Palmer and Marion Talbot to place women at the center of university life. Believing in the value of women's culture to the university, Talbot helped to create a situation where she supervised not only women's, but men's student life, thus ensuring a more positive approach to gender relations than on other coeducational campuses. Men and women had separate student activities, with the men dominating campus life, but the hostility men students directed toward women at California, Cornell, Rochester, Wesleyan, and Stanford did not exist at Chicago. And yet, when Chicago's male faculty became upset over women's prominence on their campus, they turned to further separatism as the answer and voted for classroom segregation.

Founders and proponents of single-sex colleges viewed them as the most desirable way to educate women. By attending women's colleges, female students would have all the advantages of higher education, while maintaining social separatism. Even in the earliest days, however, the exposure of women to men's curricula turned single-sex colleges into places where women learned to think and act like men. Student activities like debate, athletics, drama, mock political campaigns, self-government, and journalism functioned much as they did at men's colleges. And although women's colleges never gave intermural competition a central role in campus life, their students competed with other institutions in debate, field hockey, and basketball.

Here, too, separatism functioned creatively; in the absence of male students, women took on leadership roles not available to them elsewhere and enjoyed the full attention of faculty who encouraged graduate study, professional careers, and political activism. Campus life at the eastern Seven Sisters colleges best exemplified this unexpected outcome of single-sex higher education, but the same trends existed at southern women's colleges. Resisting familial demands to keep their daughters' loyalties directed toward the home, students at Agnes Scott and Sophie Newcomb Colleges developed strong ties to their schools, participated in debate, athletics, drama, literary societies, and student government, and worried over the future of educated women. Yet students at women's colleges ultimately had the same problems as their coeducated sisters. Beyond the gates of their single-sex institutions, men refused to accept them as equals. Tulane's administration, for example, stoutly resisted Newcomb women's demands for graduate and professional education within the university.

In the nineteenth century, on the campus and elsewhere, separatism and women's culture constituted, as Gerda Lerner has noted, "the ground upon which women stand in their resistance to patriarchal dominance and their assertion of their own creativity in shaping society." For one hundred years before passage of the Nineteenth Amendment, American women had slowly acquired educations, skills, organizational expertise, and a voice in social institutions, mostly by asserting society's need for womanly influence.[1]

Separatism, however, had always been a double-edged sword; its ideology and rhetoric used as often to hold women back as for their advancement. Marion Talbot had achieved much for women at the University of Chicago through her advocacy of social separatism; yet its existence supported William Rainey Harper's case for classroom segregation. Thus, during the Progressive Era, women's culture and the separatist ideology behind it reached the height of their utility and slowly became obsolescent, leading college women to demand equality.

Moreover, the concepts of separate spheres did not mean as much to the second generation of college women, who having grown up in the late nineteenth century, experienced less gender separation and wider opportunities than their mothers and grandmothers. As women went to college, worked at a variety of occupations and professions, headed national organizations, became active in social reform causes, traveled, spoke in public, and planned political campaigns, their lives and desires became more like men's. Increasingly, they rejected the bonds of womanhood, the concept of womanliness, and the idea of choosing between domesticity and career.

During the Progressive Era, the politics of separatism and women's culture evolved into the politics of equality. Modern feminism, with its emphasis on individual fulfillment, gender egalitarianism, and freedom of heterosexual expression, eventually captured the imagination of the younger generation, while the derogation of women's relationships with each other as "deviant" disrupted the role modeling and influence of their elders.

Women students of the Progressive Era experienced these cultural and political shifts during their college years. Caught between two worlds and two styles of women's politics, they absorbed the precepts of both. They admired and respected their mentors and teachers, believed that women had unique missions in public life, established close female communities on their campuses, and participated in social service and reform organizations. At the same time, this generation looked for careers outside the traditional service routes of teaching and social work and felt drawn to men as companions and future husbands. They engaged in separatist politics on their campuses but increasingly pushed for equality with men students.

The case studies in this book detailed significant institutional differences, particularly between the campus lives of coeducated women students and those attending single-sex schools. Unquestionably, women's colleges provided a superior social and educational atmosphere. Marion Talbot, Lucy Sprague, and Alice Freeman Palmer understood this and consciously built student culture at Chicago and Berkeley to resemble that of Radcliffe and Wellesley. In the 1970s, physiologist M. Elizabeth Tidball claimed that an unusually high number of twentieth-century women "achievers" had graduated from women's colleges. She hypothesized that the presence of female role models on the faculty, the freedom from restraints imposed by the presence of male students, the organizational expertise developed in extracurricular activities, and the students' choice of nontraditional (for women) majors, such as math, economics, and science, led to such career results. Although these conclusions influenced a number of women's colleges—including Wellesley, Smith, Mount Holyoke, and Barnard—not to coeducate as Vassar did, more recent research questions Tidball's findings. The distinctive impact of women's colleges on their students' postgraduate lives remains an open issue.[2]

Today, few single-sex colleges remain; Catholic institutions of higher education, the men's Ivy League schools, the service academies, and southern state universities have coeducated, receiving much public praise for doing so. As we have seen, however, institutional access does not guarantee women campus equality or positive educational experiences. During the Progressive Era, women faculty and students organized to maximize their opportunities and to demand administrative support. Building an intergenerational female community enhanced the lives of coeducated women, but coeducational institutions, then and now, have largely failed to respond to women's needs by providing mechanisms to ensure gender equality.

In the absence of such safeguards, the declining number of women's colleges is disturbing. After one hundred years of educating both sexes, coeducational colleges and universities remain bastions of inequality and male-dominated culture, both professionally and academically. Campus atmosphere and professional norms continue to define *student* and *faculty* in male terms, to perceive women as "the other," and to view difference as inferiority.

College women need to be active in strategies for changing the campus climate, as they were during the Progressive Era. But while the initiative for achieving gender equality on coeducational campuses may come from women faculty and students, they will not be successful without the vigorous public and private support of male administrators and faculty.

Colleges and universities resemble other social institutions in their resistance to change and replication of conservative attitudes. And yet as educational institutions, committed to research, teaching, and the development of an intellectual community, colleges and universities possess unique resources to address issues of discrimination, gender distinctiveness, and human behavior. A historical perspective on women's higher education teaches us about the need for activist policies. Today's universities need to use the curriculum to promote egalitarianism, possibly through women's studies programs; to hire women faculty and administrators interested in supporting female students; to appoint male faculty and administrators who can deal intelligently with gender issues; and to examine carefully the nature of undergraduate life. Until coeducational institutions adopt these and other measures, they will be replicating a culture of gender oppression and passing it on, intact, to the next generation.

However they differed as individuals, as graduates of a particular college, or alumnae of a certain type of institution, college women of the Progressive Era shared a generational consciousness. And although higher education may have created eager anticipation and great expectations for life outside the college gates, it also produced, as we have seen, concerns and fears. The widening generation gap between women students and their teachers made it difficult to deal with worries about the incompatibility of public and private aspirations. Because pioneer college women generally chose between marriage and career, they thought younger women should do the same. Students' documents indicate that they did not want to choose public over private life, or vice versa, but also believed they would have to do so.

Perhaps greater feminist consciousness during the Progressive Era would have averted or mitigated the troubles of women students. Why did women college students, the nation's female intellectual and preprofessional elite, have only a minimal impact on the suffrage movement before the formation of the College Equal Suffrage League in 1906? Advocates of women's rights and suffrage did not concern themselves with the issues troubling women students. Feminism, as it developed during the 1910s, did address issues of personal and sexual liberation and was more popular on college campuses, but the connections between higher education and feminism remained tenuous. Administrators of both single-sex and coeducational institutions denied any connections between women's higher education and the women's rights movement; at some schools, like Vassar, officials forbade organized suffrage activities. Fear of adverse public reaction and possible diminishing enrollments as well as, in many cases, their own belief in separate spheres caused presidents and deans to insist that college women should be and would be a conservative social force.

The unofficial relationship between higher education and women's rights is more complex. Some students, encouraged by the faculty, took an interest in the issues, sponsoring speakers, campus discussions, debates, and suffrage clubs; but many did not, and others openly opposed the movement. Female students at the University of Rochester knew of Susan B. Anthony's role in opening the institution's doors to them. On the day of the trustees' favorable decision, they crowded into her home to congratulate and thank her. Later they invited Anthony to campus parties, hung her portrait next to Mary Lyon's in a university building, dedicated the first issue of their yearbook to her, and served as honorary pallbearers at her funeral in 1906. And yet, many Rochester students felt uncomfortable in Anthony's presence and with her legacy of women's activism on their own behalf. As Julia Crowe Maxfield, class of 1903, put it: "When I was in college I was an ardent anti-suffragist. That seems incredible to me now, when one of my most priceless memories is of the day when Susan B. Anthony put her arm around me and called me "one of her girls." She little knew what a viper she was pressing to her bosom, and how I squirmed under her embrace. . . . In my college days I didn't believe in coeducation either."[3]

Sociologist Mirra Komarovsky has pointed to a similar situation among today's college women in her book-length study, *Women In College: Shaping New Feminine Identities* (1985). The students Komarovsky interviewed and surveyed planned active public and professional commitments combined with satisfying personal lives. And yet only 37 percent of the freshmen in her sample "sympathized greatly" with women's liberation, while an even lower number (15 percent) had participated in the movement.

Several factors may explain this lack of interest in organized women's rights and feminist activities among women college students of the Progressive Era and the 1980s. In each case, these students constituted a second generation, one that did not have to struggle for access to education and the professions and that could take for granted a certain degree of acceptance for women's achievements. Many had not yet experienced the conflicts and prejudices they would later encounter while seeking jobs, promotions, and trying to reconcile family and career. The task of reaching out to young men and developing viable heterosexual relationships seemed more problematic and compelling than feminist causes. Many, then and now, equate feminists with unattractive "man-haters," a label young college women wish to avoid.

More important than the question of why they were not all feminists, however, is the impact of higher education on students' beliefs and behavior. At the University of California, women students displayed almost no interest in women's rights until discrimination and hostility on their own campus caused them to take a more activist stance. Separatism and the resulting creation of a women's community were the preconditions making such a shift possible. Similarly, at Chicago, women faculty, students, and alumnae acted as a community to preserve educational equality when President Harper proposed gender-segregated instruction, and Vassar students demonstrated a marked increase in suffrage activity from freshmen to seniors. In Komarovsky's sample, seniors showed an increase of 11 percent in active feminism (from 15 percent to 26 percent) and an approval rate for women's liberation of 52 percent (up from 37 percent). However the factors of curriculum, peer influence, faculty example, personal experiences, and off-campus events interacted to produce such changes, higher education promoted, for women students of these two generations, approval and advocacy of women's rights and feminism.[4]

Like other American educational institutions, colleges and universities conserve the social order, serving society as a safe conduit for young people from the family to the adult world. At the same time, commitments to intellectual life, democratic values, research, and academic integrity, although never absolute, foster liberalism and creativity in higher education and campus life. Over the past one hundred years, for example, colleges have educated, sometimes against their will, diverse types of students for professional, political, and cultural leadership. And during certain eras, these institutions have, often unintentionally, encouraged idealism and a sense of social mission among their students. Progressive Era college women had to struggle for campus recognition and resources. Ultimately, however, it was society, not education, that failed to appreciate and utilize their potential for transforming American life.

EPILOGUE: THE FATE OF THE
SECOND GENERATION

In this book I have focused on women's experiences in colleges and universities; I have not made a longitudinal or demographic study of the second generation. Still, higher education and the curriculum were not ends in themselves or ways of passing time, but preparation for life. What, then, of that life and the connection, for women, between higher education and society?

College women of the Progressive Era experienced the turn-of-the-century backlash against women's achievements, especially on coeducational campuses. Off campus, however, the critics were harsher, the criticism more strident. This resistance intensified during the 1920s, 1930s, and 1940s, with a combination of political conservatism, the absence of an active feminist movement, the Great Depression, World War II, and the insistence by social scientists that "normal" women found their greatest happiness in heterosexual relationships and companionate marriages. And as the reform imperative and women's culture waned, so did women's opportunities to affect public and professional life.[5]

Although few colleges have good alumnae records, sociologists, economists, and historians have begun to analyze the lives of the second generation of college women. Based, for the most part, on surveys administered by Seven Sisters colleges to their graduates, such statistics should be used cautiously, because they tell us very little about the far more numerous graduates of coeducational institutions, or even non–Seven Sisters women's colleges. Still, this research suggests the broad outlines of the lives of educated women in mid-twentieth century America.

In their work on the alumnae of Wellesley and Mount Holyoke Colleges, Janet Z. Giele, Pamela J. Perun, and Mary E. Cookingham found that the marriage rate of graduates rose dramatically after the turn of the twentieth century. For women students of the first generation, especially those graduating between 1880 and 1890, the marriage rate was quite low—50 to 60 percent for college graduates in the northeast. By 1910, according to Perun and Giele, only 10 percent of Wellesley graduates remained unmarried throughout their lives; Cookingham found similar results for Mount Holyoke alumnae.

At the same time, low fertility rates continued to separate college graduates from women in the general population. Cookingham has pointed out that despite the greatly increased rate of marriage, college women continued to average 1.2 children per graduate, a number almost as low as those produced during the late nineteenth century, the period of the lowest marriage rate. Married college women, then, chose not to bear children at all or to have very small families, a demographic characteristic that continued through the 1930s.

In spite of their marital status, and perhaps because of their low fertility rate, second generation women college graduates actively participated in the labor force. Like the pioneers, the majority (over 80 percent) worked before marriage, and very few worked between the births of children. Unlike their predecessors, however, who left salaried positions when they married, many Progressive Era college women did not do so until the birth of their first child and then returned to work after completing their families. As Giele and Perun noted, the "either marriage or employment dichotomy" was "an illusion" for the second generation of college women. Instead, they entered, left, and reentered the labor market throughout their adult lives.

Cookingham linked college women's marriage rate and labor force participation to changing demands and opportunities in teaching, the occupation of most alumnae, although she also pointed to World War I and the growing need for clerical workers as incentives for educated women workers. Teaching remained the favored profession of college women because they could enter and leave the classroom according to the demands of their private lives, without penalty or the need to keep up with changes in the field. As districts abandoned laws prohibiting married women from teaching (although many revived such statutes during the Great Depression), it became possible for college women to combine professional and personal achievement. Women with children found school vacations a particularly attractive incentive to make teaching their career. And, although the demographers have not studied volunteerism, college women in the twentieth century continued to join, work for, and lead numerous service organizations.[6]

Through lives as independent, single, professional women, many first-generation college women had developed an alternative to domesticity, choosing between marriage and career. Strongly drawn both to public life and traditional families, the second generation dreaded making such stark choices. Apparently many found ways to combine work and marriage—by having no children or small families and by carefully choosing an occupation, teaching, allowing maximum flexibility.

In spite of their creativity in fashioning complex lives, college women of the second generation faced externally imposed limitations on their public accomplishments. In the more socially conservative atmosphere of America after 1920, graduate and professional schools, corporations, hospitals, and other places of training and employment restricted women's entry and advancement. Women's participation in business, in the more lucrative and prestigious professions, and in politics thus diminished steadily from the mid-1920s and early 1930s through the 1950s. The profession of teaching, with its low pay, lack of autonomy, and dearth of opportunities for promotion, hampered women's enjoyment of their work and their ability to do it well. And even the few women married to liberal, progressive males, with sufficient funds to pay for housekeepers and child care, found it difficult to maintain egalitarian personal relationships and public commitments. Nor could the feminist movement, which foundered on the rock of the Equal Rights Amendment in the 1920s, provide leadership and guidance.[7]

In their recent study of women in the professions, Penina Migdal Glazer and Miriam Slater pointed to the Progressive Era as a time "when many were dazzled by the expansion of new opportunities, the culture of social reform, and the growing enthusiasm for technical expertise." Access to collegiate and graduate education, "the formation of new associations, and the creation of new positions" gave women "a sense of possibility and entitlement and provided a focus for their ambition and growing expertise."[8]

At the turn of the century, women professionals often worked in separate spheres, such as single-sex colleges and medical schools, settlement houses (where most, though not all, of the residents were females), and agencies like the U.S. Children's Bureau, bringing the values of women's culture, particularly service and empathy, and the social-reform ideals of progressivism to the practice of their professions. During the politically conservative era following World War I, however, women's progressive vision diminished, and separate institutions disappeared or lost their distinctive values. The coalition of organized women, progressive educators, labor, settlement workers, immigrant and ethnic leaders, academics, and other reformers broke apart, transforming communal goals into programs for the welfare of particular groups and specific individuals. The National Woman's Party proposal for an Equal Rights Amendment, for example, of great benefit to women professionals, might have undermined protective labor legislation for working-class women. Concomitantly, postwar professionalism moved away from the emphasis on service and reform of the Progressive Era. Stressing instead the supremacy of science and rationality over empathy and sensibility, and individual achievements over communal enterprises, twentieth-century doctors, lawyers, academics, and social workers developed conservative social attitudes and individualistic outlooks.[9]

Similarly, feminism of the 1920s took on an individualistic and thus more socially conservative stance. As Dorothy Dunbar Bromley described her, the "new-style" feminist was "intensely self-conscious whereas older feminists were intensely sex-conscious." She "professes no loyalty to women en masse, although she staunchly believes in individual women." Joyce Antler, Elaine Showalter, Sara Alpern, and others have noted the tendency of prominent women in the mid-twentieth century to look for individual solutions to the problems of managing work and family and to believe that hard work and individual merit would overcome any lingering sexism.[10]

As demonstrated in this book, separatism as a political strategy reached its limits during the Progressive Era, but individual equality without a separate power base, gender consciousness, and a reform ideology did not work well for women in the early and mid-twentieth century. Penina Glazer and Miriam Slater discuss several "coping" strategies for professional women in a "man's world," including superperformance, subordination, (working as assistants to men), innovation, separatism (working in different organizations than men, and devising creative ways of doing their jobs under difficult conditions). Although some women had successful professional experiences using these strategies, most fell victim to discrimination and underemployment.[11]

We have very little information as to how this generation viewed the relationship of their college years to their postgraduate lives. Undoubtedly many found satisfaction in family life, work, and volunteer activities, or some combination of the three. Still, ambitious women educated in a more idealistic era found postwar America disappointing, and their options limited. When Marjorie Nicolson, class of 1914 at the University of Michigan and professor of English at Smith College and Columbia University, looked back in the 1930s on her generation's experiences, she commented:

> As I look back upon the records, I find myself wondering whether our generation was not the only generation of women that ever really found itself. We came late enough to escape the self-consciousness and belligerence of the pioneers, to take education and training for granted. We came early enough to take equally for granted professional positions in which we could make full use of our training—the millennium had come; it did not occur to us that life could be different. Within a decade, shades of the prison house began to close, not upon the growing boy, but upon the emancipated girls.[12]

Nicolson's prison house metaphor indicated the depth of college women's idealism and their disillusionment. And although she did not say so, women's lack of a distinctive voice and public influence in the mid-twentieth century negatively affected the social fabric of American life.

NOTES

INTRODUCTION

1. Examples of seminal works in higher education that pay little heed to students include Bledstein, *The Culture of Professionalism,* and Veysey, *The Emergence of the American University.* For the view that college life has always been oppositional to academic culture, see Horowitz, *Campus Life.*

2. For the "status anxiety" thesis see Hofstadter, *The Age of Reform;* for the modernization theory, Wiebe, *The Search for Order.*

3. Diner, *A City and Its Universities.*

4. Lagemann, "The Challenge of Jane Addams"; Morantz-Sanchez, *Sympathy and Science;* Costin, *Two Sisters for Social Justice;* Rousmaniere, "Cultural Hybrid in the Slums."

5. See, e.g., Solomon, *In The Company of Educated Women.*

6. For evidence on students' social class, see Rogers, *Vassar Women;* Gordon, "Smith College Students: The First Ten Classes"; Rota, "Between True Women and New Women: Mount Holyoke Students, 1837–1908"; Solomon, *In the Company of Educated Women* 62–77; Kilman, "Southern Collegiate Women."

7. Newcomer, *A Century of Higher Education for American Women,* 52.

8. "Little Edens of liberty" quoted from Emily James Smith, dean of Barnard College, "Some Further Considerations of College Curricula," Association of Collegiate Alumnae *Publications* (December 1908): 29–31.

9. Discussion of the long-lasting effects of college life may be found in Feldman and Newcomb, *The Impact of College on Students;* and Newcomb, *Persistence and Change.* Longitudinal studies of specific alumnae are virtually nonexistent, and

Newcomb's work on Bennington does not discuss women's attitudes on gender roles.

CHAPTER 1: FROM SEMINARY TO UNIVERSITY

1. Cott, *The Bonds of Womanhood,* provides an excellent description of the emerging cult of domesticity and the development of woman's sphere. The other critical book on this subject, stressing intellectual and theological history, is Sklar, *Catharine Beecher.* The essays of Carroll Smith-Rosenberg, collected in her *Disorderly Conduct,* are indispensable for understanding the origins, development, and decline of Victorian women's culture. See especially "The Female World of Love and Ritual: Relations Between Women in Nineteenth Century America," 53–76. Examples of Victorian women using domesticity to subvert the social order may be found in Glenda Gates Riley, "The Subtle Subversion"; Smith-Rosenberg, "Beauty, the Beast, and the Militant Woman," in *Disorderly Conduct,* 109–28; Anne Firor Scott, "The Ever-Widening Circle." On the values of women's culture in the public sphere, see Rousmaniere, "Cultural Hybrid in the Slums," and Lynn D. Gordon, "Women and the Anti-Child Labor Movement in Illinois, 1890–1920." For discussion and conceptualization of the liberal-conservative debate over women's nature and social roles, see Rosalind Rosenberg, *Beyond Separate Spheres,* especially the introduction and chap. 1.

2. The classic statement of the relationship between women's education, the American Revolution and republicanism is Kerber, *Women of the Republic.* See also Kerber, "Daughters of Columbia: Educating Women for the Republic, 1787–1805," in *The Hofstadter Aegis;* Glenda Gates Riley, "Origins of the Argument for Improved Female Education," *History of Education Quarterly* 4 (Winter 1969): 470; and Hoffman, ed., *Woman's True Profession.*

3. For general descriptions of nineteenth-century academy and seminary education, including detailed accounts of curricula and institutions, see Woody, *A History of Women's Education in the U.S.,* especially vol. 1; Solomon, chap. 2. More specific and thematic studies include Sklar, *Catharine Beecher;* Sklar, "The Founding of Mount Holyoke College"; Scott, "The Ever-Widening Circle"; Scott, "What, Then, Is the American, This New Woman?" Green, *Mary Lyon and Mount Holyoke;* and Kerns, "Farmers' Daughters." For a critical assessment of the literature on women's secondary education, see Schwager, "Educating Women in America."

4. Scott, "The Ever-Widening Circle"; Sklar, *Catharine Beecher;* Rota, "Between True Women and New Women"; Kerns, "Farmers' Daughters;" Allmendinger, "Mount Holyoke Students Encounter the Need For Life-Planning."

5. Clinton, "Equally Their Due;" Fox-Genovese, *Within The Plantation Household;* Friedman, *The Enclosed Garden;* Blandin, *History of Higher Education of Women in the South Prior to 1870.*

6. Stowe, "The *Thing,* Not Its Vision"; Stowe, "The Not-So-Cloistered Academy."

7. M. Carey Thomas, "Present Tendencies in Women's College and University Education," Association of Collegiate Alumnae *Publications* (February 1908).

8. Brown, "Golden Girls"; Schwager, "Arguing For the Higher Education of Women"; Wallach, "The Dilemmas of Coeducation."

9. Hogeland, "Coeducation of the Sexes at Oberlin College"; Schwager, "Arguing for the Higher Education of Women"; Rury and Harper, "The Trouble With Coeducation."

10. Lori Ginzberg, "The Joint Education of the Sexes: Oberlin's Original Vision," in *Coeducation in A Changing World*, ed. Carol Lasser (Urbana: University of Illinois Press, 1987): 67–80.

11. Clarke, *Sex in Education*, and Clarke, *Building a Brain*.

12. Thomas, "Present Tendencies," 49.

13. Scott, *The Southern Lady*, especially chapter on post–Civil War South; Mayo, *Southern Women in the Recent Educational Movement in the South*. See especially, the introduction by Dan T. Carter and Amy Friedlander to the new edition of Mayo's work (Baton Rouge: Louisiana State University Press, 1978): xi–xxiii.

14. Butcher, "Education For Equality: Women's Rights Periodicals and Women's Higher Education"; Duffey, *No Sex in Education;* Brackett, ed., *The Education of American Girls;* Howe, ed., *Sex and Education*. For a fascinating discussion of Clarke's work and its impact, see Morantz-Sanchez, 54–55, 206. On Laura Clay, see Fuller, *Laura Clay and the Woman's Rights Movement*.

15. Florence Kelley, "When Co-education Was Young," *The Survey* 57 (1 February 1927): 557–61, 600–02.

16. Palmieri, "In Adamless Eden": Scarborough and Furumoto, *Untold Lives*.

17. Rogers, *Vassar Women*.

18. Letters from William Campbell Preston Breckinridge to Sophonisba Breckinridge, 20 September 1884–30 March 1885, in Breckinridge Papers, Library of Congress, Washington, D.C. Quoted in Horowitz, "With More Love Than I Can Write." I am grateful to Natalie Zemon Davis for the reference to this source.

19. D. McIntyre, Luke H. Parsons, and B. L. Baxter, "Report on the Admission of Females," 29 September 1858, *Regents' Proceedings*, 795.

20. McGuigan, *A Dangerous Experiment*, 19–22.

21. Curti and Carstensen, *The University of Wisconsin 1848–1925*, 1: 369–81; Olin, *The Women of a State University;* Hague, "What If the Power Does Lie Within Me?"

22. Conable, *Women at Cornell*.

23. Haines, "Coeducation and the Development of Leadership Skills in Women."

24. May, "History of the University of Rochester," unpublished MS; Harper, *The Life and Work of Susan B. Anthony*, vol. 4.

25. Ihle, "The Development of Co-Education in Major Southern Universities."

26. For a lively account of women's admission and campus experiences at one land grant university, see Treichler, "Alma Mater's Sorority."

27. Anderson, *An American Girl and Her Four Years in A Boys' College.*

28. Ibid., 52.

29. Newcomer, *Century of Higher Education,* 49.

30. Rudolph, *Curriculum;* Boas, *Woman's Education Begins,* 256–58.

31. Horowitz, *Alma Mater,* 9–55.

32. Davis, *American Heroine,* 29; Lagemann, "The Challenge of Jane Addams."

33. Solomon, *In the Company of Educated Women,* 62–77; Rogers, *Vassar Women;* Sarah H. Gordon, "Smith College Students"; Rota, "From True Women to New Women."

34. Palmieri, "In Adamless Eden," chap. 1 and 2.

35. Rota, "From True Women to New Women"; Shea, "Mount Holyoke College, 1875–1910"; Glazer and Slater, *Unequal Colleagues,* chap. 2.

36. Abbott, "A Generation of College Women" and "The College Woman and Matrimony"; Shinn, "The Marriage Rate of College Women" and "Etc.," Thwing, "What Becomes of College Women"; Olin, *The Women of A State University.* For a modern assessment of the first generation's choices, see Cookingham, "Bluestockings, Spinsters, and Pedagogues."

37. Rousmaniere, "Cultural Hybrid in the Slums"; Gordon, "Women and the Anti-Child Labor Movement."

38. Campbell, *The Liberated Woman of 1914.*

39. Shinn, "The Marriage Rate of College Women" and "Etc.", Sicherman, *Alice Hamilton;* Dobkin, *The Making of a Feminist;* Herman, "Loving Courtship or the Marriage Market?" Davis, "Why They Failed to Marry."

40. Smith-Rosenberg, "Female World of Love and Ritual"; Palmieri, "In Adamless Eden."

41. Davis, *Factors in the Sex Life of 2200 Women.*

42. Criticism of the second generation of college women can be found in Mathews, *The Dean of Women;* Talbot, *The Education of Women;* and Talbot, *More Than Lore.*

43. Horowitz, *Alma Mater* and *Campus Life.*

44. Brown, "Golden Girls," chap. 1; Morantz-Sanchez, *Sympathy and Science.*

45. Rudolph, *The American College and University.*

46. Rossiter, *Women Scientists in America.* My own view of the home economics movement is more positive than Rossiter's. See also Vincenti, "A History of the Philosophy of Home Economics"; Marion Talbot, "The Vocational and Cultural Value of Domestic Science," *Journal of Home Economics* 5: 3 (1913): 232–36; Talbot, *The Education of Women.*

47. Institutional efforts to broaden women's career opportunities are described in subsequent chapters of this book. See also the Association of Collegiate Alumnae's *Publications,* 1898–1911. For a discussion of the professionalization of social

work, see Roy Lubove, *The Professional Altruist: The Emergence of Social Work As A Career* (Cambridge: Harvard University Press, 1965).

48. Briscoe, "Bryn Mawr College Traditions."

49. Jean Webster, *When Patty Went to College* (New York: Grosset and Dunlap, 1903), 53–57.

50. Victoria Bissell Brown, "Golden Girls," chap. 1.

51. Nancy Sahli, "Smashing"; Filene, *Him/Her/Self*; Simmons, "Companionate Marriage and the Lesbian Threat"; Smith-Rosenberg, "The New Woman as Androgyne: Social Disorder and Gender Crisis, 1870–1936," in *Disorderly Conduct*, 245–96.

52. Cott, *The Grounding of Modern Feminism*.

53. Brett, "A Different Kind of Being."

54. Wechsler, "An Academic Gresham's Law."

55. Mathews, *Dean of Women*, 160. For a theoretical discussion of women's separatism in the nineteenth and early twentieth centuries, see Freedman, "Separatism as Strategy."

56. Hobson, *Laura Z,* 16, 64–66.

57. Memoir dated 21 December 1962, box 36, file 2, no. 26, in Gregoria Fraser Goins Papers, Moorland-Spingarn Research Center, Howard University, Washington, D.C.

58. Woody, *A History of Women's Education in the United States,* 2: 280–94.

59. Morantz-Sanchez, *Sympathy and Science,* 64–89, discusses the debate over medical coeducation and women physicians' concept of their professional mission.

60. For a useful description of one institution's response to the coeducational crisis, see Knight, "The Quails." My thanks to Rosalind Rosenberg for drawing my attention to this source.

61. Emily James Smith, "Some Further Considerations."

62. Slater, *Rhees of Rochester;* May, "History of the University of Rochester."

63. James Monroe Taylor to Harriet Elizabeth Giles, 1900, "Racial Matters" file, Spelman College Archives; transcript of interview with Susie Williams Jones, 11 April 1977, p. 20, by Merze Tate, Black Women's Oral History Project, Columbia University.

64. Durr, "A Southern Belle Comes North." My thanks to Leah Fygetakis for sending me this article.

65. Wechsler, *The Qualified Student;* Gordon, "Annie Nathan Meyer and Barnard College."

66. Hurwitz, "Coming of Age at Wellesley."

67. Dutton, "History of the Southern Association of College Women"; Lemmon, "Elizabeth Avery Colton"; *Proceedings of the Southern Association of College Women,* 1912, 1913.

68. McCandless, "Preserving the Pedestal."

69. Kilman, "Southern Collegiate Women."

CHAPTER 2: WOMEN AT THE UNIVERSITY OF
CALIFORNIA, 1870–1920

1. Stadtman, *The University of California, 1868–1968,* discusses the opening of the university but passes over the admission of women. See also Mary McLean Olney, "Oakland, Berkeley, and the University of California," especially 130–39. Olney said no one expected women to attend the university; consequently no plans were made to keep them out. Information on the Regents' resolution is from the *Occident* 8: 4 (6 February 1885): 29. For enrollment statistics, see Stadtman, ed., *The Centennial Record of the University of California,* 212–19.

2. Stadtman, *Centennial Record,* 113–17, describes student traditions.

3. Joy Lichtenstein, *For the Blue and Gold.* The only statistics available on the social origins of Berkeley students deal with a somewhat later period and may be found in Benjamin Ide Wheeler, *Report of the President of the University,* 1905–06, 20–21. According to this source, 20.3 percent of the university's students came from farming families, 21.5 percent had fathers who were businessmen, 10.2 percent mechanics or laborers, 8.5 percent bankers or realtors, 7.4 percent clerks, 5.4 percent lawyers, 5.5 percent doctors or dentists, 3.2 percent clergy, 3.6 percent teachers, 3.6 percent miners. Thus, students coming from middle- or upper-middle-class professional and white-collar homes made up around half of the student body. Novels, comments of deans, and interviews with former students confirm a gulf between the wealthy students in the sororities and fraternities and others.

4. Lichtenstein's book is one of many college novels idealizing the democracy and meritocracy of men's campus life; the most famous is Owen Johnson, *Stover at Yale* (New York: Grosset and Dunlap, 1911).

5. Wheeler, *Report of the President of the University,* 1900–02, 23, cites 71.9 percent of students living on campus. In Wheeler, ibid., 1913–14, Dean of Women Lucy Ward Stebbins stated that 50 percent of women students lived at home. Because such statistics were not kept on a regular basis, we do not know how many men lived at home in 1913–14. It seems safe to assume, however, that most women students were commuters and most men students were not and that this distinction held for the earlier years of the university as well.

6. Scarborough and Furumoto, *Untold Lives,* 53–69; Burnham, "Milicent Washburn Shinn," in *Notable American Women,* 3: 285–86. Skelley, "*The Overland Monthly* under Milicent Washburn Shinn, 1883–1894."

7. *Blue and Gold,* 1900, 9.

8. Deutsch, ed., *The Abundant Life,* 111.

9. Paul, "Phoebe Apperson Hearst," in *Notable American Women,* 2: 171–73. For personal recollections of Hearst's interaction with women students, see *The Prytaneans,* 1: 14, 49, 78, 131.

10. Adeline Grace Smith, undated; Tillie Browning, 6 October 1903; Nina Beebe, 6 October 1903; Rhoda Orgren, 5 October 1903; Marion Schneider, 7

October 1903; E. Virginia Judy, undated; Helen Azalia Staples, 5 October 1903; all to Phoebe Apperson Hearst in "Letters from Hearst Domestic Industries Students," Phoebe Apperson Hearst (hereafter PAH) Papers, carton 1, Bancroft Library, Berkeley, California.

11. Christine B. Labarraque, 30 October 1906; Bessie M. Sessions, 7 January 1901; Ella Castillo Bennett, 28 September and 11 October 1911; Jeanette Shafer, 1 September and 16 November 1913, 17 and 23 May 1913; all to PAH in "Letters from Hearst Domestic Industries Students," PAH Papers, carton 1. Milicent W. Shinn to PAH, 20 June 1911, PAH Papers, Correspondence, "Milicent W. Shinn" file; and PAH Papers, Correspondence, "Julia Morgan" file. See also Elinor Richey, "Julia Morgan," in *Notable American Women: The Modern Period* eds. Barbara Sicherman and Carol Hurd Green (Cambridge: Harvard University Press, 1980): 499–501.

12. PAH to Hon. James H. Budd, 1897, in PAH Papers, Letters of PAH, 1889–1918; May Treat Morrison to PAH, 11 September 1897, in PAH Papers, Correspondence, 11 January 1889–14 August 1903, "May Treat Morrison" file.

13. Katharine C. Felton '95 in the *Berkeleyan* 3: 2, 15–16.

14. Horace Davis, *Report of the President of the University,* 1891, 16. Martin Kellogg, *Report of the President of the University,* 1898, 20.

15. Ritter, *More Than Gold in California,* 205.

16. Ibid., 212–14. Each year the *Blue and Gold* published a list of fraternities, sororities, and residence clubs.

17. *Berkeleyan* 4: 6.

18. *Handbook of the Associated Women Students,* 1915, University of California Archives. The point system began some years earlier, and the distribution of points to various offices frequently changed.

19. Mary Bennet Ritter to PAH, 10 February 1905; 15 January, no year; May 1904; 15 August and 6 January 1904 in PAH Papers, Correspondence, "Mary Bennett Ritter" file.

20. Charlotte Anita Whitney (Wellesley '89) to PAH, undated (probably November 1904) in PAH Papers, Correspondence, "Charlotte Anita Whitney" file.

21. Office of PAH to Benjamin Ide Wheeler, 13 November 1902, in PAH Papers, Correspondence, 11 January 1889–14 August 1903.

22. Lucy Sprague Mitchell, "Pioneering in Education," transcript, 44–47; Chambers, "Jessica Blanche Peixotto," in *Notable American Women,* 3: 42–43; "Jessica Peixotto," *University of California in Memoriam* (1941), University of California Archives.

23. Mitchell, *Two Lives,* 134. Antler, *Lucy Sprague Mitchell,* chaps. 1–5.

24. Mitchell, *Two Lives,* 192–93.

25. Mitchell, "Pioneering in Education," 44–47; Sally Schwager, "Harvard Women."

26. "Women's Department," *Occident* 51 (October 1906): 88. See also Lucy Sprague, "A Suggestion," *Women's Occident* 50 (22 February 1906): 222–25.

27. Mitchell, *Two Lives,* 199–200; "Pioneering," 44–45.

28. Mitchell, "Pioneering," 77–82.

29. The University of California Archives contain scripts for the Partheneia of 1912–17 and 1919. The pageant was suspended during the war years and discontinued after 1919.

30. Antler, *Lucy Sprague Mitchell,* 106.

31. *Blue and Gold,* 1912, 40. Stebbins's questionnaire and description of her project's results may be found in Files of the Office of the President, University of California Archives. See also Lucy Ward Stebbins, "Report of the Dean of Women," in Benjamin Ide Wheeler, *Report of the President of the University,* 1914, 197.

32. See articles by May Shepard Cheney '83 in *Alumni Magazine,* 6 February, 13 March, and 11 September 1909; and "A Demand For Home Economics," Women's Department, *Occident* 52 (May 1907): 29–30.

33. Mitchell, "Report of the Dean of Women," in Benjamin Ide Wheeler, *Report of the President of the University,* 1907, 105–09; Stebbins, "Report of the Dean of Women," in Benjamin Ide Wheeler, *Report of the President of the University,* 1912–13, 160–61.

34. Braden, "Child Welfare and Community Service," 37.

35. Ida L. Jackson, "Ida L. Jackson, Educator," in *There Was Light,* ed. Irving Stone, 249–66.

36. *Daily Californian,* 21 August 1906.

37. Edward B. Clapp, "The Adjustment to Co-Education," address reprinted in *The University Chronicle,* November 1899, 333–45.

38. Gus Keane '05, *Blue and Gold,* 1905, introductory essay, no pagination.

39. Benjamin Ide Wheeler, *Report of the President of the University,* 1904, 9–11.

40. Wheeler's speech reported in the *Daily Californian,* 1 September 1904. See also Wheeler, *The Writings of Benjamin Ide Wheeler* (no publishing information) 5: 18 (20 August 1909), University of California Archives; "Lillian Moller Gilbreth, Industrial Engineer," in Stone, *There Was Light,* 83; Gilbreth, *Time Out For Happiness,* 2.

41. Stephens's remarks reported in the *Daily Californian,* 23 February 1910.

42. *Daily Californian,* 2 November 1910.

43. Ibid., 8 September 1908.

44. Ibid.

45. *Pelican,* October 1909.

46. *Blue and Gold,* 1893, no pagination.

47. Ibid., 1900, 158.

48. Harold C. Bradley, *From a Packrat's Files: Autobiography of Harold C. Bradley For His Sons* (copyright Ruth Bradley, 1976), n.p. Chapter on Berkeley days courtesy of the University of California Archives. For a similar view of the proper approach to romance, this time by a woman student, see Mary Carolyn Davies, "The Girl Just Made For Jones," *Occident* 64 (13 February): 37–47.

49. "The Old Story," *Occident* 8 (15 May 1885): 135–37.

50. Kathleen Thompson, "The Parting Paths," *Occident* 44 (12 May 1903): 422; Zoe Riley '07, "The Way of A Sister," *Occident* 52 (February 1907): 34–36. For a history of the *Occident* see Robert Cross '11, "The *Occident*," *Occident* 57 (March 1910): 33–36.

51. W. H. R. '05, "Tom's Final Ex," *Occident* 47 (26 September 1904): 234–40; Essie Tobriner '04, "The Inconsistency of Man," *Occident* 46 (1 April 1904): 289–91.

52. "A Man's Work," *Occident* 60 (February 1911): 10–15.

53. Effie Sackville, "Little Miss Fixit," *Occident* 71 (March 1917): 259–61.

54. Ruth Hamilton, "Three Maids Errant and a Blushing Knight," *Occident* 73 (June 1919): 381–92.

55. Rose Gardner '11, "Straws," *Occident* 62 (February 1912): 19–22.

56. Robert Hood '06, "How She Gave Her Consent," *Occident* 49 (17 August 1905): 34–38.

57. Annie Dale Biddle, "Student Reorganization," *Occident* 54 (February 1908): 33–35. See also other articles in the same issue and "ASUC and AWS," *Occident* 51 (October 1906): 65; "Separation and the AWS," *Occident* 54 (February 1908): 20–21; Annie Dale Biddle '08, "The Proposed Separation of AWS from ASUC," *Occident* 53 (November 1907): 27; Mary Ada Pence '10, "Readjustment," *Occident* 58 (February 1911): 8–11.

58. Interview of Katherine Amelia Towle '20, transcript, 23.

59. *Student Opinion,* 24 August 1915.

60. Ibid., 21 September 1915.

61. *Daily Californian,* 16 March 1916; *Daily Californian,* 1 December 1915; *Brass Tacks,* 4 November and 19 September 1915. For further information on the proposed ASUC–AWS merger, see *Daily Californian,* 10 March 1916; 21 March 1916; 10 February 1916; 11 February 1916; and *Brass Tacks,* cartoon, 1916.

62. Interview of Josephine Miller Powell '16 by Margaret Marshall, April 1969, in the *Prytanean Oral History,* transcript, 199–204; *Daily Californian,* 6 March 1916.

63. Elsie McCormick '16, "An Etiquette for Coeds," *Brass Tacks,* March 1916.

64. Lucy Ward Stebbins, "The Attendance of Women," *California Alumni Fortnightly* 10: 184–87. Stebbins assured the university community that the "problem" was not as serious as they feared. Only a 10 percent increase in the percentage of women students had occurred because of the war; *Raspberry Press,* 6 February and 26 October 1917.

65. *Daily Californian,* 8 February 1918.

66. Ibid.

67. Figures on college enrollments during the war years from the *California Alumni Fortnightly,* 11:58. Ella Barrows Hagar '19, interview by Lynn D. Gordon, December 1977, Berkeley, California.

68. Interview of Dorothy Rieber Joralemon '15 by Joy Cox Hussey '59, 9 April 1970, Berkeley, California, in *Prytanean Oral History, 1901–1920,* transcript, 167–79.

69. "Once A Pelican," *California Alumni Fornightly* 10: 85–86.

70. "The Double Standard Among College Men," *Brass Tacks,* 13 October 1915. For the comments on the tenderloin district and women students' moral responsibilities, see *Daily Californian,* 19 February 1914.

71. *Pelican,* September 1907.

72. *California Alumni Fortnightly,* 10: 86.

CHAPTER 3: THE UNIVERSITY OF CHICAGO, 1892–1920

1. The two histories of the university are Goodspeed, *A History of the University of Chicago,* and Storr, *Harper's University.* See Storr, chap. 2, for a discussion of the nationwide turn-of-the-century reaction against coeducation.

2. Storr, *Harper's University,* 35–56.

3. Ibid., 76. The policy of requiring entrance examinations changed rapidly because Chicago found it difficult to attract as many high-caliber Junior College students as it wanted. By 1905 more than two-thirds of the undergraduates entered on certificates. See Wechsler, *The Qualified Student,* 219.

4. Herrick, *Chimes,* 15–16.

5. Contemporaries were fascinated by the compartments, divisions, and rankings Harper devised and considered them important educational innovations. See Goodspeed, 130–57; Talbot, *More Than Lore,* 13–20. Bledstein, *The Culture of Professionalism,* 53–65, discusses middle-class interest in dividing time and space.

6. Talbot, *More Than Lore,* 18, quotes Harper's first report to the Board of Trustees. For information and correspondence on the establishment of fraternities at Chicago, see the Presidents' Papers, 1889–1925, box 26, folders 1–5, Special Collections, Joseph Regenstein Library, University of Chicago, Chicago, Illinois.

7. Harper quoted in Goodspeed, *University of Chicago,* 138. For information on women at the old university see Rosalind Rosenberg, "The Academic Prism: The New View of American Women," in *Women of America,* 318–41; and Lydia Aurelia Dexter '84, "The Women of the University of Chicago, 1867–1886," *Chicago Alumni Magazine,* March 1908, 7–9.

8. Weimann, "A Temple to Women's Genius."

9. Rousmaniere, "Cultural Hybrid in the Slums," and Gordon, "Women and the Anti-Child Labor Movement in Illinois." For a more detailed analysis of connections between academics and social reformers, see Diner, *A City and Its Universities.* Discussion of Jane Addams's complex relationship with the University of Chicago can be found in Deegan, *Jane Addams and the Men of the Chicago School, 1892–1918.*

10. *Chicago Inter-Ocean,* 10 July 1892; Presidents' Papers 1889–1925, box 34, folder 16, clipping dated 7 October 1892, newspaper unknown.

11. Palmer, *The Life of Alice Freeman Palmer,* 132–33; Solomon, "Alice Freeman Palmer," in *Notable American Women,* 3: 4–8.

12. Palmieri, "In Adamless Eden"; Wells, *Miss Marks and Miss Woolley.* For an account different from my own, see Frankfort, *Collegiate Women,* and less scholarly books by Baker, *I'm Radcliffe! Fly Me!;* Kendall, *Peculiar Institutions.* For statistics on women graduate students, Marion Talbot, "The Women of the University," in *The President's Report, 1892–1902* (Chicago: University of Chicago Press, 1902).

13. Wallace, *The Unending Journey,* 50–58.

14. Sophonisba Breckinridge Autobiography (unpublished MS), folder 9, Special Collections, Joseph Regenstein Library.

15. Ibid., folders 6 and 10.

16. Storr, "Marion Talbot," in *Notable American Women,* 3: 423–24.

17. Talbot, *The Education of Women,* 22.

18. Talbot, *More Than Lore,* 6.

19. Presidents' Papers, 1889–1925, box 24, folders 3 and 13.

20. Talbot, *More Than Lore,* 7–11; diary of Demia Butler, Special Collections, Joseph Regenstein Library. Entries in the diary are often undated, and pages unnumbered.

21. Breckinridge Autobiography, folder 10.

22. Marion Talbot Papers, box 4, folder 3, Special Collections, Joseph Regenstein Library. For correspondence on the high cost of university housing, see Presidents' Papers, 1889–1925, box 31, folder 4.

23. Talbot, *The Education of Women,* 203.

24. Marion Talbot Papers, box 4, folder 1.

25. Marion Talbot to Harry Pratt Judson, 8 September 1906, Presidents' Papers, 1889–1925, box 24, folder 13.

26. Harry Pratt Judson to George MacLean, 8 January 1906, Presidents' Papers, 1889–1925, box 61, folder 9.

27. Talbot, *More Than Lore,* 62; diary of Demia Butler, undated entry.

28. Talbot, *More Than Lore,* 65.

29. Parke Ross to William Rainey Harper, 9 March 1900; Marion Talbot to William Rainey Harper, 13 March 1900; Marion Talbot to William Rainey Harper, undated; Presidents' Papers, 1889–1925, box 26, folder 1. In the opening chapter of Robert Herrick's *Chimes* he contrasts "Gertrude Porridge" (Talbot) with the lovely and charming former dean of women, Edith Crandall (Alice Freeman Palmer).

30. William Rainey Harper to Marion Talbot, box 31, folder 5, Presidents' Papers, 1889–1925.

31. James R. Angell to Marion Talbot, 1 April 1919; unnamed correspondent to Marion Talbot, undated; Marion Talbot Papers, box 4, folder 1.

32. Irma H. Gross, "Miss Marion Talbot, 1892–1924," in *History of the Department of Home Economics at the University of Chicago,* ed. Marie Dye (Chicago: Home Economics Alumnae Association, n.d.), 162.

33. Marion Talbot to Emily Talbot, 12 October 1892, Marion Talbot Papers, box 1, folder 12.

34. Talbot discussed the Club of Women Fellows annually in her report to the president. See also her memo to the Board of Student Organizations, 7 May 1898, Marion Talbot Papers, box 4, folder 1.

35. Marion Talbot, "The Women of the University," *President's Report* (Chicago: University of Chicago Press, 1904–06).

36. Alice Greenacre, "The Chicago Alumnae Club," *Cap and Gown,* 1914, unpaginated.

37. For correspondence dealing with Sophonisba Breckinridge's rank and salary, see the Presidents' Papers, 1889–1925, box 24, folder 12; also Marion Talbot to William Rainey Harper, 16 December 1896 (urging that Katherine Bates of the Department of English be given a salary larger than five hundred dollars a year), Presidents' Papers, 1889–1925, box 24, folder 11. For details of Talbot's feuds with Professor Julia Bulkley and Commons Manager Cora Colburn, see the Presidents' Papers, 1889–1925, box 24, folder 14, and Marion Talbot Papers, box 5, folder 1.

38. Talbot, *The Education of Women,* viii.

39. O'Neill, *Everyone Was Brave* (Chicago: Quadrangle, 1969).

40. Dye, *History of the Department of Home Economics at the University of Chicago,* 2.

41. Ibid., 160.

42. University of Chicago *Register,* 1892–93, 48.

43. Dye, *History of the Department of Home Economics,* 30–39.

44. Marion Talbot, "The Women of the University," in the *Presidents' Reports,* 1892–1920 (Chicago: University of Chicago Press). See especially her essay in the *Decennial President's Report, 1892–1902* (Chicago: University of Chicago Press, 1902).

45. Rosenberg, *Beyond Separate Spheres,* chap. 3.

46. "Graduating Pot-Pourri," *University Weekly* 2: 35 (21 June 1894), 7.

47. Report of the Senior Council to the University Council, 4 August 1898, Presidents' Papers, 1889–1925, box 25, folder 18.

48. "Day Boarders," *University Weekly* 7: 19 (23 February 1899), 200.

49. "Gallantry or Custom?" *University Weekly* 7: 41 (3 August 1899), 444.

50. Editorial, *University Weekly* 7: 39 (20 July 1899), 422.

51. "Prexy Said It," *University Weekly* 8: 9 (7 December 1899), 99, 102.

52. "The 1904–1905 Rush and Results," *University Weekly* 10: 6 (7 November 1905), 130.

53. Editorial, *University Weekly* 12: 43 (23 August 1894), 5.

54. *University News,* 1 November 1892.

55. "Some Women Good Students," *University Weekly* 4: 12 (19 December 1895), 675.

56. *University News,* 22 March 1893.

57. Floyd W. Reeves and John Dale Russell, *The Alumni of the Colleges* (Chicago: University of Chicago Press, 1933), 7–33.

58. "The Story of Martha Lavinia Gray," *Cap and Gown,* 1900, 281–86.

59. Letters to Marion Talbot from Florence Kelley, Isabel Howland, Mrs. Mary Roberts Smith, Jane Bancroft Robinson, all from February–December 1896, Marion Talbot Papers, box 2, folder 1.

60. Marion Talbot to Emily Talbot, 1896, Marion Talbot Papers, box 2, folder 1.

61. Reeves and Russell, 48ff.

62. Sheean, *Personal History,* 9–24. For attendance figures of the Junior and Senior Colleges, 1893–1908, see Marion Talbot, "The Women of the University," in *The President's Report* (Chicago: University of Chicago Press, 1908), 102. Each year *Cap and Gown* listed fraternities and secret clubs, with names of members.

63. For statistics and comments on students' racial and religious backgrounds, see Theodore Soares and Harold Lasswell, "Social Survey of Undergraduates, University of Chicago, 1920," Special Collections, Joseph Regenstein Library. *Chicago Tribune,* 27 July 1907, contains the story on Cecelia Johnson. See also Albion Small to Cecelia Johnson, July 1907, and Small to Harry Pratt Judson, 26 July 1907, Presidents' Papers, 1889–1925, "Racial Questions" folder.

64. Reeves and Russell, *Alumni of the Colleges,* 48 ff.

65. All organizations are listed in *Cap and Gown.* Most showed remarkable stability, lasting throughout the Progressive Era.

66. Fanny Burling, "In Camp," *University Weekly* 7: 37 (6 July 1899), 397–98; *University Weekly,* 29 October 1899, 713; Fanny Burling, "Mercedes or Dora?" *University Weekly* 8: 46, (13 September 1900), 533–34.

67. "One Recitation in the Spring Elective," *Cap and Gown,* 1900, 258–66.

68. I. D. Iot, "Questions and Answers," *University Weekly* 11: 16 (25 January 1894), 6.

69. "Points of View," *Cap and Gown,* 1899, 273–79.

70. Arthur Sears Henning, "The Game of Tennis," *University Weekly* 5:22 (4 March 1897), 217–19; "The Awakening," *University Weekly* 7: 35 (15 June 1899), 375; Fanny Burling '99, "Once Again," *University Weekly* 17: 29 (4 May 1899), 301.

71. *University News,* 7 December 1893.

72. Goodspeed, *University of Chicago,* 407.

73. Marion Talbot, "The Women of the University," *Decennial President's Report 1892–1902* (Chicago: University of Chicago Press, 1902), 139.

74. Herrick, *Chimes,* 2.

75. According to the key to Herrick's novel, Jessica Stowe is modeled on sociologist Elsie Clews Parsons. Key is located in Special Collections, Joseph Regenstein Library. For further information on Parsons, see Rosenberg, *Beyond Separate Spheres,* chap. 6; interview information from the *Daily Maroon,* 22 October 1902.

76. "A Co-Educational Episode," *Cap and Gown,* 1899; University Weekly, 13 December 1901, 988.

77. *University Weekly,* 13 December 1901, 108.

78. Nathaniel Butler to William Rainey Harper; Edward Capps to William Rainey Harper, box 60, folder 11, Presidents' Papers, 1889–1925. This folder contains statements on the segregation issue, written at Harper's request that the faculty give him their views.

79. Unsigned letter to William Rainey Harper, Presidents' Papers, 1889–1925, box 60, folder 11.

80. Harry Pratt Judson to William Rainey Harper, Presidents' Papers, 1889–1925, box 60, folder 11.

81. Albion Small to William Rainey Harper, Presidents' Papers, 1889–1925, box 60, folder 11.

82. Marion Talbot to William Rainey Harper, 16 January 1902, Presidents' Papers, 1889–1925, box 60, folder 11.

83. John Dewey to William Rainey Harper, Presidents' Papers, 1889–1925, box 60, folder 11.

84. William G. Hale to William Rainey Harper, Presidents' Papers, 1889–1925, box 60, folder 11.

85. Pamphlet of the Chicago Alumnae Club, Presidents' Papers, 1889–1925, box 60, folder 11.

86. Madeleine Wallin Papers, Special Collections, Joseph Regenstein Library.

87. Mineola Graham Sexton to Thomas W. Goodspeed, 13 October 1902, Presidents' Papers, 1889–1925, box 24, folder 1. For additional correspondence from women's groups, see box 24, folder 3.

88. *University Weekly* 10: 38 (3 July 1902), 861–62.

89. Marion Talbot to Jacob Gould Schurman, 3 May 1916, Marion Talbot Papers, box 2, folder 8; *President's Report* (Chicago: University of Chicago Press), 1902–04, 92–93; 1906–07, 62; 1907–08, 96–97; 1909–10, 1916–17, 1917–19, 1919–20. See also *Annual Register of the University of Chicago,* 1902–20.

90. *Daily Maroon,* 1 January 1907.

91. Ibid., 14 November 1902 and 8 December 1906.

92. Reeves and Russell, *Alumni of the Colleges,* 57; Marion Talbot, "The Women of the University," in *President's Report* (Chicago: University of Chicago Press, 1908–1909), 96.

93. Talbot, *More Than Lore,* 131–43.

94. *Daily Maroon,* 9 April 1912.

95. Ibid., 8 January 1907; 6 November 1910 and subsequent issues; February 1907.

CHAPTER 4: VASSAR COLLEGE, 1865–1920

1. Matthew Vassar, *Communications to the Board of Trustees,* quoted in Dorothy Plum '22 et al., *The Magnificent Enterprise,* 1, 5; Harriet Raymond Lloyd, ed., *Life*

and Letters of John Howard Raymond, 584–85, 601–02, 683–84, 734; *Prospectus* quoted and discussed in Herman, "College and After, 28–31.

2. Plum, *Magnificent Enterprise,* 9–10.

3. Wood, *Earliest Years at Vassar,* 21, 29, 41; Agnes Rogers, *Vassar Women,* 58.

4. Norris, *The Golden Age of Vassar,* 75–76.

5. Wood, *Earliest Years,* 82.

6. Mitchell quoted in Stephen M. Clement, "Aspects of Student Religion at Vassar College, 1861–1914" (Ed.D. diss., Harvard University, 1977), 77.

7. Rogers, 38; Blatch and Lutz, *Challenging Years,* 35–40.

8. Plum, *Magnificent Enterprise,* 1–29; letter of Matthew Vassar, dated 28 April 1868, quoted, 12.

9. Helen Dawes Brown '78, *Two College Girls.*

10. Ibid., 289–97.

11. Description and analysis of the sibyls' prophecies in Herman, chap. 2; marriage statistics in Mabel Newcomer and Evelyn Gibson, "Vital Statistics From Vassar College," *Vassar Quarterly* 9: 2 (February 1924), table 1, 102.

12. These articles on women's careers appeared in the *Vassar Miscellany* and the *Vassar Alumnae Monthly* between 1892 and 1914.

13. Simpson, "Helen Lockwood's College Years, 1908–1912," 13–14.

14. Morris, ed., *Miss Wylie of Vassar,* 78.

15. Rubin, *Constance Rourke and American Culture,* 8–26.

16. Louise Fargo Brown, *Apostle of Democracy,* 101, 102. Brown, Salmon's colleague in the Vassar Department of History used no footnotes in this biography, based on the Lucy Salmon Papers, Vassar College Archives, Vassar College, Poughkeepsie, New York.

17. Ibid., 108.

18. Ibid., 214.

19. Ibid., 140.

20. Ibid., 141.

21. Margaret (Peggy) Shipp '05 to May Louise (Mamie) Shipp, 25 January 1902, Vassar Student Letters Collection, 1865–1935, Vassar College Archives.

22. Ruth Adams '04 to her parents, 16 January 1903, Vassar Student Letters Collection.

23. Brown, *Apostle of Democracy,* 212–13. Appendices to this biography give sample examination questions from Salmon's courses.

24. Mills, ed., *College Women and the Social Sciences,* 300–02.

25. Ibid., xiii.

26. Dorothy Smith Gruening '09, "Recollections of the Vassar Graveyard Suffrage Meeting," tape at Arthur and Elizabeth Schlesinger Library of Women's History, Radcliffe College, Cambridge, Massachusetts. See also Boyer, "Inez Milholland Boissevain," in *Notable American Women,* 1: 188–90, and Kendall, *Peculiar Institutions.*

27. *Report of the President of Vassar College,* 1904, 15.

28. Ibid., 1905, 17.

29. Simpson, "Helen Lockwood's College Years, 1908–1912."

30. MacCracken, *The Hickory Limb,* 30.

31. Ibid., 25.

32. For data on the Vassar faculty during Taylor's administration, see *Report of the President of Vassar College,* 1905 and 1912. Taylor's achievements are described in Plum, *Magnificent Enterprise.*

33. MacCracken, *Hickory Limb,* 64–74.

34. *The Vassarion,* 1902 and in other years, lists student organizations. See also, Plum, *Magnificent Enterprise,* for discussion and listing of student activities. A "bacon-bat" is a picnic where students cooked bacon by winding it around a baseball bat and holding it over a campfire.

35. Adelaide Claflin '97 to her family, 17 January 1895; Dorothy Hawley ex-'14 to her family, 7 November 1910, Vassar Student Letters Collection. Students who left college without graduating were referred to as "ex" members of their class.

36. Adelaide Claflin '97 to her family, 12 November 1893; Dorothy Hawley ex-'14 to her mother, 15 January 1911, Vassar Student Letters Collection.

37. Solomon, 62–70; *Ladies' Home Journal,* April 1890, 8.

38. Information on tuition, room and board fees from Plum, *Magnificent Enterprise.* On the subject of student allowances at the turn of the century, see Simpson, "Helen Lockwood's College Years," 3–4. For information on students' socio-economic status, see Rogers, *Vassar Women,* 31–32. Her statistics show very little change between 1871 and 1922 in the occupations of the fathers of Vassar students. In contrast, Helen Horowitz argues in *Alma Mater* that Seven Sisters students came from more elite, wealthier homes after the turn of the century.

39. MacCracken, *Hickory Limb,* 41–46.

40. "Dean's Report," in *Report of the President of Vassar College,* 1914–15.

41. Virginia Nisbet Heard '01 to her mother, November 1897; Ruth Crippen '04 to her father, December 1900; Ruth Adams '04 to her family, 25 May 1903; Dorothy Hawley ex-'14 to her mother, 27 March 1911, 7 November 1911, spring 1912; Ruth Adams '04 to her family, 4 October 1900; Muriel Tilden Eldridge '14 to her mother, 26 February 1912, Vassar Student Letters Collection.

42. *Vassarion,* 1914, foreword.

43. Schwartz, *Elinor's College Career.*

44. Adelaide Claflin '97 to her mother, 14 January 1894, Vassar Student Letters Collection; James Monroe Taylor to Harriet E. Giles, 1900, Spelman College Archives.

45. Ruth Adams '04 to her parents, 29 October 1900; Adelaide Claflin '97 to her mother, 26 January 1896; Dorothy Hawley ex-'14 to her family, 10 March 1912, Vassar Student Letters Collection.

46. Julia Schwartz, "In Search of Experience," *Vassar Studies,* no pagination.

47. Ruth Adams '04 to her family, 22 February 1903, Vassar Student Letters Collection.

48. Ibid., 26 May 1902; Plum, *Magnificent Enterprise,* describes student customs and class traditions.

49. Maude Louise Ray '00, "In the Course of a Year," *Vassar Miscellany,* 1899–1900, 93–105.

50. *Vassar Miscellany,* fiftieth anniversary issue, October 1915, 96, 150.

51. *Vassar Miscellany,* 1907–08, 270.

52. Ibid., 1911–12, 519–20.

53. *Daily Princetonian,* 27 January 1916, reprinted and answered in the *Vassar Miscellany,* 5 February 1916.

54. *Vassar Miscellany,* fiftieth anniversary issue, October 1915.

55. Clement, "Aspects of Student Religion," discusses the changing role of the Student Christian Association at Vassar. See also the *Vassarion,* 1902; the *Vassar Miscellany,* fiftieth anniversary issue, October 1915; Plum, *Magnificent Enterprise,* Editorial in the *Vassar Miscellany,* 1908–09, 204.

56. Dorothy Phillips '14, "Bulging Thoughts," *Vassar Miscellany,* March 1913, 401–02.

57. Katherine Krom Merritt '08, "The Social Status," *Vassar Miscellany,* February 1908, 21–44.

58. Muriel Tilden Eldridge '14 to her mother, 26 September 1913, Vassar Student Letters Collection.

59. *Vassar Miscellany,* 5 June 1918; 28 September 1918; 26 October 1918; 10 November 1920. See also Hubbard, "War and the Women's College," 285–87; MacCracken, "Girls Who Want to Go to France," 248; Mills, "College Women and Nursing," 94–95; Johnson, "Is the Woman's College Essential in Wartime?" 586–91; Elliot, "How War Strikes Home to a Woman's College," 470–73. Mary Culver Pollock '17 to her family, 30 September 1913; 10 January 1916; 16 February 1916; 8 March 1916, Vassar Student Letters Collection.

60. Blatch and Lutz, *Challenging Years,* 113–14; Cheney, *Millay in Greenwich Village.* See also MacCracken, *Hickory Limb,* for a description of Boissevain's visit to the campus.

61. Adelaide Claflin '97 to her sister Edith, 10 December 1893; Muriel Tilden Eldridge '14 to her mother, 17 March 1912; Dorothy Danforth Compton '17 to her family, 15 January 1914, Vassar Student Letters Collection.

62. Dorothy M. Baldwin '12, "The Opinion of the Vassar Students on Woman Suffrage," *Vassar Miscellany,* May 1911, 599.

63. Margaret Shipp '05 to May Louise (Mamie) Shipp, 25 October and 1 November 1903, Vassar Student Letters Collection.

64. Julia Schwartz, "Heroic Treatment," in *Vassar Studies,* no pagination.

65. Ruth Adams '04 to her family, 1 May 1903; Margaret Shipp '05 to her family,

6 December 1901 and 3 May 1903; Adelaide Claflin '97 to her mother, 21 January 1894, Vassar Student Letters Collection.

66. *Vassarion,* 1902, 70.

67. Marjorie Lewis Prentiss '03, "The Critic and the Criticised," *Vassar Miscellany,* 1902–03, 15–22.

68. Mary D. Stewart '02, "A Girl I Have Known", *Vassar Miscellany,* 1899–1900, 106–09.

69. Alice Lovett Carson '04, "A Woman's Point of View," *Vassar Miscellany,* 1903–04, 99–104.

70. Louise Elizabeth Dutton '05, "Miss Carter, Critic," *Vassar Miscellany,* 1904–05, 264–70.

71. Marjorie McCoy '11 to her parents, 22 May 1910, Vassar Student Letters Collection.

72. Coolidge, "Enemies of the Republic: Are the Reds Stalking Our College Women?" 10–11. For information on the Intercollegiate Socialist Society, see Horn, *The Intercollegiate Socialist Society, 1905–1921.*

73. Bennett, "Seven Colleges—Seven Types," 13.

74. *Vassar Miscellany,* 18 January 1919, 13 October 1920, 3 November 1917, 6 March 1918; Horn, *Intercollegiate Socialist Society,* 25, 76, 95–96.

75. *Vassar Miscellany,* 2 March 1918; Marion Willard Everett '13 to her brother Grant, no date, Vassar Student Letters Collection.

76. Dale Mezzacappa '72, "Vassar College and the Suffrage Movement," *Vassar Alumnae Quarterly,* 2ff.; Mary Culver Pollock '17 to her family, Fall 1913, Fall 1914, March 1914, 26 April 1915, 22 September 1915, 16 October 1915, Vassar Student Letters Collection.

77. Marion Willard Everett '13 to her mother, 1 February 1911; Mrs. Willard to her husband, 15 May 1913, Vassar Student Letters Collection.

78. Letter from alumna, class of 1908, in *Vassar Miscellany News,* 1917, quoted in Mezzacappa, "Vassar College and the Suffrage Movement," 6.

79. Dorothy Danforth Compton '17 to her family, 13 October 1915, Vassar Student Letters Collection.

80. "The First Year Out of College," *Vassar Alumnae Monthly,* June and July 1910.

81. *Vassar Miscellany,* 7 and 18 February 1920.

82. Violet L. Pike '07, "The First Year Out of College and the Bureau of Occupations," *Vassar Alumnae Monthly,* special no. 1912.

83. Mary Culver Pollock '17 to her family, 30 September 1913, 10 January 1916, 16 February 1916, 8 March 1916, Vassar Student Letters Collection.

84. Dorothy Danforth Compton '17 to her family, 13 February 1914; Mary Culver Pollock '17 to her family, 6 November 1914; Marion Willard Everett '13 to her mother, 20 April 1913, Vassar Student Letters Collection.

85. Muriel Tilden Eldridge '14 to her family, 19 February 1912, Vassar Student Letters Collection.

86. Muriel Tilden Eldridge '14 to her parents, 18 February 1913, Vassar Student Letters Collection.

87. *Vassar Miscellany,* April, May, and June 1913.

88. Ibid., December 1919.

89. Dorothy Sanburn Phillips '14, "The Prom," *Vassar Miscellany,* April 1914.

90. Edna St. Vincent Millay '17, "The Wall of Dominoes," *Vassar Miscellany,* May 1917. This story was Vassar's entry in the literary competition of the Association of Northern College Magazines.

91. *Vassarion,* 1917, no pagination.

CHAPTER 5: SOPHIE NEWCOMB AND
AGNES SCOTT COLLEGES, 1887–1920

1. Dixon, *A Brief History of the H. Sophie Newcomb Memorial College, 1887–1919,* 58; Dyer, "Education in New Orleans," in *The Past as Prelude,* 116–45; Dyer, *Tulane.*

2. Ormond and Irvine, *Louisiana's Art Nouveau,* 3–14.

3. Dixon gives a full account of the founding of Newcomb College in his book. He took pride in the fact that Newcomb was the country's first coordinate women's college. In 1888 a committee from New York City visited New Orleans to investigate the coordinate arrangement and went home to found Barnard College within Columbia University. Although Radcliffe College has also been called coordinate, its original name, The Harvard Annex, more accurately describes its dependent existence on Harvard University's faculty and resources. For an account of the founding of Radcliffe, see Schwager, "Harvard Women." On Barnard, see Meyer, *Barnard Beginnings.*

4. Dixon, *A Brief History,* 32–39.

5. Biographical files in the Tulane University Archives, Howard Tilton Memorial Library, New Orleans, Louisiana, contain a limited amount of information on the Newcomb faculty—usually little more than a vita. See also, Dyer, *Tulane,* 98.

6. *Tulane University Catalogue,* 1902–03; John Duffy, "Pestilence in New Orleans," in *Past As Prelude,* 88–115. See Dixon for an account of his recruiting efforts and of the effects of yellow fever scares on the college.

7. James Ross McCain, "The Growth of Agnes Scott College, 1889–1955," 1–6; Friedlander, "Not a Veneer or a Sham, 33–44.

8. Alston, "The Significance of the Life of George Washington Scott," in Alston, ed., *Colonel George Washington Scott,* 4–5.

9. McCain, "Agnes Scott College," 2–3, 6; *Student Handbook* (Decatur, Georgia: Student Government Association, Agnes Scott College, 1917), 46ff.; "Religious Traditions at Agnes Scott," notes for chapel talk by James Ross McCain, 23 February 1952, Agnes Scott Notebooks, Agnes Scott College Archives, Agnes Scott College, Decatur, Georgia. In the 1960s Agnes Scott's reputation as a liberal arts institution conflicted with its Christian mission. The college rejected the application of Kathryn

Harris, a doctoral candidate from Emory University, for a position in the Department of English, because she was Jewish. President Wallace Alston told newspapers that he had taken an oath to bring "only professing Christians" onto the faculty; Gene Roberts, "Atlanta College Bars Jews On Faculty," *New York Times,* 16 February 1967. See also *Atlanta Constitution,* 16 February 1967; *Atlanta Journal,* 17 October 1968.

10. McCain, "Agnes Scott College," 4.

11. *Catalogue of Agnes Scott Institute,* 1898–99; 1903–04, 75–76; 1906–07; 1910–11; 1918–19.

12. *Student Handbook,* Agnes Scott College, 1912–1913.

13. Information on the faculty, including degrees and ranks, may be found in the *Catalogue of Agnes Scott Institute* and *Catalogue of Agnes Scott College.*

14. *Daily Picayune,* 14 June 1894; Edwin Alderman quoted in *Daily Picayune,* 28 April 1903, Newcomb College Scrapbooks, Tulane University Archives.

15. Right Reverend Hugh Miller Thompson, Bishop of Mississippi, speech at Newcomb College Commencement, 1892, source of clipping unknown; *World's Fair Advocate,* 18 March 1893; Judge W. W. Howe quoted in the *Daily Picayune,* 30 June 1898; all in Newcomb College Scrapbooks.

16. Edwin Alderman, quoted in the *Daily Picayune,* 28 April 1903, Newcomb College Scrapbooks.

17. Report of the Registrar of H. Sophie Newcomb Memorial College, 1914–15, Tulane University Archives, and Amelie Roman Faculty File, Tulane University Archives. Between 1890 and 1920 the college awarded 492 B.A. degrees; between 1893 and 1901, 29 B.S. degrees; between 1897 and 1920, 39 B.Des. (art) degrees; between 1913 and 1920, 24 B.Mus. (music) degrees; and between 1913 and 1925, 181 B.A.'s in education. Domestic science students who stayed for four years received a B.A. in education. Attendance figures were higher than the number of degrees warranted, indicating that many women stayed only for two years. In 1915, for example, with 89 students in the art school, the college awarded one degree in art. Figures on degrees awarded from statement prepared by Horace Renegar, Public Relations Director, Tulane University for *Mademoiselle* magazine, no date, Tulane University Archives. See also Mayo, *Southern Women in the Recent Educational Movement in the South,* 167. Irvine and Ormond, *Louisiana's Art Nouveau,* describe the art school, pottery shops, etc. at Newcomb College. In an appendix, they list art school graduates and information on their subsequent employment. It is not clear how many women needed to support themselves. Josephine Newcomb's bequest assumed an economic need, but Irvine and Ormond commented that the famous decorators came from the New Orleans gentry, free to attend college and work at the guild after graduation because their services were not needed at home (p. 71). See also Ellsworth Woodward, "Art in Colleges," *Arcade,* 1915–16, 26–31.

18. *Jambalaya,* 1896, 159.

19. Margaret Sterling Lea, "According to Cable," *The Tulanian,* February 1905, 71–72; "The Tragedy of a Bow of Blue Ribbon," *The Tulanian,* April 1906, 64–69.

20. Letter from Dixon to Newcomb parents quoted in unknown newspaper, 10 February 1892, Newcomb College Scrapbooks.

21. Dixon to "My Dear B—," ca. 1891, quoted in *Newcomb 1886–1986,* a pictorial history published by the college, 1987, no pagination.

22. Dixon, *A Brief History,* 32–33.

23. Delie Bancroft '14, "The Gospel of Work," *Arcade,* June 1913, 21–27.

24. Mildred Renshaw '17, "To Thine Ownself Be True," *Arcade,* April 1916, 28–31.

25. *Daily Picayune,* 8 April 1911 and 30 March 1912; *Times-Democrat,* 15 March 1914; *Times-Picayune,* 11 November 1914, Newcomb College Scrapbooks.

26. Dixon, *A Brief History,* 33.

27. L. E. Zimmerman, "Jean Margaret Gordon," and "Kate M. Gordon," in *Notable American Women,* 2: 64–68; Allen F. Davis, "Eleanor Laura McMain," *Notable American Women,* 2: 474–76.

28. "The New Economics Course," *Arcade,* June 1911, 71–72.

29. Doris Kent '17, "A History of Varsity Debating at Newcomb," *Arcade,* April 1917, 257–61. For Agnes Scott students' version of the same event see account by Emma Jones Smith in Agnes Scott Notebooks, Agnes Scott College Archives: "The Newcomb girls felt that we took an unfair advantage of the judges because we wore evening dresses whereas they marched forth to battle clad in sensible white skirts and shirtwaists."

30. Elizabeth McFetridge '12, "The Point of View," monologue given by Ethel Perkins '92 at the Alumnae Vaudeville Show, printed in the *Arcade,* undated, 40–43.

31. "'12," "The Newcomb News At Home," and "More Newcomb News," *Arcade,* undated, 35–40 and 47–55.

32. Ihle, "Co-Education at Major Southern Universities;" *Daily Picayune,* 10 June 1906; 27 October 1907; *Mobile Register,* 14 September 1907; a New York newspaper, 24 November 1907; *Times-Democrat,* 20 July 1911, 17 December 1911, 22 November 1909; *Times-Picayune,* 15 December 1914, all in Newcomb College Scrapbooks.

33. *Arcade,* March 1909, 64–65.

34. "'12," "A Meeting of the Tulane Board," *Arcade,* 73–79.

35. Friedlander, 38–39; Louise McKinney quoted in *Atlanta Constitution,* 20 December 1961; interview by Lynn Gordon with Prof. E. W. McNair, December 1980.

36. Emma Jones '18, "Not In The Catalogue," *Agnes Scott Bulletin,* series 14, 19 April 1917, no pagination; "How The Spring Holidays Came to Be," *Agonistic,* 29 March 1919.

37. *Agnes Scott Institute Catalogue,* 1896–1897, 63; ibid., 1904–05, 85.

38. "Senior Sketches," *Aurora,* 1899, 177–83; Mabel McKowen, "Looking Backward," ibid., May 1905, 420–22.

39. Lillian Harper '15, "Her Last Game," *Aurora,* January 1912, 115–18. Mattie L. Tilly '04, "How Clare Got First Honor," *Aurora,* October 1902, 22–24.

40. "Washington Irving's Conception of Woman," *Mnemosynean* 3: 9 (May 1894), 12–13.

41. Mary Mel Neel, "Valedictory, " *Mnemosynean* 3: 9 (May 1894), 1–3.

42. "Mnemosynean Prophecy," *Aurora,* 1897, 137–39.

43. "Senior Decisions," *Aurora,* 1899, 143–49; Teddy '05, "Marguerite's Success," *Aurora,* December 1904, 139–45; "A Romance," *Mnemosynean,* January 1899, 8; Mary Dillard, "Grandmother," *Aurora,* April 1907, 7–8; Laura E. Candler '04, "The North or the South," *Aurora,* March 1903, 189–92; Lottie May Blair '14, "Violets and A Mournful Man," *Aurora,* December 1911, 6–8; Polly, "Mistaken Identity," *Aurora,* December 1904, 173–74.

44. *The Alumnae of Agnes Scott College;* "What Happened to Us In China," *Agnes Scott Alumnae Quarterly,* June 1927, 7–8; and "The Spires of Oxford"; Vivian Little, "A Student In Paris"; Leslie Gaylord, "Eternal Rome"; Carla Hinman, "Studying French in Geneva"; Marion Green, "The University of Grenoble"; "Doing Graduate Work in the South"; Isabel Ferguson, "The Beginner in Graduate Work at Chicago"; Frances Harper, "History At Louisiana State University"; Ivylyn Girardeau, "Medicine at Tulane"; Leone Bowers Hamilton, "A Summer At An Art Academy"; Helen Lane Comfort, "Specializing In New York City"; and "What Price Graduate Work?" all in *Agnes Scott Alumnae Quarterly,* November 1927, 3–19. For a complete listing of Agnes Scott graduates, 1893–1924, see *Agnes Scott College Catalogue,* 1924–25, 162–91. The catalogue also lists graduate degrees and married names through the class of 1921. Combining this information with career lists from the *Agonistic,* 5 April 1922, it is possible to get at least a limited picture of Agnes Scott alumnae's postgraduate lives.

45. *Agnes Scott Bulletin,* ser. 11, no. 3, 27 March 1914, 8–10; "The Woman's College and Women," *Agnes Scott Bulletin,* series 13, no. 7, April 1916; *Student Handbook,* 1918, 10.

46. *Agonistic,* 30 March 1917 and 25 October 1921; *Agnes Scott College Catalogue,* 1918–19, 73–74; *Student Handbook* (Student Government Association: Agnes Scott College), 1917; ibid., 1919, 10.

47. *Agonistic,* 25 October 1921. The citizens of Atlanta did not encourage women's reform and political activities. See, for example, Taylor, "Woman Suffrage Activities in Atlanta," 45–53; Newman, "The Role of Women in Atlanta's Churches, 1865–1906," 17–30; Roth, "Matronage.

48. Janie Curry '04, "What Margie Learned At Sabbath-School," *Aurora,* January 1903, 132–33.

CHAPTER 6: CONCLUSION

1. Ellen C. DuBois et al., "Politics and Culture in Women's History."

2. Tidball and Kistiakowsky, "Baccalaureate Origins of American Scientists and Scholars"; Oates and Williamson, "Women's Colleges and Women Achievers."

3. Julia Crowe Maxfield '03 to Helen Rogers '03, Women's College Records, Department of Rare Books and Special Collections, Rush Rhees Library, University of Rochester, Rochester, New York.

4. Komarovsky, *Women in College*.

5. Simmons, "Companionate Marriage and the Lesbian Threat"; Hummer, *The Decade of Elusive Promise*.

6. Cookingham, "Bluestockings, Spinsters, and Pedagogues," "Working After Childbearing in Modern America," and "Combining Marriage, Motherhood and Jobs Before World War II"; Giele, "Cohort Variations in Life Patterns of Educated Women"; Giele and Perun, "Life After College"; Stricker, "Cookbooks and Law Books."

7. Cott, *The Grounding of Modern Feminism;* Hummer, *Decade of Elusive Promise;* Glazer and Slater, *Unequal Colleagues;* Dan C. Lortie, *Schoolteacher* (Chicago: University of Chicago Press, 1974); Stricker, "Cookbooks and Law Books;" Showalter, ed., *These Modern Women*.

8. Glazer and Slater, *Unequal Colleagues,* 209.

9. Lawrence Cremin, *The Transformation of the School* (New York: Vintage Books, 1961), discusses the breakdown of the progressive coalition. See Cott, *Grounding of Modern Feminism,* for discussion of the controversy over the Equal Rights Amendment. The transformation of social work is discussed in Glazer and Slater, *Unequal Colleagues,* 165–208; and in Costin, *Two Sisters For Social Justice*.

10. Dorothy Dunbar Bromley, "Feminist—New Style"; Antler, "Feminism As Life-Process"; Alpern, *Freda Kirchwey;* Showalter, ed., *These Modern Women*.

11. Glazer and Slater, *Unequal Colleagues,* 213–31.

12. Nicolson, "The Rights and Privileges Pertaining Thereto," 136.

BIBLIOGRAPHY

AGNES SCOTT COLLEGE

Agnes Scott College Archives, Agnes Scott College, Decatur, Ga.

The Agonistic, 1916–25.

The Alumnae of Agnes Scott. Decatur, Ga.: Agnes Scott Alumnae Assn.

Agnes Scott Alumnae Quarterly, 1927.

Agnes Scott Bulletin, 1900–20, 1956.

Agnes Scott Notebooks.

Agnes Scott Student Handbooks, Student Government Assn., 1912–15, 1917, 1919.

The Aurora, 1895–1920.

Catalogues of Agnes Scott Institute and Agnes Scott College, 1887–1920.

Mnemosynean, 1894, 1899.

Books, articles, and interviews

Alston, Wallace M., ed. *Colonel George Washington Scott.* Decatur, Ga.: Agnes Scott College, n.d.

Friedlander, Amy. "Not a Veneer or a Sham: The Early Days at Agnes Scott." *Atlanta Historical Journal* (Winter 1979–80): 33–44.

McCain, James Ross. "The Growth of Agnes Scott College, 1889–1955." *Agnes Scott College Bulletin,* ser. 53, no. 2, April 1956.

McNair, W. Edward. Interviewed by Lynn D. Gordon, December 1980, Decatur, Georgia.

Newman, Harvey K. "The Role of Women in Atlanta's Churches, 1865–1906." *Atlanta Historical Journal* (Winter 1979–80): 17–30.

Bibliography

❖

Taylor, A. Elizabeth. "Woman Suffrage Activities in Atlanta." *Atlanta Historical Journal* (Winter 1979–80): 45–53.

UNIVERSITY OF CALIFORNIA

University of California Archives, The Bancroft Library, Berkeley, Calif.

The Berkeleyan, 1874–97.

The Blue and Gold, 1890–1920 (1906 unavailable).

Brass Tacks, 1913–16.

The California Alumni Fortnightly, 1916–20.

The California Alumni Weekly, 1911–15.

The California Pelican, 1903–20.

The Daily Californian, 1897–1920.

The Dill Pickle, 1916, 1935.

Dornin, May. "Biographies of Women Having Residence Halls Named for Them."

Files of the Office of the President, selected papers.

Handbook of the Associated Women Students, 1915.

Phoebe Apperson Hearst Papers.

The Occident, 1885–1920.

The Partheneia (scripts), 1912–17, 1919.

The Raspberry Press, February 12, 1915–March 26, 1934.

Report of the President of the University, 1890–1920.

Student Opinion, August 17, 1915–April 17, 1916.

Student Scrapbook Collection.

The University of California Magazine, 1895–1904.

Interviews

Braden, Amy Steinhart. "Child Welfare and Community Service." Interviewed by Edna Tartaul Daniel, 1965. University of California Oral History Project, Berkeley, Calif.

Coffin, Irene. Interviewed by Lynn D. Gordon, December 1977. Oakland, Calif.

Drew, James Edward. Interviewed by Lynn D. Gordon, December 1977. San Francisco, Calif.

Hagar, Ella Barrows. Interviewed by Lynn D. Gordon, December 1977. Berkeley, Calif.

Huntington, Emily. "A Career in Consumer Economics and Social Insurance." Interviewed by Alice Greene King, 1971. University of California Oral History Project, Berkeley, Calif.

Mitchell, Lucy Sprague. "Pioneering in Education." Interviewed by Irene Prescott, 1962. University of California Oral History Project, Berkeley, Calif.

Olney, Mary McLean. "Oakland, Berkeley, and the University of California." Interviewed by Willa Baum, 1973. University of California Oral History Project, Berkeley, Calif.

Bibliography

❖

Parrish, Mila Clearley. Interviewed by Lynn D. Gordon, January 1978. San Francisco, Calif.

Towle, Katherine Amelia. Interviewed by Harriet Nathan, 1970. University of California Oral History Project, Berkeley, Calif.

Books and articles

Bradley, Harold C. *From a Packrat's Files: Autobiography of Harold C. Bradley.* Copyright Ruth Bradley, 1976. University of California Archives.

Burnham, John C. "Milicent Washburn Shinn." *Notable American Women,* vol. 3, 285–86. Cambridge: Harvard University Press, 1971.

Chambers, Clarke. "Jessica Blanche Peixotto." *Notable American Women,* vol. 3, 42–43. Cambridge: Harvard University Press, 1971.

Deutsch, Monroe, ed. *The Abundant Life.* Berkeley: University of California Press, 1926.

Gilbreth, Frank B., Jr. *Time Out for Happiness.* New York: Thomas Y. Crowell, 1970.

Lichtenstein, Joy. *For the Blue and Gold.* San Francisco: A. M. Robertson, 1901.

Mitchell, Lucy Sprague. *Two Lives: The Story of Wesley Clair Mitchell and Myself.* New York: Simon and Schuster, 1953.

Paul, Rodman Wilson. "Phoebe Apperson Hearst." *Notable American Women,* vol. 2, 171–73. Cambridge: Harvard University Press, 1971.

The Prytaneans: An Oral History of the Prytanean Society, Its Members and Their University. 2 vols. Berkeley: University of California Press, 1933.

Ritter, Mary B. *More Than Gold in California.* Berkeley: University of California Press, 1933.

Skelley, Grant Teasdale. "*The Overland Monthly* under Milicent Washburn Shinn 1883–1894: A Study in Regional Publishing." Ph.D. diss., University of California, 1968.

Solomons, Selina. *How We Won the Vote in California.* San Francisco: New Woman, 1911.

Stadtman, Verne, ed. *The Centennial Record of the University of California.* Berkeley: University of California, 1967.

Stadtman, Verne. *The University of California, 1868–1968.* New York: McGraw Hill, 1970.

Stone, Irving, ed. *There Was Light: Autobiography of a University: Berkeley, 1868–1968.* Garden City, N.Y.: Doubleday, 1970.

Webb, Catherine Janes. *A Family History of California.* Berkeley: Type-Ink Press, 1975.

Wheeler, Benjamin Ide. *The Writings of Benjamin Ide Wheeler.* 8 vols. (no publication information given).

UNIVERSITY OF CHICAGO

University of Chicago Archives, Special Collections, Joseph Regenstein Library, Chicago, Ill.

Sophonisba Breckinridge Autobiography.
The Cap and Gown, 1895–1920.

Bibliography

❖

The Daily Maroon, 1895–96, 1902–20.

Diary of Demia Butler.

The Presidents' Papers, 1889–1925.

The President's Reports, 1892–1920.

Marion Talbot Papers.

University News, 1892–93.

University of Chicago Register, 1892–1920.

University Weekly, 1893–1902.

Madeleine Wallin Papers.

Books and articles

Clements, Ellen Bell. "Marion Talbot and the College Woman." Senior essay, University of Chicago, 1977.

Dye, Marie. History of the Department of Home Economics at the University of Chicago. Home Economics Alumnae Association, n.d.

Goodspeed, Thomas Wakefield. A History of the University of Chicago: The First Quarter Century. 1916. Reprint. Chicago: University of Chicago Press, 1972.

Herrick, Robert. Chimes. New York: Macmillan, 1926.

Reeves, Floyd W., and John Dale Russell. The Alumni of the Colleges. Vol. 6 of The University of Chicago Survey. Chicago: University of Chicago Press, 1933.

Sheean, Vincent. Personal History. Boston: Houghton Mifflin, 1934.

Solomon, Barbara Miller. "Alice Freeman Palmer." Notable American Women, vol. 3, 4–8. Cambridge: Harvard University Press, 1971.

Storr, Richard. Harper's University: The Beginnings. Chicago: University of Chicago Press, 1966.

———. "Marion Talbot." Notable American Women, vol. 3, 423–24. Cambridge: Harvard University Press, 1971.

Talbot, Marion. The Education of Women. Chicago: University of Chicago Press, 1910.

———. More Than Lore: The Reminiscences of Marion Talbot, Dean of Women at the University of Chicago, 1892–1925. Chicago: University of Chicago Press, 1936.

Tannler, Albert. One In Spirit. Chicago: University of Chicago Library, 1973.

Wallace, Elizabeth. The Unending Journey. University of Minnesota Press, 1952.

Weimann, Jeanne Madeline. "A Temple to Women's Genius: The Women's Building of 1893." Chicago History (Spring 1977): 23–33.

SOPHIE NEWCOMB COLLEGE

Tulane University Archives, Howard-Tilton Memorial Library, New Orleans, La.

The College Spirit, 1894–97.

Faculty Biographical Files, Newcomb College.

The Jambalaya, 1896–1920.

The Newcomb Arcade, 1909–20.

Bibliography

❖

Josephine Newcomb Biographical Files.

Newcomb College Scrapbooks.

The Olive and Blue, 1896–1904.

Horace Renegar, Public Relations Director, Report for *Mademoiselle,* n.d.

Report of the Registrar of the H. Sophie Newcomb Memorial College, 1914–15.

Tulane University Catalogue, 1900–20.

The Tulanian, 1904–07.

Books and articles

Carter, Hodding, ed. *The Past as Prelude: New Orleans 1718–1968.* New Orleans: Pelican, 1968.

Davis, Allen F. "Eleanor Laura McMain." *Notable American Women,* vol. 2, 474–76. Cambridge: Harvard University Press, 1971.

Dixon, Brandt Van Blarcom. *A Brief History of the H. Sophie Newcomb Memorial College 1887–1919.* New Orleans: Hauser, 1928.

Dutton, Emily Helen. "History of the Southern Association of College Women." Schlesinger Library, Cambridge, Mass., n.d.

Dyer, John. *Tulane: The Biography of a University 1834–1965.* New York: Harper and Row, 1966.

Hall, Jacquelyn Dowd. *Revolt Against Chivalry: Jessie Daniel Ames and the Women's Campaign Against Lynching.* New York: Columbia University Press, 1979.

Lemmon, Sarah McCulloh. "Elizabeth Avery Colton." *Notable American Women,* vol. 1, 364–65. Cambridge: Harvard University Press, 1971.

Mayo, Reverend A. D. *Southern Women in the Recent Educational Movement in the South.* Bureau of Education, Circular of Information, no. 1, 1892.

Newcomb 1886–1986. New Orleans: Upton, 1986 (publication of the Newcomb Pictorial History Committee).

Ormond, Suzanne, and Mary E. Irvine. *Louisiana's Art Nouveau: The Crafts of the Newcomb Style.* Gretna, La.: Pelican, 1976.

Southern Association of College Women. *Proceedings.* 1912, 1913. Schlesinger Library, Cambridge, Mass.

Zimmerman, L. E. "Jean Margaret Gordon," "Kate M. Gordon." *Notable American Women,* vol. 2, 64–68. Cambridge: Harvard University Press, 1971.

VASSAR COLLEGE

Vassar College Archives, Vassar College Library, Poughkeepsie, N.Y.

The Report of the President of Vassar College, 1890–1920.

The Vassar Alumnae Monthly, 1890–1920.

The Vassarion, 1890–1920.

The Vassar Miscellany, 1890–1920.

Vassar Student Letters Collection, 1865–1935.

Bibliography

❖

Books and articles

Bacon, Marion, ed. *Life at Vassar: 75 Years in Pictures*. Poughkeepsie: Vassar Cooperative Bookshop, n.d.

Blatch, Harriot Stanton, and Alma Lutz. *Challenging Years: The Autobiography of Harriot Stanton Blatch*. New York: Putnam's, 1940.

Brown, Helen Dawes. *Two College Girls*. Boston: Ticknor, 1886.

Brown, Louise Fargo. *Apostle of Democracy: The Life of Lucy Maynard Salmon*. New York: Harper Brothers, 1943.

Boyer, Paul S. "Inez Milholland Boissevain." *Notable American Women*, vol. 1, 188–90. Cambridge: Harvard University Press, 1971.

Cheney, Anne. *Millay in Greenwich Village*. University, Ala.: University of Alabama Press, 1975.

Clement, Stephen M. "Aspects of Student Religion at Vassar College, 1861–1914." Ed.D. diss., Harvard University, 1977.

Cleveland, Anne, and Jean Anderson. *The Educated Woman in Cartoon and Caption*. New York: Dutton, 1960.

Gruening, Dorothy Smith. Taped Recollections of Graveyard Suffrage Meeting, 1908. Schlesinger Library, Cambridge, Mass.

Herman, Debra. "College and After: The Vassar Experiment in Women's Education: 1861–1924." Ph.D. diss., Stanford University, 1979.

Lloyd, Harriet Raymond, ed. *The Life and Letters of John Howard Raymond*. New York: Fords, Howard and Hulbert, 1881.

McCarthy, Mary. *The Group*. New York: Harcourt Brace Jovanovich, 1954.

MacCracken, Henry Noble. *The Hickory Limb*. New York: Scribner's, 1950.

Mills, Herbert E., ed. *College Women and the Social Sciences*. New York: John Day, 1934.

Morris, Elizabeth Woodbridge, ed. *Miss Wylie of Vassar*. New Haven: Yale University Press, 1934.

Norris, Mary Harriot. *The Golden Age of Vassar*. Poughkeepsie: Vassar College, 1915.

Plum, Dorothy, George Dowell, and Constance Ellis. *The Magnificent Enterprise: A Chronicle of Vassar College*. Poughkeepsie: Vassar College, 1961.

Rogers, Agnes. *Vassar Women: An Informal Study*. Poughkeepsie: Vassar College, 1940.

Schwartz, Julia. *Elinor's College Career*. Boston: Little, Brown, 1906.

———. *Vassar Studies*. New York: Putnam's, 1899.

Simpson, Alan. "Helen Lockwood's College Years 1908–1912." Convocation Address, May 6, 1977. Printed by Vassar College.

Swain, Barbara. *Helen Drusilla Lockwood: A Memoir and Appreciation*. Printed by Vassar College, May 6, 1977.

Webster, Jean. *When Patty Went to College*. New York: Grosset and Dunlap, 1903.

Wood, Frances A. *Earliest Years at Vassar*. Poughkeepsie: Vassar College, 1909.

Bibliography

GENERAL

Monographs and unpublished papers

Allmendinger, David. *Paupers and Scholars: The Transformation of Student Life in the Nineteenth Century.* New York: St. Martin's, 1975.

Alpern, Sara. *Freda Kirchwey: A Woman of the Nation.* Cambridge: Harvard University Press, 1987.

Antler, Joyce. *Lucy Sprague Mitchell: The Making of a Modern Woman.* New Haven: Yale University Press, 1986.

———. "The Educated Woman and Professionalization: The Struggle for a New Feminine Identity, 1890–1920." Ph.D. diss., State University of New York at Stony Brook, 1977.

Baker, Liva. *I'm Radcliffe! Fly Me!: The Seven Sisters and the Failure of Women's Education.* New York: Macmillan, 1976.

Banner, Lois W. *American Beauty: A Social History Through Two Centuries of the American Idea, Ideal, and Image of the Beautiful Woman.* New York, Random House, 1983.

———. *Women in Modern America.* New York: Harcourt Brace Jovanovich, 1974.

Berg, Barbara. *The Remembered Gate: Origins of American Feminism.* New York: Oxford University Press, 1978.

Bernard, Jessie. *Academic Women.* New York: New American Library, 1964.

Blair, Karen. *The Clubwoman as Feminist: True Womanhood Redefined, 1868–1914.* New York: Holmes and Meier, 1980.

Blandin, Isabella M. E. *History of Higher Education of Women in the South Prior to 1870.* New York: Neale, 1909.

Bledstein, Burton J. *The Culture of Professionalism: The Middle Class and the Development of Higher Education in America.* New York: W. W. Norton, 1976.

Boas, Louise Schutz. *Women's Education Begins: The Rise of the Women's Colleges.* Norton, Mass.: Wheaton College Press, 1935.

Brickman, William, and Lehrer, Stanley, eds. *A Century of Higher Education.* Westport, Conn.: Greenwood Press, 1962.

Briscoe, Virginia Wolf. "Bryn Mawr College Traditions: Women's Rituals as Expressive Behavior." Ph.D. diss., University of Pennsylvania, 1981.

Brown, Victoria Bissell. "Golden Girls: Female Socialization in Los Angeles, 1880–1920." Ph.D. diss., University of California at Los Angeles, 1985.

Brubacher, John, and Willis Rudy. *Higher Education in Transition: An American History, 1636–1956.* New York: Harper and Row, 1958.

Campbell, Barbara Kuhn. *The Liberated Woman of 1914.* Ann Arbor, Mich.: University Microfilms Research Press, 1979.

Carroll, Berenice, ed. *Liberating Women's History.* Urbana: University of Illinois Press, 1978.

Carver, Marie Negri. *Home Economics as an Academic Discipline.* Phoenix: Center for the Study of Higher Education, University of Arizona, May 1979.

Chafe, William H. *The American Woman: Her Changing Social, Economic, and Political Role, 1920–1970*. New York: Oxford University Press, 1972.

Clark, Thomas D. *Indiana University: Midwestern Pioneer*. 2 vols. Bloomington: Indiana University Press, 1970.

Conable, Charlotte. *Women at Cornell: The Myth of Equal Education*. Ithaca: Cornell University Press, 1977.

Costin, Lela B. *Two Sisters for Social Justice: A Biography of Grace and Edith Abbott*. Urbana: University of Illinois Press, 1983.

Cott, Nancy F. *The Bonds of Womanhood: Woman's Sphere in New England, 1780–1835*. New Haven: Yale University Press, 1977.

———. *The Grounding of Modern Feminism*. New Haven: Yale University Press, 1987.

Cross, Barbara M., ed. *The Educated Woman in America*. New York: Teachers College Press, 1965.

Crunden, Robert M. *Ministers of Reform: The Progressives' Achievement in American Civilization, 1889–1920*. Urbana: University of Illinois Press, 1984.

Curti, Merle, and Vernon Carstensen. *The University of Wisconsin 1848–1925: A History*. Madison: University of Wisconsin Press, 1949.

Davis, Allen. *American Heroine: The Life and Legend of Jane Addams*. New York: Oxford University Press, 1973.

———. *Spearheads for Reform: The Social Settlements and the Progressive Movement, 1890–1914*. New York: Oxford University Press, 1967.

Deegan, Mary Jo. *Jane Addams and the Men of the Chicago School, 1892–1918*. New Brunswick, N.J.: Transaction, 1988.

Degler, Carl N. *At Odds: Women and the Family in America from the Revolution to the Present*. New York: Oxford University Press, 1980.

Diner, Steven J. *A City and Its Universities: Public Policy in Chicago 1892–1919*. Chapel Hill: University of North Carolina Press, 1980.

Dobkin, Marjorie Housepian. *The Making of a Feminist: Early Journals and Letters of M. Carey Thomas*. Kent, Ohio: Kent State University Press, 1979.

Dulles, Eleanor Lansing. *Chances of a Lifetime: A Memoir*. Englewood Cliffs, N.J.: Prentice-Hall, 1980.

Eagan, Eileen. *Class, Culture, and the Classroom*. Philadelphia: Temple University Press, 1981.

Ephron, Nora. *Crazy Salad*. New York: Alfred A. Knopf, 1972.

Erenberg, Lewis. *Steppin' Out: New York Nightlife and the Transformation of American Culture 1890–1930*. Westport, Conn.: Greenwood Press, 1980.

Fass, Paula S. *The Damned and the Beautiful: American Youth in the 1920s*. New York: Oxford University Press, 1977.

Feldman, Kenneth A., and Theodore M. Newcomb. *The Impact of College On Students: An Analysis of Four Decades of Research*, vol. 1. San Francisco: Jossey-Bass, 1973.

Filene, Peter. *Him/Her/Self: Sex Roles in Modern America*. New York: Harcourt Brace Jovanovich, 1974.

Flexner, Eleanor. *Century of Struggle*. Rev. ed. Cambridge: Harvard University Press, 1975.

Fox-Genovese, Elizabeth. *Within the Plantation Household: Black and White Women of the Old South*. Chapel Hill: University of North Carolina Press, 1988.

Frankfort, Roberta. *Collegiate Women: Domesticity and Career in Turn-of-the-Century America*. New York: New York University Press, 1977.

Friedan, Betty. *The Feminine Mystique*. New York: Dell, 1963.

Friedman, Jean E. *The Enclosed Garden: Women and Community in the Evangelical South*. Chapel Hill: University of North Carolina Press, 1985.

Fuller, Paul E. *Laura Clay and the Woman's Rights Movement*. Lexington: University Press of Kentucky, 1975.

Gitlin, Todd. *The Sixties: Years of Hope, Days of Rage*. New York: Bantam, 1987.

Glazer, Penina Migdal, and Miriam Slater. *Unequal Colleagues: The Entrance of* *Women into the Professions, 1890–1940*. New Brunswick: Rutgers University Press, 1987.

Gluck, Sherna, ed. *From Parlor to Prison: Five American Suffragists Talk about Their Lives*. New York: Vintage, 1976.

Gordon, Linda. *Woman's Body, Woman's Right: A Social History of Birth Control in America*. New York: Grossman, 1976.

Gordon, Lynn D. "Women with Missions: Varieties of College Life in the Progressive Era." Ph.D. diss., University of Chicago, 1980.

Grantham, Dewey W. *Southern Progressivism: The Reconciliation of Progress and Tradition*. Knoxville: University of Tennessee Press, 1983.

Green, Elizabeth Alden. *Mary Lyon and Mount Holyoke: Opening the Gates*. Hanover, N.H.: University Press of New England, 1979.

Haller, John S., Jr., and Robin M. Haller. *The Physician and Sexuality in Victorian America*. Urbana: University of Illinois Press, 1974.

Handlin, Oscar, and Mary Handlin. *Facing Life: Youth and the Family in American History*. Boston: Little, Brown, 1971.

Harper, Ida Husted. *The Life and Work of Susan B. Anthony*, 4 vols. Indianapolis: Hollenbeck, 1898–1908.

Hartman, Mary, and Lois Banner, eds. *Clio's Consciousness Raised: New Perspectives in the History of Women*. New York: Harper and Row, 1974.

Hayden, Tom. *Reunion: A Memoir*. New York: Random House, 1988.

Health Resources Administration, Department of Health, Education and Welfare. *100 Years of Marriage and Divorce Statistics in the United States, 1867–1967*, Washington, D.C.: Government Printing Office, 1973.

Hobson, Laura Z. *Laura Z.: The Early Years and Years of Fulfillment*. 2 vols. in 1. New York: Donald I. Fine, 1986.

Hoffman, Nancy, ed. *Woman's True Profession: Voices from the History of Teaching*. New York: Feminist Press, 1979.

Hofstadter, Richard. *The Age of Reform*. New York: Vintage Books, 1955.

Horn, Max. *The Intercollegiate Socialist Society, 1905–1921: Origins of the Modern American Student Movement*. Boulder, Colo.: Westview Press, 1979.

Horowitz, Helen Lefkowitz. *Alma Mater: Design and Experience in the Women's Colleges from their Nineteenth Century Beginnings to the 1950s*. New York: Alfred A. Knopf, 1984.

———. *Campus Life: Undergraduate Cultures from the End of the Eighteenth Century to the Present*. New York: Alfred A. Knopf, 1987.

Howe, Florence. *Myths of Co-education: Selected Essays, 1964–1983*. Bloomington: University of Indiana Press, 1984.

Hummer, Patricia M. *The Decade of Elusive Promise: Professional Women in the United States, 1920–1930*. Ann Arbor, Mich.: University Microfilms Research Press, 1979.

Ihle, Elizabeth Lee. "The Development of Co-Education in Major Southern Universities." Ed.D. diss., University of Tennessee at Knoxville, 1976.

Kendall, Elaine. *Peculiar Institutions*. New York: Putnam's, 1975.

Kennedy, David M. *Birth Control in America: The Career of Margaret Sanger*. New Haven: Yale University Press, 1970.

Kerber, Linda K. *Women of the Republic: Intellect and Ideology in Revolutionary America*. Chapel Hill: University of North Carolina Press, 1980.

Kett, Joseph. *Rites of Passage: Adolescence in America 1790 to the Present*. New York: Basic, 1977.

Kilman, Gail Apperson. "Southern Collegiate Women: Higher Education at Wesleyan Female College and Randolph Macon Women's College, 1893–1907." Ph.D. diss., University of Delaware, 1984.

King, Mary Elizabeth. *Freedom Song: A Personal Story of the 1960s Civil Rights Movement*. New York: William Morrow, 1987.

Knight, Louise Wilby. "The 'Quails': The History of Wesleyan University's First Period of Co-Education, 1872–1912." B.A. honors thesis, Wesleyan University, 1972.

Komarovsky, Mirra. *Dilemmas of Masculinity*. New York: Norton, 1976.

———. *Women in College: Shaping New Feminine Identities*. New York: Basic, 1985.

Lagemann, Ellen Condliffe. *A Generation of Women: Education in the Lives of Progressive Reformers*. Cambridge: Harvard University Press, 1979.

Lasser, Carol, ed. *Educating Men and Women Together: Co-Education in a Changing World*. Urbana: University of Illinois Press, 1987.

Leach, William. *True Love and Perfect Union: The Feminist Reform of Sex and Society*. New York: Basic, 1980.

Lemons, J. Stanley. *The Woman Citizen: Social Feminism in the 1920s*. Urbana: University of Illinois Press, 1973.

234

Lever, Janet, and Pepper Schwartz. *Women at Yale: Liberating a College Campus.* Indianapolis, Ind.: Bobbs-Merrill, 1971.

Levine, Daniel. *Jane Addams and the Liberal Tradition.* Madison: The State Historical Society of Wisconsin, 1971.

Lopate, Carol. "Ellen Richards and the Home Economics Movement: Women with a Partial Vision." Paper delivered at the Berkshire Conference on Women's History, Mt. Holyoke College, August 1978.

Lyons, John O. *The College Novel in America.* Carbondale: Southern Illinois University Press, 1962.

McGuigan, Dorothy G. *A Dangerous Experiment: 100 Years of Women at the University of Michigan.* Ann Arbor, Mich.: Center for Continuing Education of Women, 1970.

Mather, Linda Lee. "The Education of Women: Images from Popular Magazines." Ed.D. diss., University of Pennsylvania, 1977.

May, Arthur J. "History of the University of Rochester." Department of Rare Books and Special Collections, Rush Rhees Library, University of Rochester, Rochester, New York.

May, Elaine Tyler. *Great Expectations: Marriage and Divorce in Post-Victorian America.* Chicago: University of Chicago Press, 1980.

May, Henry F. *The End of American Innocence.* Chicago: Quadrangle, 1959.

May, Lary. *Screening Out the Past: The Birth of Mass Culture and the Motion Picture Industry.* New York: Oxford University Press, 1980.

Messerli, Jonathan. *Horace Mann.* New York: Alfred A. Knopf, 1972.

Morantz-Sanchez, Regina Markell. *Sympathy and Science: Women Physicians in American Medicine.* New York: Oxford University Press, 1985.

Newcomb, Theodore M. *Persistence and Change: Bennington College and Its Students After Twenty-Five Years.* New York: John Wiley, 1967.

Newcomer, Mabel. *A Century of Higher Education for American Women.* New York: Harper Brothers, 1959.

Nickerson, Marjorie L. *A Long Way Forward: The First 100 Years of the Packer Collegiate Institute.* Brooklyn, N.Y.: Packer Collegiate Institute, 1945.

O'Neill, William. *Divorce in the Progressive Era.* New Haven: Yale University Press, 1967.

———. *Everyone Was Brave: A History of Feminism in America.* Chicago: Quadrangle, 1969.

Palmieri, Patricia A. "In Adamless Eden: A Portrait of Academic Women at Wellesley College, 1875–1920." Ed.D. diss., Harvard University, 1981.

Peterson, George. *The New England College in the Age of the University.* Amherst, Mass.: Amherst College Press, 1964.

Rosenberg, Rosalind. *Beyond Separate Spheres: Intellectual Roots of Modern Feminism.* New Haven: Yale University Press, 1982.

Rossiter, Margaret W. *Women Scientists in America: Struggles and Strategies to 1940.* Baltimore: Johns Hopkins University Press, 1982.

Rota, Tiziana F. "Between True Women and New Women: Mount Holyoke Students, 1837–1908." Ph.D. diss., University of Massachusetts at Amherst, 1983.

Roth, Darlene Rebecca. "Matronage: Patterns in Women's Organizations, Atlanta, Georgia, 1890–1940." Ph.D. diss., George Washington University, 1978.

Rothman, Ellen. *Hands and Hearts: A History of Courtship in America.* New York: Basic, 1984.

Rothman, Sheila. *Woman's Proper Place.* New York: Basic, 1978.

Rubin, Joan Shelley. *Constance Rourke and American Culture.* Chapel Hill: University of North Carolina Press, 1980.

Rudolph, Frederick. *The American College and University.* New York: Vintage, 1972.

———. *Curriculum: A History of the American Undergraduate Course of Study Since 1636.* San Francisco: Jossey Bass, 1977.

Ryan, Mary P. *Womanhood in America.* New York: New Viewpoints, 1975.

Sanford, Nevitt, ed. *The American College: A Psychological and Social Interpretation of Higher Education.* New York: John Wiley, 1962.

Scarborough, Elizabeth, and Laurel Furumoto. *Untold Lives: The First Generation of Women Psychologists.* New York: Columbia University Press, 1987.

Schwager, Sally. "Arguing for the Higher Education of Women: Early Experiences with Co-Education." Qualifying paper, Harvard University, 1979.

———. "Harvard Women: A History of the Founding of Radcliffe College." Ed.D. diss., Harvard University, 1982.

Scott, Anne Firor. *The Southern Lady: From Pedestal to Politics, 1830–1930.* Chicago: University of Chicago Press, 1970.

———. *Making the Invisible Woman Visible.* Urbana: University of Illinois Press, 1984.

Shea, Charlotte K. "Mount Holyoke College, 1875–1910: The Passing of the Old Order." Ph.D. diss., Cornell University, 1983.

Showalter, Elaine, ed. *These Modern Women: Autobiographical Essays from the Twenties.* Old Westbury, N.Y.: Feminist Press, 1978.

Sicherman, Barbara. *Alice Hamilton: A Life in Letters.* Cambridge: Harvard University Press, 1984.

Sklar, Kathryn Kish. *Catharine Beecher: A Study in American Domesticity.* New Haven: Yale University Press, 1973.

Slater, John Rothwell. *Rhees of Rochester.* New York: Harper Brothers, 1946.

Smith-Rosenberg, Carroll. *Disorderly Conduct: Visions of Gender in Victorian America.* New York: Alfred A. Knopf, 1985.

Solberg, Winton U. *The University of Illinois 1867–1894: An Intellectual and Cultural History.* Urbana: University of Illinois Press, 1968.

Solomon, Barbara Miller, *In the Company of Educated Women: A History of Women and Higher Education in America.* New Haven: Yale University Press, 1985.

Trilling, Diana. *We Must March My Darlings.* New York: Harcourt Brace Jovanovich, 1964–77.

Van Voris, Jacqueline, ed. *College: A Smith Mosaic*. West Springfield, Mass.: M. J. O'Malley, 1975.

Veysey, Laurence R. *The Emergence of the American University*. Chicago: University of Chicago Press, 1965.

Vicinus, Martha. *Independent Women: Work and Community for Single Women in England, 1850–1920*. Chicago: University of Chicago Press, 1985.

Vincenti, Virginia Brambe. "A History of the Philosophy of Home Economics." Ph.D. diss., Pennsylvania State University, 1981.

Wallach, Stephanie. "Dilemmas of Coeducation: Past and Present." Master's thesis, University of Chicago, 1977.

Walsh, Mary Roth. *Doctors Wanted: No Women Need Apply. Sexual Barriers in the Medical Profession 1835–1975*. New Haven: Yale University Press, 1977.

Ware, Susan. *Beyond Suffrage: Women in the New Deal*. Cambridge: Harvard University Press, 1981.

Wechsler, Harold S. *The Qualified Student: A History of Selective College Admission in America*. New York: John Wiley, 1977.

Wells, Anna Mary. *Miss Marks and Miss Woolley*. Boston: Houghton Mifflin, 1978.

Welter, Barbara. *Dimity Convictions: The American Woman in the Nineteenth Century*. Athens: Ohio University Press, 1976.

White, Lynn, Jr. *Educating Our Daughters*. New York: Harper Brothers, 1950.

Wiebe, Robert. *The Search for Order, 1877–1920*. New York: Hill and Wang, 1967.

Williamson, Harold F., and Wild, Payson S. *Northwestern University: A History 1850–1975*. Evanston: Northwestern University, 1976.

Wolters, Raymond. *The New Negro on Campus: Black College Rebellions of the 1920s*. Princeton: Princeton University Press, 1975.

Woody, Thomas. *A History of Women's Education in the United States*. 2 vols. New York: Science Press, 1929.

Books and Articles

Allmendinger, David F. "Mount Holyoke Students Encounter the Need for Life-Planning, 1837–1850." *History of Education Quarterly* 19 (Spring 1979): 27–46.

Antler, Joyce. "After College, What? New Graduates and the Family Claim." *American Quarterly* 32 (Fall 1980): 409–34.

———. "Feminism as Life-Process: The Life and Career of Lucy Sprague Mitchell." *Feminist Studies* 7 (Spring 1981): 134–57.

———. "Culture, Service, and Work: Changing Ideals of Higher Education for Women." In *The Undergraduate Woman: Issues in Educational Equity*, edited by Pamela J. Perun, 15–41. Lexington, Mass.: Lexington, 1982.

Brett, Sally. "A Different Kind of Being." In *Stepping Off the Pedestal: Academic Women in the South,* edited by Patricia A. Stringer and Irene Thompson, 13–22. New York: Modern Language Association, 1982.

Brumberg, Joan and Nancy Tomes. "Women in the Professions: A Research Agenda for American Historians." *Reviews in American History* 5 (June 1982): 275–96.

Bunkle, Phillida. "Sentimental Womanhood and Domestic Education, 1830–1870." *History of Education Quarterly* 14 (Spring 1974): 13–30.

Burnham, John. "Progressive Era Revolution—American Attitudes on Sex." *Journal of American History* 59 (March 1973): 885–903.

Butcher, Patricia Smith. "Education for Equality: Women's Rights Periodicals and Women's Higher Education, 1849–1920." *History of Higher Education Annual* 6 (1986): 63–79.

Carter, Susan B. "Academic Women Revisited: An Empirical Study of Changing Patterns in Women's Employment as College and University Faculty, 1890–1960." *Journal of Social History* 14 (Summer 1981): 675–99.

———. "Women's Educational History: A Labor Market Perspective." *Academy Notes* 13, no. 2 (Winter 1983): 25–27.

Clifford, Geraldine Joncich. "Shaking Dangerous Questions from the Crease: Gender and American Higher Education." *Feminist Issues* 3, no. 2 (Fall 1983): 3–62.

Clinton, Catherine. "Equally Their Due: The Education of the Planter Daughter in the Early Republic." *Journal of the Early Republic* 2 (April 1982): 39–60.

Conway, Jill K. "Coeducation and Women's Studies: Two Approaches to the Question of Woman's Place in the Contemporary University." *Daedalus* 103 (Fall 1974): 239–49.

———. "Perspectives on the History of Women's Education in the United States." *History of Education Quarterly* 14 (Spring 1974): 1–12.

Cook, Blanche Wiesen. "Female Support Networks and Political Activism: Lillian Wald, Crystal Eastman, Emma Goldman." *Chrysalis* 3 (1977): 43–61.

Cookingham, Mary E. "Bluestockings, Spinsters, and Pedagogues: Women College Graduates, 1865–1910." *Population Studies* 38 (November 1984): 349–64.

———. "Combining Marriage, Motherhood and Jobs Before World War II: Women College Graduates, Classes of 1905–1935." *Journal of Family History* 9 (Summer 1984): 349–64.

———. "Working After Childbearing in Modern America." *The Journal of Interdisciplinary History* 14 (Spring 1984): 773–92.

DuBois, Ellen, Mari Jo Buhle, Temma Kaplan, Gerda Lerner, Carroll Smith-Rosenberg, and Judith Walkowitz. "Politics and Culture in Women's History: A Symposium." *Feminist Studies* 6 (Spring 1980): 26–33.

Durr, Virginia Foster. "A Southern Belle Comes North." *Wellesley Alumnae Magazine,* Spring 1986: 11–14, 41–43.

Degler, Carl N. "What Ought to Be and What Was: Women's Sexuality in the Nineteenth Century." *American Historical Review* 79 (December 1974): 1467–90.

Fletcher, Robert S. "Oberlin and Co-Education." *Ohio State Archaeological and Historical Quarterly* 47 (1938): 1–19.

Freedman, Estelle B. "Separatism as Strategy: Female Institution Building and American Feminism, 1870–1930." *Feminist Studies* 5 (Fall 1979): 512–29.

Fritschner, Linda Marie. "Women's Work and Women's Education: The Case of Home Economics 1870–1920." *Sociology of Work and Occupations* 4 (May 1977): 209–34.

Giele, Janet Z. "Cohort Variation in Life Patterns of Educated Women, 1911–1960." *Western Sociological Review* 13 (1982): 1–24.

Giele, Janet Z., and Pamela J. Perun. "Life After College: Historical Links Between Women's Education and Women's Work". In *The Undergraduate Woman: Issues in Educational Equity*, edited by Pamela J. Perun, 375–98. Lexington, Mass.: Lexington, 1982.

Gordon, Ann D. "The Young Ladies' Academy of Philadelphia." In *Women of America*, edited by Carol R. Berkin and Mary Beth Norton, 68–91. Boston: Houghton Mifflin, 1979.

Gordon, Lynn D. "Annie Nathan Meyer and Barnard College: Mission and Identity in Women's Higher Education, 1889–1950." *History of Education Quarterly* 26 (Winter 1986): 503–22.

———. "Co-Education on Two Campuses: Berkeley and Chicago, 1890–1912." In *Woman's Being, Woman's Place*, edited by Mary Kelley, 171–93. Boston: G. K. Hall, 1979.

———. "The Gibson Girl Goes to College: Popular Culture and Women's Higher Education in the Progressive Era, 1890–1920." *American Quarterly* 39 (Summer 1987): 211–30.

———. "In the Shadow of SDS: Writing the History of Twentieth Century College Students." *History of Education Quarterly* 26 (Spring 1986): 131–39.

———. "Katharine Bement Davis." In *Biographical Dictionary of Social Welfare in America*, edited by Walter I. Trattner, 207–10. Westport, Conn: Greenwood Press, 1986.

———. "Women and the Anti-Child Labor Movement in Illinois 1890–1920." *Social Service Review* 51 (June 1977): 228–48.

Gordon, Sarah H. "Smith College Students: The First Ten Classes 1879–1888." *History of Education Quarterly* 15 (Summer 1975): 147–67.

Graham, Patricia A. "Expansion and Exclusion: A History of Women in American Higher Education." *Signs* 3 (Summer 1978): 759–73.

———. "So Much to Do: Guides for Historical Research on Women in Higher Education." *Teachers College Record* 76 (February 1975): 421–29.

Hague, Amy. "What if the Power Does Lie Within Me?: Women Students at the University of Wisconsin, 1875–1900." *History of Higher Education Annual* 4 (1984): 78–100.

Haines, Patricia Foster. "Co-Education and the Development of Leadership Skills in Women: Historical Perspectives from Cornell University, 1868–1900." In *Women and Educational Leadership*, edited by Sari Knopp Biklen and Marilyn B. Brannigan, 113–28. Lexington, Mass.: D. C. Heath, 1980.

Herman, Sondra R. "Loving Courtship or the Marriage Market? The Ideal and Its Critics, 1871–1911." In *Our American Sisters,* edited by Jean E. Friedman and William G. Shade, 233–51. Boston: Allyn and Bacon, 1976.

Higham, John. "The Re-Orientation of American Culture in the 1890s." In *The Origins of Modern Consciousness,* edited by John Weiss, 25–48. Detroit: Wayne State University Press, 1965.

Hogeland, Ronald W. "Co-Education of the Sexes at Oberlin College: A Study of Social Ideas in Mid-Nineteenth Century America." *Journal of Social History* 6 (Winter 1972–73): 160–76.

Horowitz, Helen Lefkowitz. "With More Love Than I Can Write: A Nineteenth Century Father to His Daughter." *Wellesley Alumnae Magazine* 65 (Fall 1980): 16–20.

Jenkins, William D. "Housewifery and Motherhood: The Question of Role Change in the Progressive Era." In *Woman's Being, Woman's Place,* edited by Mary Kelley, 142–53. Boston: G. K. Hall, 1979.

Keller, George C., and Gene R. Hawes. "Where the Girls Are." *Esquire* 61 (June 1964): 119–23.

Kerber, Linda. "Daughters of Columbia: Educating Women for the Republic, 1787–1805." In *Hofstadter Aegis: A Memorial,* edited by Stanley Elkins and Eric McKitrick, 36–59. New York: Alfred A. Knopf, 1974.

Kerns, Kathryn. "Farmer's Daughters: The Education of Women at Alfred Academy and University Before the Civil War." *History of Higher Education Annual* 6 (1986): 11–28.

Kohlstedt, Sally Gregory. "Single-Sex Education and Leadership: The Early Years of Simmons College." In *Women and Educational Leadership,* edited by Sari Knopp Biklen and Marilyn B. Brannigan, 93–112. Lexington, Mass.: D. C. Heath, 1980.

Lagemann, Ellen Condliffe. "The Challenge of Jane Addams: A Research Note. *History of Higher Education Annual* 6 (1986): 51–61.

Lears, T. J. Jackson, "From Salvation to Self-Realization." In *The Culture of Consumption: Critical Essays in American History, 1880–1980,* edited by T. J. Jackson Lears and Richard Wightman Fox, 1–38. New York: Pantheon, 1983.

McCandless, Amy Thompson. "Preserving the Pedestal: Restrictions on Social Life at Southern Colleges for Women, 1920–1940." *History of Higher Education Annual* 7 (1987): 45–67.

McGovern, James R. "The American Woman's Pre-World War I Freedom in Manners and Morals." *Journal of American History* 58 (September 1968): 315–33.

Newton, Esther. "The Mythic Mannish Lesbian: Radclyffe Hall and the New Woman." *Signs* 9 (Summer 1984): 557–75.

Palmieri, Patricia A. "But Is It Progress? The Status of Women in Higher Education." *Harvard Graduate School of Education Bulletin* 23 (Winter 1978–79): 5.

———. "Here was Fellowship: A Social Portrait of Academic Women at Wellesley

College, 1880–1920." *History of Education Quarterly* 23 (Summer 1983): 195–214.

———. "Paths and Pitfalls: Illuminating Woman's Educational History." *Harvard Educational Review* 49 (November 1979): 534–41.

———. "Patterns of Achievement of Single Academic Women at Wellesley College, 1880–1920." *Frontiers* 5 (Spring 1980): 63–68.

———. "Placing Women in Higher Educational History." *Academy Notes* 13, no. 2 (Winter 1983): 22–25.

Riesman, David. "Two Generations." In *The Woman in America,* edited by Robert Jay Lifton, 72–97. Boston: Beacon Press, 1964–65.

Riley, Glenda Gates. "The Subtle Subversion: Changes in the Traditionalist Image of the American Woman." *Historian* 32 (February 1970): 210–27.

Rosenberg, Rosalind. "The Academic Prism: The New View of American Women." In *Women of America,* edited by Carol R. Berkin and Mary Beth Norton, 318–41. Boston: Houghton Mifflin, 1979.

———. "The Limits of Access: The History of Co-Education in America." In *Women and Higher Education in American History,* edited by John Mack Faragher and Florence Howe, 107–29. New York: W. W. Norton, 1988.

Rossiter, Margaret W. "Women Scientists in America Before 1920." *American Scientist* 62 (May–June 1974): 312–23.

Rousmaniere, John P. "Cultural Hybrid in the Slums: The College Woman and the Settlement House 1889–1894." *American Quarterly* 22 (Spring 1970): 45–66.

Rury, John, and Glenn Harper. "The Trouble with Co-Education: Mann and Women at Antioch." *History of Education Quarterly* 26 (Winter 1986): 481–502.

Sahli, Nancy. "Smashing: Women's Relationships Before the Fall." *Chrysalis* 17 (Summer 1979): 679–703.

Schwager, Sally. "Educating Women in America." *Signs* 12 (Winter 1987): 333–72.

Scott, Anne Firor. "The Ever Widening Circle: The Diffusion of Feminist Values from the Troy Female Seminary." *History of Education Quarterly* 19 (Spring 1979): 3–25.

———. "What, Then, Is the American, This New Woman?" *Journal of American History* 65 (December 1978): 679–703.

Scott, Joan W. "Gender: A Useful Category of Historical Analysis." *American Historical Review* 91 (December 1986): 1053–75.

Searles, Patricia, and Janet Mickish. "A Thoroughbred Girl: Images of Female Gender Roles in Turn-of-the-Century Media." *Women's Studies* 10 (1984): 261–81.

Simmons, Christina. "Companionate Marriage and the Lesbian Threat." *Frontiers* 4 (1979): 54–59.

Sklar, Kathryn Kish. "The Founding of Mount Holyoke College." In *Women in America,* edited by Carol R. Berkin and Mary Beth Norton, 177–201. Boston: Houghton Mifflin, 1978.

Smith, Daniel Scott. "Dating the American Sexual Revolution: Evidence and Interpretation." In *The American Family in Social-Historical Perspective,* 2d ed., edited by Michael Gordon, 426–38. (New York: St. Martin's Press, 1978).

Spitzer, Alan B. "The Historical Problem of Generations." *American Historical Review* 73 (December 1973): 1353–85.

Stricker, Frank. "Cookbooks and Law Books: The Hidden History of Career Women in 20th Century America." *Journal of Social History* 10 (Fall 1976): 1–19.

Stowe, Steven M. "The *Thing* Not Its Vision: A Woman's Courtship and Her Sphere in the Southern Planter Class." *Feminist Studies* 9 (Spring 1983): 113–30.

———. "The Not-So-Cloistered Academy: Elite Women's Education and Family Feeling in the Old South." In *The Web of Southern Social Relations: Women, Family, and Education,* edited by Walter J. Fraser, Jr., Frank Saunders, Jr., and Jon L. Wakelyn, 90–106. Athens: University of Georgia Press, 1985.

Susman, Warren I. "Personality and the Making of Twentieth Century Culture." In *Culture as History: The Transformation of American Society in the Twentieth Century,* edited by Warren I. Susman, 271–85. New York: Pantheon, 1984.

Tidball, M. Elizabeth, and Vera Kistiakowsky. "Baccalaureate Origins of American Scientists and Scholars." *Science* 193 (August 1976): 646–50.

Treichler, Paula A. "Alma Mater's Sorority: Women and the University of Illinois, 1890–1925." In *Alma Mater: Theory and Practice in Feminist Scholarship,* edited by Paula A. Treichler, Cheris Kramarae, and Beth Stafford, 5–61. Urbana: University of Illinois Press, 1985.

Vicinus, Martha. "Distance and Desire: English Boarding-School Friendships." *Signs* 9 (Summer 1984): 600–22.

Wechsler, Harold S. "An Academic Gresham's Law: Group Repulsion As a Theme in American Higher Education." *Teachers College Record* 82 (Summer 1981): 567–88.

———. "The Rationale for Restriction: Ethnicity and College Admission in America, 1910–1980." *American Quarterly* 36 (Winter 1984): 643–67.

Williamson, Susan, and Mary Oates. "Women's Colleges and Women Achievers." *Signs* 3 (Summer 1978): 795–806.

Wilson, Christopher P. "The Rhetoric of Consumption." In *The Culture of Consumption: Critical Essays in American History, 1880–1980,* edited by T. J. Jackson Lears and Richard Wightman Fox, 39–64. New York: Pantheon, 1983.

Zimmerman, Joan G. "Daughters of Main Street: Culture and the Female Community at Grinnell 1884–1917." In *Woman's Being, Woman's Place,* edited by Mary Kelley, 154–70. Boston: G. K. Hall, 1979.

Primary sources

Abbott, Frances M. "A Generation of College Women." *Forum* 20 (November 1895): 377–84.

———. "The College Woman and Matrimony: Again." *Century* 51 (March 1896): 796–98.

———. "Three Decades of College Women." *Popular Science Monthly* 75 (August 1904): 350–59.

Abernethy, Julian W. "The Anomaly of Co-Education." *School and Society* 9 (1 March 1919).

Addams, Jane. *Twenty Years at Hull House.* New York: Macmillan, 1910.

Allinson, Anne C. E. "The Present and Future of Collegiate Co-Education." *The Nation* 88 (22 April 1909): 404–06.

Anderson, Olive San Louis. *An American Girl and Her Four Years in a Boys' College.* New York: D. Appleton, 1878.

Angell, James B. "Coeducation at Michigan University." *Pennsylvania School Journal* 29 (1881): 281.

———. "Coeducation in Relation to Other Types of College Education for Women." NEA *Proceedings* (1904): 548–49.

Angell, James R. "Some Reflections upon the Reaction from Coeducation." *Popular Science Monthly* 62 (November 1902): 5–26.

Angell, Pauline. "Matthew Vassar, Feminist." *Harper's Weekly* 61 (2 October 1915): 320–21.

Association of Collegiate Alumnae, *Journal,* 1911–20.

Association of Collegiate Alumnae, *Publications,* 1890–1911.

Austin, Annette, and Abby Merchant. "College Girls Preferred." *Good Housekeeping* 50 (June 1910): 727–31.

Bennett, Helen M. "Seven Colleges—Seven Types." *Woman's Home Companion* 47 (November 1920): 13.

Bevier, Isabel. "Recollections and Impressions of the Beginnings of the Department of Home Economics at The University of Illinois." *Journal of Home Economics* 32 (May 1940): 291–97.

Bolce, Harold. "Away from Ancient Altars." *Cosmopolitan* 48 (March 1910): 519–28.

———. "The Crusade Invisible." *Cosmopolitan* 48 (February 1910): 310–20.

———. "Does the College Rob the Cradle?" *Delineator* 77 (March 1911): 169–70.

Brackett, Anna C., ed. *The Education of American Girls.* New York: Putman's, 1874.

Brande, Dorothea. "Cinderella in Industry." *The New Republic* 24 (24 November 1920): 323–25.

Bromley, Dorothy Dunbar. "Feminist—New Style." *Harper's Magazine* 155 (October 1927): 552–60.

Brooks, Ruth Steele. "College and Sorority." *School and Society* 14 (24 September 1921): 199–205.

Brownell, Louise Sheffield. "Government of Women Students in Colleges and Universities." *Educational Review* 20 (December 1900): 475–98.

Canfield, Dorothy. *The Bent Twig.* New York: Henry Holt, 1915.

The Century, vol. 85 (November 1912–February 1913).

Chamberlin, Roy B. "Letter to the Editor." *The Independent* 66 (25 March 1909): 648–49.

Christy, Howard Chandler. *The American Girl.* 1906. Reprint. New York: Da Capo Press, 1976.

Clarke, Edward M. *Sex in Education or A Fair Chance for the Girls.* Boston: J. R. Osgood, 1873.

Coates, Mary Isabel. "Getting Vassared." *Delineator* 80 (September 1912): 136–37.

Cockerell, T. D. A. "War Work of College Women in the West." *School and Society* 6 (15 December 1917): 699–705.

"Co-Education of the Sexes." Committee on the Education of Girls. NEA *Proceedings* (1890): 338–43.

"The College Girls' Budget." *The Independent* 85 (6 March 1916): 330.

"College Girls' Number." *Good Housekeeping* 40 (June 1905).

"College Girls Under Fire." *The Independent* 94 (11 May 1918): 241–42.

"Comrades and Sweethearts." *The Independent* 67 (28 October 1909): 989–91.

Coolidge, Calvin. "Enemies of the Republic: Are the Reds Stalking Our College Women?" *Delineator* 98 (June 1921): 10–11.

Crawford, Mary Caroline. *The College Girls of America.* Boston: L. C. Page, 1904.

Crow, Martha Foote. "Will the Co-Educated Co-Educate Their Children?" *The Forum* 17 (July 1894): 582–94.

Curtis, Henry S. "Pedagogy and Matrimony." *School and Society* 8 (20 July 1918): 79–82.

Curtis, Wardon A. The Movement Against Co-Education at the University of Wisconsin." *The Independent* 65 (6 August 1908): 323–26.

Davis, Charles Belmont. "Court Circles at Wisconsin." *Collier's* 45 (23 July 1910): 14–16.

Davis, Katharine Bement. *Factors in the Sex Lives of 2200 Women.* New York: Harper Brothers, 1929.

———. "Why They Failed to Marry." *Harper's Magazine* (March 1928): 460–69.

Dealey, Hermione L. "The Problem of the College Sorority." *School and Society* 4 (11 November 1916): 735–40.

"The Distractions of College Fraternities." *The Independent* 60 (15 February 1906): 391–94.

Draper, Andrew. "Coeducation in the United States." *Educational Review* 25 (February 1903): 109–29.

Duffey, Mrs. Eliza B. *No Sex in Education: Or, An Equal Chance for Both Boys and Girls.* Philadelphia: J. M. Stoddart, 1874.

Eliot, Charles William. "The Higher Education for Women." *Harper's Bazar* 42 (June 1908): 519–22.

Elliot, Gabrielle. "How War Strikes Home to a Woman's College." *Outlook* 117 (21 November 1917): 470–73.

Engelmann, George J. "Education Not the Cause of Race Decline." *Popular Science Monthly* 63 (June 1903): 172–84.

Fallows, Alice Katharine. "The Girl Freshman." *Munsey's Magazine* 25 (September 1901): 818–28.

———. "The Practical Religion of the College Girl." *Outlook* 74 (1 August 1903): 819–24.

———. "Self-Government for College Girls." *Harper's Bazar* 38 (July 1904): 698–705.

———. "Working One's Way Through Women's Colleges." *The Century* 62 (July 1901): 323–41.

Frost, M. A., and J. H. Caverno. "What It Costs to Send a Girl Through College." *Outlook* 59 (7 May 1898): 82–83.

Gaines, Ruth. "The First Mass at Grecourt." *The Survey* 39 (10 November 1917): 142.

Gardner, George E. "College Women and Matrimony." *Education* 20 (January 1900): 285–91.

Goldsberry, Louise Dunham. "We," pt. 2. *The Independent* 72 (11 April 1912): 774–76.

Goodloe, Abbe Carter. *College Girls*. New York: Scribner's, 1895.

Goodsell, Willystine. *The Education of Women*. New York: Macmillan, 1923.

"The Grind Peril in a Girls' College." *Scribners' Magazine* 62 (December 1917): 766–68.

Hall, G. Stanley. *Adolescence*. 2 vols. New York: D. Appleton, 1905.

———. "The Question of Co-Education." *Munsey's Magazine* 34 (February 1906): 588–92.

Hall, G. Stanley, and Theodate Smith. "Marriage and Fecundity of College Men and Women." *The Pedagogical Seminary* (September 1903): 275–314 (later *The Journal of Genetic Psychology*).

Hamilton, Edith. *The New Republic* 10 (10 February 1917): 45–46.

Harkness, Mary Leal. "The College Course for Women." *The Independent* 73 (1 August 1912): 240–43.

Harper, Carrie A. "A Feminine Professorial Viewpoint." *The Educational Review* 46 (June 1913): 47–51.

Harper, Ida Husted, and Susan B. Anthony. *History of Women's Suffrage*. Vol. 6. Indianapolis, Ind.: Hollenbeck Press, 1906–11.

Harvey, Lorenzo D. "The Education of Girls." NEA *Proceedings* (1912): 425–30.

Hatch, Mary R. P. "Nan's Career." *New England Magazine* 42 (June–July 1910): 440–47, 561–63.

Hollingsworth, Leta S. "Phi Beta Kappa and Women Students." *School and Society* 4 (16 December 1916): 932–33.

Howe, Julia Ward. *Sex and Education*. Boston: Roberts Brothers, 1874.

Howes, Annie G. *Health Statistics of Women College Graduates*. Boston: Wright and Potter, 1885.

Hubbard, Grace A. "War and the Woman's College." *The New Republic* 15 (6 July 1918): 285–87.

Hurwitz, Ruth Sapin. "Coming of Age at Wellesley." *The Menorah Journal* 38 (Fall 1950): 220–36.

———. "The Jewish Girl at College." *The Menorah Journal* 2 (1916): 294–300.

Johnson, Burges. "Is the Woman's College Essential in War Time?" *The Outlook* 118 (10 April 1918): 586–91.

———. "The Question of Co-Education." *Munsey's Magazine* 34 (March 1906): 683–88.

The Ladies' Home Journal Vols. 3–37 (1886–1920).

Latimer, Caroline. "Scientific Instruction in Girls' Schools." *Popular Science Monthly* 53 (June 1898): 246–54.

Lee, Jennette. "The College Woman in the Community." *Good Housekeeping* 59 (September 1914): 364–68.

———. "With A College Education" *Good Housekeeping* 58 (June 1914): 796–805.

MacCracken, Henry Noble. "The Cause of Learning." *School and Society* 2 (30 October 1915): 613–19.

———. "Girls Who Want to Go to France." *The Independent* 94 (11 May 1918): 248.

———. "Off to College." *Good Housekeeping* 63 (September 1916): 43.

McConn, Max. "Co-Education and Spring." *The New Republic* 22 (12 May 1920): 338–39.

McIntyre, D., Luke H. Parsons, and B. L. Baxter. "Report on the Admission of Females," September 29, 1858. *Regents' Proceedings*, 795, Michigan Historical Collection, Ann Arbor, Michigan.

Martin, Gertrude S. "The Education of Women and Sex Equality." American Academy of Political and Social Science *Annals* 56 (November 1914): 38–46.

Mathews, Lois Kimball. *The Dean of Women*. Boston: Houghton Mifflin, 1915.

Mearkle, A. L. "The Higher Education of Women: Education and Marriage." *The Arena* 33 (June 1900): 285–91.

Meyer, Annie Nathan. *Barnard Beginnings*. Boston: Houghton Mifflin, 1935.

Mills, Herbert Elmer. "College Women and Nursing." *The Survey* 40 (10 November 1917): 142.

Morris, Edith L. "Typical Rooms in Women's Colleges." *Harper's Bazar* 33 (25 August 1900): 1050–54.

Nicolson, Marjorie. "The Rights and Privileges Pertaining Thereto." *Journal of the American Association of University Women* 31 (April 1938): 135–42.

Nielson, William Allan. "The Inaugural Address of the President of Smith College." *School and Society* 8 (20 July 1918): 61–68.

"Of Feminine Achievement." *The New Republic* 14 (20 April 1918): 343–44.

Olin, Helen R. *The Women of a State University: An Illustration of the Workings of Co-Education in the Middle West*. New York: Putnam's, 1909.

The Outlook 83 (30 June 1906): 511–12; (11 August 1906): 895–96. Unsigned, untitled articles.

Paine, Grace Elizabeth. "The Maids' Club at Vassar." *Good Housekeeping* 56 (June 1913): 809–11.

Palmer, Alice Freeman. "A Review of the Higher Education of Women." *The Forum* (September 1891): 28–40.

Palmer, George Herbert. *The Life of Alice Freeman Palmer.* Boston: Houghton Mifflin, 1908.

Parkhurst, Genevieve. "Does This Mean Sex War?" *Delineator* 98 (March 1921): 7, 62.

Picard, J. L. "Co-Education in Colleges." *Education* 13 (January 1893): 259–66.

Piper, P. F. "Secret Societies in Women's Colleges." *Harper's Bazar* 35 (October 1901): 580–84.

Pomeroy, Sarah Gertrude. "The Service of the Women's Fraternities." *The Independent* 79 (21 September 1914): 413–14.

Porter, Elizabeth Crane. "How Mt. Holyoke Freed Itself from Secret Societies." *The Independent* 74 (2 January 1913): 26–28.

Powell, Reverend Lyman. "Religious Influences in College Life." *Good Housekeeping* 52 (April 1911): 420–28.

Ralph, Julian. "A Recent Journey Through the West." *Harper's Weekly* 39 (17 August 1895): 775–77.

Reppelier, Agnes. "The Girl Graduate." *The Century* 80 (June 1910): 227–30.

Rice, Richard, Jr. "The Educational Value of Co-Education." *The Independent* 73 (5 December 1912): 1304–06.

Richards, Mrs. Ellen. "Domestic Science as a Synthetic Study for Girls." NEA *Proceedings* (1898): 766–73.

"R.O." "The Pros and Cons of Co-Education." *The Nation* 76 (2 April 1902): 267–68.

Robinson, Mabel Louise. *The Curriculum of the Woman's College.* U.S. Bureau of Education Bulletin, no. 13, 1918.

Rolker, A. W. "The College Woman in Business." *Good Housekeeping* 53 (August 1911): 147–53.

Salmon, Lucy M. "Education in the Household." *New England Magazine* 10 (April 1894): 185–88.

———. "Recent Progress in the Study of Domestic Science." *The Atlantic Monthly* 96 (November 1905): 628–35.

School and Society 12 (16 October 1920): 348–49. Unsigned, untitled article on opening of Harvard Graduate School of Education.

Scoville, S., Jr. "Athletic Vassar." *The Outlook* 54 (4 July 1896): 17–19.

"Segregated Chicago." *The Independent* 61 (2 October 1906): 1004–06.

"The Shame of Wesleyan." *The Independent* 66 (4 March 1909): 494–95.

Sherwood, Margaret. "Undergraduate Life at Vassar." *Scribners' Magazine* 23 (June 1898): 643–60.

Shinn, Milicent W. "Etc." *The Overland Monthly* 15 (April 1890): 443–45.

———. "The Marriage Rate of College Women." *Century* 50 (October 1895): 946–48.

"The Size of Families of College Graduates." *Popular Science Monthly* 64 (April 1904): 570–71.

Small, Albion. NEA *Proceedings* (1903): 288–97. Untitled article.

Smith, Mary Roberts. "Statistics of College and Non-College Women." American Statistical Association, *Publications* 7 (March–June 1900): 1–26.

Talbot, Marion. "The College, the Girl, and the Parent." *North American Review* 192 (September 1910): 349–58.

Thomas, Martha Carey. *The Education of Women*. U.S. Department of Education, 1899. Schlesinger Library, Cambridge, Mass.

Thwing, Charles F. "The Advantage of the Co-Ordinate (Annex) Method in Education." NEA *Proceedings* (1904): 547–48.

———. "What Becomes of College Women." *North American Review* 161 (November 1895): 546–53.

Van der Warker, Ely. "Is the Education of Women With Men a Failure?" *Harper's Weekly* 48 (20 August 1904): 1288–89.

Welch, Margaret Hamilton. "Club Life in Women's Colleges." *Harper's Bazar* 33 (16 June 1900): 436–38.

Wells, Kate Gannett. "Why More Men Do Not Marry." *North American Review* 165 (July 1897): 123–28.

"What Girls Can Do for Girls." *Good Housekeeping* 56 (June 1913): 783–84.

White, Hannah Hastings. "Rolling Pins, Fruit Trees and Shoes." *The Independent* 01 (11 August 1917): 226–27.

Wilcox, Suzanne. "The Conduct of College Girls." *The Independent* 75 (7 August 1913): 320–22.

Wilson, Elizabeth. *Fifty Years of Association Work Among Young Women*. New York: National Board of the YWCA, 1916.

Wolfs, Marie L. "The Last to Leave." *The Independent* 94 (23 June 1918): 470–71, 485.

Woolley, Mary Emma. "The Status of Women: Preparation of Women for Twentieth Century Life." NEA *Proceedings* (1914): 56–60.

INDEX